ALL'S WELL THAT ENDS WELL

The RSC Shakespeare

Edited by Jonathan Bate and Eric Rasmussen

Chief Associate Editors: Jan Sewell and Will Sharpe

Associate Editors: Trey Jansen, Eleanor Lowe, Lucy Munro,
Dee Anna Phares, Héloïse Sénéchal

All's Well That Ends Well

Textual editing: Eric Rasmussen

Introduction and Shakespeare's Career in the Theater: Jonathan Bate

Commentary: Eleanor Lowe and Héloïse Sénéchal

Scene-by-Scene Analysis: Jan Sewell

In Performance: Maria Jones (RSC stagings) and Jan Sewell (overview)

The Director's Cut (interviews by Jan Sewell and Kevin Wright):
Gregory Doran and Stephen Fried
Guy Henry on Playing Parolles

The RSC Shakespeare

William Shakespeare

ALL'S WELL THAT ENDS WELL

Edited by Jonathan Bate and Eric Rasmussen

Introduction by Jonathan Bate

The Modern Library
New York

2011 Modern Library Paperback Edition

Copyright © 2007, 2011 by The Royal Shakespeare Company

Published in the United States by Modern Library, an imprint of
The Random House Publishing Group, a division of
Random House, Inc., New York.

The version of *All's Well That Ends Well* and the corresponding footnotes
that appear in this volume were originally published in *William Shakespeare:
Complete Works,* edited by Jonathan Bate and Eric Rasmussen, published
in 2007 by Modern Library, an imprint of The Random House
Publishing Group, a division of Random House, Inc.

ISBN 978-0-8129-6937-5
eBook ISBN 978-1-58836-884-3

Printed in the United States of America

www.modernlibrary.com

2 4 6 8 9 7 5 3 1

CONTENTS

INTRODUCTION

"HE WEARS HIS HONOUR IN A BOX UNSEEN"

All's Well That Ends Well is one of Shakespeare's least performed and least loved comedies. It is also one of his most fascinating and intriguingly modern works. The play presents a battlefield of opposing value systems: abstract codes jostle against material commodities, words are undermined by actions, generation argues with generation, and a sex war rages.

The language of sexual relations is persistently intermingled with that of warfare. The key word, deployed with equal force in conversations about the bedroom, the court, and the battlefield, is "honour." The atmosphere feels very different from that of Shakespeare's comic green world. *All's Well* shares the darker view of human nature and the more troubling preoccupations of three other plays written at the end of Queen Elizabeth I's reign and the beginning of James I's: *Troilus and Cressida, Othello,* and *Measure for Measure.*

In the very first scene, virginity is described by Parolles as woman's weapon of resistance. But man will besiege it, "undermine" it, and "blow up" his foe—make her pregnant. Like honor, virginity may variously be seen as a mystical treasure, a mark of integrity, a marketable commodity, and a kind of nothing. Traditional wisdom suggests that it is something a girl must preserve with care. But the play is full of proverbs and moral maxims that are found wanting, "undermined" by the demands of the body. Lavatch, Shakespeare's most cynical and lascivious fool, is on hand to remind us of this. "I am driven on by the flesh," he remarks, suggesting that the story of the sexes boils down to "Tib's rush for Tom's forefinger." "Tib" was a generic name for a whore; the "rush" is a rudimentary wedding ring fashioned from reeds, but a woman's "ring" is also the place where she is penetrated by a man's nether finger.

"War," says Bertram, "is no strife / To the dark house and the detested wife." For a young man in search of action, a wife is but a "clog," a block of wood tied to an animal to prevent it from escaping. Parolles voices the same sentiment in the tumble of language that is his hallmark:

> . . . To th'wars, my boy, to th'wars!
> He wears his honour in a box unseen
> That hugs his kicky-wicky here at home,
> Spending his manly marrow in her arms,
> Which should sustain the bound and high curvet
> Of Mars' fiery steed. To other regions,
> France is a stable, we that dwell in't jades:
> Therefore, to th'war!

"Kicky-wicky" is an abusive term for a wife, the "box unseen" is the vagina, and "marrow" is the essence of manliness (according to ancient physiology, semen was distilled from the marrow in the backbone). A proper man, Parolles suggests, should be off riding a "fiery steed" into battle, in the spirit of Mars, god of war; those who stay at home are no better than female horses, good only for breeding and sexual indulgence ("jade" was another slang term for whore).

All's Well is in the mainstream of comedy insofar as it is about young people and the process of growing up. Bertram is like most young men of every era: he wants to be one of the boys, to prove his manhood. Enlistment in the army provides the ideal opportunity. He wants to sow some wild oats along the way, but is not ready for marriage. Critics hate him for not loving the lovely humble Helen from the start. "I cannot reconcile my heart to Bertram," wrote Dr. Johnson with characteristic candor and forthrightness, "a man noble without generosity, and young without truth; who marries Helen as a coward, and leaves her as a profligate: when she is dead by his unkindness, sneaks home to a second marriage, is accused by a woman whom he has wronged, defends himself by falsehood, and is dismissed to happiness."[1] Of course there is something obnoxious in the snobbery with which Bertram first dismisses Helen on the grounds of her low status, but when he goes on to say that he is simply not in love with her, he reveals a kind of integrity. He bows to the King's will and marries her, but since his heart does not belong to her he refuses to give her his body. If a woman were forced to marry in this way, we would rather admire her for withholding sexual favors from her husband.

THE NEW CODE OF THE SELF

Bertram represents modernity in that he acts according to an existential principle: he follows his own self, not some preexistent code of duty, service to his monarch, or obligation to the older generation. One word for this code is indeed integrity. Another is selfishness. It is the prerogative of the old, especially mothers, to know, to suffer, and still to forgive the selfishness of their young. Bertram's mother, the widowed Countess of Rossillion, who treats the orphaned Helen like a daughter and is only too happy to accept her as a daughter-in-law, regardless of her lowly background, was described by George Bernard Shaw as "the most beautiful old woman's part ever written" (though she could perfectly well be in her forties). Since female parts were written for young male actors, strong maternal roles such as this are exceptional in Shakespeare. The only analogous parts are the more overbearing figures of Queen Margaret in the *Henry VI* plays, Tamora in *Titus Andronicus*, and Volumnia in *Coriolanus*. The serenity of the Countess has meant that the principal reason for modern revivals of *All's Well* has been the opportunity to showcase actresses such as Edith Evans, Peggy Ashcroft, and Judi Dench in their later years.

One of the key debates in the play is that between nature and nurture. The Countess of Rossillion believes that her son is a fundamentally good boy who has fallen into bad company, as embodied by the worthless Parolles. Helen, meanwhile, has strong natural qualities (the "dispositions she inherits") reinforced by a loving and responsible upbringing (the "education" she has received first from her doctor father, then in the household of the Countess).

Parallel to the question of nature and nurture is that of divine providence and individual responsibility. Helen believes that "Our remedies oft in ourselves do lie, / Which we ascribe to heaven": like Bertram, she is a voice of modernity in her belief that individuals can carve their own destiny. She does so by means of disguise and bold solo travel: from Rossillion in southwest France to Paris, where she gains access to the King, then to Florence in the dress of a pilgrim en route to Compostela. Like Julia in *The Two Gentlemen of Verona*, Rosalind in *As You Like It*, and Viola in *Twelfth Night*, she uses her disguised self as an opportunity to talk about her true feelings. The part is the longest in the play and it gives an actor great opportunities for the portrayal of an isolated young woman's self-exploration through both soliloquy and dialogue in lucid and serpentine verse, not to mention passages of prose banter and some piercing asides.

As Dr. Johnson dryly noted, the geography seems somewhat awry when Helen undertakes her pilgrimage: in going from France to Spain via Italy, she is "somewhat out of the road." Such details did not matter to Shakespeare. For him, the pilgrim motif—taken over from the story in Boccaccio that was his source for the main plot of the play—had symbolic importance in that it associated Helen with an older value structure of reverence and self-sacrifice even as she asserts her own will. Pilgrims are people who believe in miracles, so Helen's adoption of the role allies her with the worldview voiced by the old courtier Lafew after she has cured the King: "They say miracles are past, and we have our philosophical persons to make modern and familiar, things supernatural and causeless. Hence is it that we make trifles of terrors, ensconcing ourselves into seeming knowledge when we should submit ourselves to an unknown fear."

Yet Helen is only a pretended pilgrim and the King has been cured not by a miracle but by the medical knowledge she has inherited from her father. Again and again the play takes a fairy-tale motif and turns it into something tougher, more earthly and open to philosophical debate. Lafew's generalization sets up the key scene in which Bertram rejects Helen. The idea of unquestioning obedience to the King's will is itself a thing "supernatural and causeless." It depends upon an "unknown fear," the mystique of monarchy, the idea that the King is God's representative on earth and that to challenge him will cause the entire fabric of the natural order to collapse. In a crucial rhyming couplet near the end of the play—often editorially reassigned to the Countess of Rossillion for no good textual reason—the King says that, since he has failed in his management of

Bertram's first marriage, the second had better be a success, otherwise "nature" may as well "cesse" (cease).

Shakespeare's instinctive conservatism tips the balance in favor of
the old order. The King, the Countess, and the old courtier are generous and ethically admirable, much more obviously sympathetic than
Bertram, Parolles, and Lavatch. Bertram has to be tricked out of his
sexual selfishness and Parolles out of his vainglory, but still Shakespeare the role-player and wordsmith invests huge dramatic energy
in the darker characters. He uses them to open cracks in the established order. The King tells Bertram that Helen should be viewed for
what she is within, not by way of the superficial trappings of wealth
and rank: "The property by what it is should go, / Not by the title."
Yet his own authority depends on his title, and the "go by what it is"
argument might be turned to say that if Bertram does not love Helen
he should not marry her. The King moves swiftly from reasoning to
the assertion of raw authority: "My honour's at the stake, which to
defeat, / I must produce my power." Shakespeare's intensely com-
pacted writing style makes the point. By "which to defeat," the King
means "in order to defeat the threat to my honour," but ironically
the very need to produce his "power" itself defeats the code of honor.
As so often in Shakespeare's darker plays, the figure of Niccolò
Machiavelli lurks in the shadows, whispering that fine old codes
such as honor and duty can only be underwritten by raw power.

He who asserts the new code of the self must live by that code.
Both Bertram and Parolles are found out. The two lords Dumaine are
not only mechanics in the double plot of ambush and bed trick, but
also commentators upon how their victims are brought to self-
knowledge: "As we are ourselves, what things are we! / Merely our
own traitors." The Dumaines too are young and modern in their
recognition that we cannot simply sort our kind into sheep and goats
in the manner of authoritarian religious dispensations. They propose instead that human life is shaded gray: "The web of our life is of
a mingled yarn, good and ill together: our virtues would be proud if
our faults whipped them not; and our crimes would despair if they
were not cherished by our virtues." This could be the epigraph for
Shakespeare's dramatically mingled yarn of tragicomedy.

Parolles comes to acknowledge his boastful tongue. "Simply the thing I am / Shall make me live," he vows. What, though, can this mean, given that—as his name indicates—he is made of nothing but words? Bertram, meanwhile, only comes to realize how much Helen is to be valued when she has been lost. The fiction of comedy gives him a second chance to love her. But in the modern world where there are no miracles, "all's well that ends well" *is* a fiction. Along the way we have been promised on more than one occasion that all will end well, but when it comes to the climax the King says that "all yet *seems* well" and that "*if* it end so meet" then all bitterness will be past. Those little conditional qualifiers leave open the door to the tragic world.

THE CRITICS DEBATE

Early critics regarded *All's Well* as a farce, then as a romance, then largely as a failure in psychological realism. In the nineteenth century, commentators highlighted a lack of poetry in the drama: "The style of the whole is more sententious than imaginative: the glowing colours of fancy could not with propriety have been employed on such a subject."[2]

At the turn of the nineteenth century into the twentieth, George Bernard Shaw suggested that the problem of the play was its modernity: a part such as that of Helen was "too genuine and beautiful and modern for the public."[3] In Shaw's view, Helen's independence of mind made her into a proto-feminist heroine, an anticipation of the female characters in the plays of Henrik Ibsen who sought to escape the doll's house. Shaw was reacting to the very mixed reception that had long been accorded to Helen, the fact that some had idealized her and others demonized her. Samuel Taylor Coleridge did both: on one occasion he described her as Shakespeare's "loveliest character,"[4] while on another he suggested that "Bertram had surely good reason to look upon the King's forcing him to marry Helena as a very tyrannical act. Indeed, it must be confessed that her character is not very delicate, and it required all Shakespeare's consummate skill to interest us for her."[5]

For Anna Jameson, writing in the 1830s as the first female critic to reflect at length upon Shakespeare's women, Helen exemplified the virtue of patience in the face of adversity and male infidelity: "There never was, perhaps, a more beautiful picture of a woman's love, cherished in secret, not self-consuming in silent languishment . . . but patient and hopeful, strong in its own intensity, and sustained by its own fond faith."[6] A couple of generations later, the great actress Ellen Terry begged to disagree, describing Helen as belonging to the "doormat" type: "They bear any amount of humiliation from the men they love, seem almost to enjoy being maltreated and scorned by them, and hunt them down in the most undignified way when they are trying to escape. The fraud with which Helena captures Bertram, who has left his home and country to get away from her, is really despicable."[7]

Bertram, by contrast to Helen, has always been roundly condemned by the great majority of critics. As already noted, Dr. Johnson set the tone of the debate with his remark that he could not reconcile his heart to Bertram. Coleridge tried to mount a defense, but resorted to special pleading on the grounds of status and alleged partial knowledge:

> I cannot agree with the solemn abuse which the critics have poured out upon Bertram . . . He was a young nobleman in feudal times, just bursting into manhood, with all the feelings of pride of birth, and appetite for pleasure and liberty, natural to such a character so circumstanced. Of course, he had never regarded Helena otherwise than as a dependant in the family; and of all that which she possessed of goodness and fidelity and courage, which might atone for her inferiority in other respects, Bertram was necessarily in a great measure ignorant.[8]

For twentieth-century critics, the main problem with the play was more a matter of genre and tone than of the morality of the central characters. It was suggested that there was an incongruity between the realistic characterization and the folktale or even fairy-tale plot:

Shakespeare transferred the *Decameron* story [the main source of his plot] from sunlight into shadow, not abandoning Boccaccio's naturalism, but making it problematic, turning its social and sexual givens into occasions for moral reflection and private anguish. As a result, character and motive become contradictory, and standards of judgement other than the right and natural claims of love make ironic and questionable the implications of the original.[9]

The plot contains strong folktale motifs, such as those that have been described as the Healing of the King, the Fulfillment of Tasks, and the Clever Wench. Some critics have accordingly suggested that this gives primacy to structure and plot over psychology and interior life. The play can be read as a "romantic fable" in which

the intrigues and deceptions of the plot are stressed. In order to bring out the traditional basis for the story, the movement of the play builds to three peaks, the cure of the King, the use of the bed-trick, and the redemption of Bertram. Each is accentuated as the fulfilment of a task which will lead to the resolution of the dilemma . . . Since psychological motivation is relatively unimportant, the other characters fill out the play as stock figures.[10]

Yet at the same time, a much more hard-edged reading is possible:

Considered as the basis for a serious play, the plot may expose the moral problem of birth versus merit, the social problem which explores the legitimacy of female aggression, or the domestic problems of the unwanted wife . . . If the play is regarded as satire, then cynicism infects the realism. The dark mood is established in the first scene by the stress on disease, old age and death.[11]

So it is that "the characterization of the major dramatic persons is at odds with the final tendency of the action, in which a tone of irony and often satire conflicts with the 'all's well' complacency implied by the fairy-tale elements, and in which a concrete, realistic presentation works at cross purposes with the romantic image of experience which the play seems trying to project."[12]

Such difficulties and variation in interpretation, and the perceived contradictions within both the action and the characterization, resulted in twentieth-century critics' identifying *All's Well* as one of Shakespeare's "problem" plays. This term was first used to describe the realistic dramas of the nineteenth century, those of Ibsen especially, that confronted controversial social issues by means of onstage debate, often with characters representing conflicting attitudes and points of view. The critic F. S. Boas, writing under the influence of Shaw, applied the term to *All's Well*, *Measure for Measure*, and *Troilus and Cressida*, three sex-charged plays that he thought shared an interest in social problems. Subsequent criticism applied the term more loosely, and corralled more Shakespearean plays within it, often emphasizing problems of form as well as content. *All's Well* and *Measure for Measure* in particular were seen as "problem comedies" because they did not conform to the supposed comic norm of a light touch and a happy ending. The related term "dark comedies" has also been used. So, for example, the ending was seen as a special problem. What *were* Shakespeare's intentions? Critics have fiercely debated "whether he meant Helena to be regarded as noble and admirable, or as a schemer and a harpy, why he blackened the character of Bertram and yet rewarded him at the end, and whether he meant the final reconciliation of Bertram and Helena to be taken as a prelude to future bliss, or ironically, as a union which must ultimately result in disaster."[13]

More recent criticism has continued to emphasize "problems" even as the terms of the debate have been converted into those of modern gender politics. The play has been especially amenable to analysis on these lines because it inverts the literary and dramatic norm whereby it is customarily the man who pursues the woman:

Helena has been a puzzle and provocation to critics because she occupies the masculine position of desiring subject, even as she apologises fulsomely for her unfeminine forwardness and works desperately to situate herself within the feminine position of desired object. Bertram, too, poses problems because he occupies the feminine space of the Other, even as he struggles to define himself as a man by becoming a military and sexual conqueror. He is the desired object, the end of the hero's—or in this case heroine's—gendered journey of self-fulfilment.[14]

By this account, Helen becomes one of Shakespeare's most interesting comic heroines, not least because she is given genuinely introspective soliloquies:

The intensity and extremity which have come to her from folktale . . . combine with the quality of female self-containedness with which Shakespeare seems to have been more and more concerned in the mature comedies. And from the fusion of these two things there emerges a radically new comic heroine. For Helena is *inward* . . . She is much given to secrecies and reticences.[15]

The richness of her interior life makes it surprising that the role has not been taken on by more of the major female actors of modern times.

It has long been recognized that the parallel between Bertram and Parolles is central to the structure of the play:

Both are "seemers." Grant this, and the whole sub-plot of the exposure of "Mr Words" has its place and point: Parolles is there to be stripped; and stripped at just the very moment when Bertram's fortunes reach their apogee (in his suppositious conquest of Diana) and begin to turn retrograde—towards his own exposure.[16]

With the advent of explicit feminism and the late twentieth-century war between the sexes, it became easier for critics and audiences to see not just the shadowing of Bertram in Parolles but also the broader parallelism between the sex plot and the war plot:

The shaming of Parolles runs counterpoint, in carefully matched scenes, to Bertram's attempt to seduce Diana and his own deception by the bed-trick . . . Bertram is trying to satisfy sexual relations impersonally in terms of war, translating male aggression into promiscuity, in which sex is treated as the taking and possessing of a woman's "spoil," repudiating responsibility and abandoning the woman as soon as she has surrendered.[17]

The play's explicit concern with social mobility seems equally modern in its application. Northrop Frye, one of the great twentieth-century critics, argued that *All's Well* is almost the only Shakespearean play in which there is an explicit social promotion in the foreground of the action: "It is emphasized that Helena is below Bertram in social status, and that it takes direct intervention of the king to make her marriage possible. Such a theme introduces the conception of one's 'natural place' in society, the position for which one is fitted by one's talents and social function."[18] Shakespeare perennially pitted old values and structures against new, perhaps especially so in the changed world of the first years of King James' reign, after old Queen Elizabeth's death in 1603. Northrop Frye again:

All's Well has a . . . restless feeling of social change about it, with Bertram being pulled out of the clichés of family pride in the direction of Helena's still mysterious capacities, Helena herself advancing from the background of the Roussillon household to a primary place in it, the clown Lavache turning philosophical, and the captain Parolles becoming a licensed fool in Lafeu's train . . . especially in Lavache's oracular speech, there is a faint whisper of the vision of social reversal . . . The king remains the king, of course, but when the actor playing him goes out to ask for the audience's applause, his opening line is "The king's a beggar, now the play is done."[19]

The secular social and political order jostles against an ancient, more magical and providential, way of thinking, embodied by the virtues of the older generation, who constitute Shakespeare's most striking addition to his source in Boccaccio: "The character and moral weight Shakespeare gives [the King] strengthen the effects of the Countess and Lafeu as types of old nobility: surviving exemplars of a generation, or a world, which is passing away. He is a sadly nostalgic figure."[20]

The sense of a transitional moment between two worlds helps to explain the puzzling tone of the ending. Beside the tragic potential there are elements of magical restitution and regeneration akin to those in Shakespeare's late romances such as *The Winter's Tale* and *Pericles*. There is a progression from Helen's miraculous cure of the King to her own "resurrection" and the (apparent?) moral regeneration of Bertram. As the King comes close to death and Helen is supposed to have died but returns home to become a wife, so "Parolles, who blindfolded has heard the order for his own execution, discovers when his blindfold is removed—symbolically as well as actually—that he is not really going to be killed. Bertram, too . . . is recalled from death in the course of the play."[21] *All's Well* is a complex drama of both death and new life:

> There is the current of self-wasting energy . . . symbolized by Bertram's self-will, Parolles' lack of heroism, and Lavache's vision of the great mass of people drifting to the "broad gate and the great fire." There is also the reversal of this current of energy backward into a renewed and creative life. The play opens with older characters "all in black," talking mainly about the dead; it proceeds through the healing of an impotent king . . . Helena rejuvenates the family, the king, and may even rejuvenate Bertram's fixated notions of family honour and tradition.[22]

Certainly the play offers an explicit challenge to its own title, the old comic idea of all's well that ends well:

> From a "universal" point of view, we may see the dramatic world thrown into disorder and confusion by Helena's elaborate introduction of half-truths and then miraculously restored to

order and sanity when Helena herself comes forward, returned from the dead, to dispense a spirit of love and charity. But even so, there is Bertram—deceitful, vindictive, petty—a very real and unpleasant fly in the ointment of universal forgiveness.[23]

But ultimately, in the words of John Barton, among the most critically astute of modern Shakespearean directors, "'cynical' isn't quite the right word for the ending: the tone is more one of a worldly tolerance of people."[24]

ABOUT THE TEXT

Shakespeare endures through history. He illuminates later times as well as his own. He helps us to understand the human condition. But he cannot do this without a good text of the plays. Without editions there would be no Shakespeare. That is why every twenty years or so throughout the last three centuries there has been a major new edition of his complete works. One aspect of editing is the process of keeping the texts up to date—modernizing the spelling, punctuation, and typography (though not, of course, the actual words), providing explanatory notes in the light of changing educational practices (a generation ago, most of Shakespeare's classical and biblical allusions could be assumed to be generally understood, but now they can't).

Because Shakespeare did not personally oversee the publication of his plays, with some plays there are major editorial difficulties. Decisions have to be made as to the relative authority of the early printed editions, the pocket format "Quartos" published in Shakespeare's lifetime and the elaborately produced "First Folio" text of 1623, the original "Complete Works" prepared for the press after his death by Shakespeare's fellow actors, the people who knew the plays better than anyone else. *All's Well That Ends Well* exists only in a Folio text that is problematic in some aspects and suggests a rather difficult-to-read manuscript was used as printer's copy (see "Key Facts").

The following notes highlight various aspects of the editorial process and indicate conventions used in the text of this edition:

Lists of Parts are supplied in the First Folio for only six plays, not including *All's Well That Ends Well*, so the list here is editorially supplied. Capitals indicate that part of the name used for speech headings in the script (thus "BERTRAM, Count of Rossillion").

Locations are provided by Folio for only two plays, of which *All's Well That Ends Well* is not one. Eighteenth-century editors, working in an age of elaborately realistic stage sets, were the first to provide detailed locations ("*another part of the city*"). Given that Shakespeare wrote for a bare stage and often an imprecise sense of place, we have relegated locations to the explanatory notes at the foot of the page, where they are given at the beginning of each scene where the imaginary location is different from the one before.

Act and Scene Divisions were provided in the Folio in a much more thoroughgoing way than in the Quartos. Sometimes, however, they were erroneous or omitted; corrections and additions supplied by editorial tradition are indicated by square brackets. Five-act division is based on a classical model, and act breaks provided the opportunity to replace the candles in the indoor Blackfriars playhouse which the King's Men used after 1608, but Shakespeare did not necessarily think in terms of a five-part structure of dramatic composition. The Folio convention is that a scene ends when the stage is empty. Nowadays, partly under the influence of film, we tend to consider a scene to be a dramatic unit that ends with either a change of imaginary location or a significant passage of time within the narrative. Shakespeare's fluidity of composition accords well with this convention, so in addition to act and scene numbers we provide a *running scene* count in the right margin at the beginning of each new scene, in the typeface used for editorial directions. Where there is a scene break caused by a momentary bare stage, but the location does not change and extra time does not pass, we use the convention *running scene continues*. There is inevitably a degree of editorial judgment in making such calls, but the system is very valuable in suggesting the pace of the plays.

Speakers' Names are often inconsistent in Folio. We have regularized speech headings, but retained an element of deliberate inconsistency in entry directions, in order to give the flavor of Folio. Thus BERTRAM is always so-called in his speech headings, but is often referred to as "Count of Rossillion," "Count Rossillion," or "Count" in entry directions.

Verse is indicated by lines that do not run to the right margin and by capitalization of each line. The Folio printers sometimes set verse as prose, and vice versa (either out of misunderstanding or for reasons of space). We have silently corrected in such cases, although in some instances there is ambiguity, in which case we have leaned toward the preservation of Folio layout. Folio sometimes uses contraction ("turnd" rather than "turned") to indicate whether or not the final "-ed" of a past participle is sounded, an area where there is variation for the sake of the five-beat iambic pentameter rhythm. We use the convention of a grave accent to indicate sounding (thus "turnèd" would be two syllables), but would urge actors not to overstress. In cases where one speaker ends with a verse half line and the next begins with the other half of the pentameter, editors since the late eighteenth century have indented the second line. We have abandoned this convention, since the Folio does not use it, nor did actors' cues in the Shakespearean theater. An exception is made when the second speaker actively interrupts or completes the first speaker's sentence.

Spelling is modernized, but older forms are very occasionally maintained where necessary for rhythm or aural effect.

Punctuation in Shakespeare's time was as much rhetorical as grammatical. "Colon" was originally a term for a unit of thought in an argument. The semicolon was a new unit of punctuation (some of the Quartos lack them altogether). We have modernized punctuation throughout, but have given more weight to Folio punctuation than many editors, since, though not Shakespearean, it reflects the usage of his period. In particular, we have used the colon far more than many editors: it is exceptionally useful as a way of indicating how many Shakespearean speeches unfold clause by clause in a developing argument that gives the illusion of enacting the process of thinking in the moment. We have also kept in mind the origin of punctuation in classical times as a way of assisting the actor and orator: the comma suggests the briefest of pauses for breath, the colon a middling one, and a full stop or period a longer pause. Semicolons, by contrast, belong to an era of punctuation that was only just coming in during Shakespeare's time and that is coming to an end now: we have accordingly only used them where they occur in our copy texts (and not always then). Dashes are sometimes used for parenthetical interjections where the Folio has brackets. They are also used for interruptions and changes in train of thought. Where a change of addressee occurs within a speech, we have used a dash preceded by a period (or occasionally another form of punctuation). Often the identity of the respective addressees is obvious from the context. When it is not, this has been indicated in a marginal stage direction.

Entrances and Exits are fairly thorough in Folio, which has accordingly been followed as faithfully as possible. Where characters are omitted or corrections are necessary, this is indicated by square brackets (e.g. "[*and Attendants*]"). *Exit* is sometimes silently normalized to *Exeunt* and *Manet* anglicized to "remains." We trust Folio positioning of entrances and exits to a greater degree than most editors.

Editorial Stage Directions such as stage business, asides, indications of addressee and of characters' position on the gallery stage are only used sparingly in Folio. Other editions mingle directions of this kind with original Folio and Quarto directions, sometimes marking them by means of square brackets. We have sought to distinguish what could be described as *directorial* interventions of this kind from Folio-style directions (either original or supplied) by placing them in the right margin in a different typeface. There is a degree of subjectivity about which directions are of which kind, but the procedure is intended as a reminder to the reader and the actor that Shakespearean stage directions are often dependent upon editorial inference alone and are not set in stone. We also depart from editorial tradition in sometimes admitting uncertainty and thus printing permissive stage directions, such as an ***Aside?*** (often a line may be equally effective as an aside or as a direct address—it is for each production or reading to make its own decision) or a ***may exit*** or a piece of business placed between arrows to indicate that it may occur at various different moments within a scene.

Line Numbers in the left margin are editorial, for reference and to key the explanatory and textual notes.

Explanatory Notes at the foot of each page explain allusions and gloss obsolete and difficult words, confusing phraseology, occasional major textual cruces, and so on. Particular attention is given to non-standard usage, bawdy innuendo, and technical terms (e.g. legal and military language). Where more than one sense is given, commas indicate shades of related meaning, slashes alternative or double meanings.

Textual Notes at the end of the play indicate major departures from the Folio. They take the following form: the reading of our text is given in bold and its source given after an equals sign with "F2" indicating a correction that derives from the Second Folio of 1632, "F3" a correction from the Third Folio of 1663–64, "F4" one from the Fourth Folio of 1685, and "Ed" one that derives from the subsequent editorial tradition. The rejected Folio ("F") reading is then given. Thus for Act 2 Scene 5 line 30: "**2.5.30 heard** = F2. F = hard" means we have adopted F2's "heard" instead of Folio's "hard" in the phrase "should be once heard and thrice beaten," judging that it makes better sense of the line and that "hard" was either a scribal or compositorial error.

MAJOR PARTS: (*with percentages of lines/number of speeches/scenes onstage*) Helen (16%/109/12), Parolles (13%/141/11), King of France (13%/87/4), Countess (10%/86/7), Bertram (9%/102/10), Lafew (9%/97/7), Lavatch (7%/58/6), First Lord Dumaine (5%/70/7), Second Lord Dumaine (4%/47/6), Diana (4%/44/4), First Soldier/Interpreter (3%/37/2), Widow (2%/21/5).

LINGUISTIC MEDIUM: 55% verse, 45% prose.

DATE: No external evidence to indicate when written or first performed; usually dated to early Jacobean years (1603–06) on stylistic grounds and because of similarity to *Measure for Measure*. Moments of anti-puritan satire do not help in determining a specific date.

SOURCES: Main plot derived from Giovanni Boccaccio's *Decameron* (Italian, fourteenth century) by way of William Painter's English translation, *The Palace of Pleasure* (1566); Countess and Lafew are Shakespeare's invention, as is Parolles, who is in the tradition of the braggart soldier of classical comedy—a character type of which the greatest Elizabethan examples were Falstaff in *Henry IV* and Captain Bobadil in Ben Jonson's *Every Man in His Humour*.

TEXT: First Folio of 1623 is only early printed text. Many features such as misassigned speeches, repeated speech headings, inconsistent naming, and probably misplaced lines suggest that the manuscript was not neatly prepared and that it caused confusion to the printers. Apparent authorial first thoughts suggest influence of Shakespeare's working manuscript, while music cues suggest that of the theatrical promptbook. Of the many textual problems, the most frustrating concerns the two lords/brothers Dumaine: they have several different designations, variants on "1 Lord G." and "2 Lord E.," "French E." and "French G.," "Captain G." and "Captain E." The initials are sometimes supposed to refer to actors' names. Shakespeare sometimes seems to forget whether "G." is "1" and "E." is "2" or vice versa. This means, for instance, that there is confusion over which brother leads the ambush of Parolles and which accompanies Bertram as he sets off to seduce Diana. We have adopted a solution that is dramatically consistent while requiring only minimal alteration of Folio's speech ascriptions.

ALL'S WELL THAT
ENDS WELL

LIST OF PARTS

BERTRAM, Count of Rossillion

COUNTESS of Rossillion, his mother

HELEN (occasionally known as Helena), an orphan in the protection of the countess

REYNALDO, steward to the countess

LAVATCH, clown in the countess' household

PAROLLES, a boastful follower of Bertram

KING of France

LAFEW, an old French lord

GENTLEMEN of the French court including an Astringer

FIRST LORD Dumaine ⎫
SECOND LORD Dumaine ⎬ brothers who become captains in the Florentine army
⎭

FIRST SOLDIER, who plays role of interpreter

DUKE of Florence

WIDOW, Capilet of Florence

DIANA, her daughter

MARIANA, her friend

Lords, Attendants including a Page, Soldiers, people of Florence

---

Act 1 Scene 1

Enter young Bertram, [the] Count of Rossillion, his mother [the Countess], and Helena, Lord Lafew, all in black

COUNTESS   In delivering my son from me, I bury a second husband.

BERTRAM   And I in going, madam, weep o'er my father's death anew; but I must attend his majesty's command, to whom I

5   am now in ward, evermore in subjection.

LAFEW   You shall find of the king a husband, madam, you, sir, a father. He that so generally is at all times good must of

---

List of parts   HELEN perhaps named after Helen of Troy, reputedly the most beautiful woman in the world and the cause of a great war   LAFEW some editions modernize to "lafeu" (*feu*, French for "fire")   **1.1   *Location: Rossillion (now Roussillon), ancient province in southern France, near the Pyrenees mountains*   1 delivering** sending forth (plays on the sense of "giving birth")   **4 attend** obey, heed   **5 in ward** under guardianship (as a minor who has inherited property)   **subjection** obedience, servitude as a subject/legal obligation   **6 of in   husband** i.e. protector   **7 generally** universally/to everyone necessity hold his virtue to you, whose worthiness would stir it up where it wanted rather than lack it where there is such abundance.

COUNTESS   What hope is there of his majesty's amendment?

LAFEW   He hath abandoned his physicians, madam, under whose practices he hath persecuted time with hope, and finds no other advantage in the process but only the losing of hope by time.

COUNTESS   This young gentlewoman had a father — O, that 'had'! How sad a passage 'tis! — whose skill was almost as great as his honesty, had it stretched so far, would have made nature immortal, and death should have play for lack of work. Would for the king's sake he were living! I think it would be the death of the king's disease.

LAFEW   How called you the man you speak of, madam?

COUNTESS   He was famous, sir, in his profession, and it was his great right to be so: Gerard de Narbon.

LAFEW   He was excellent indeed, madam. The king very lately spoke of him admiringly and mourningly: he was skilful enough to have lived still, if knowledge could be set up against mortality.

BERTRAM   What is it, my good lord, the king languishes of?

LAFEW   A fistula, my lord.

BERTRAM   I heard not of it before.

LAFEW   I would it were not notorious. Was this gentlewoman the daughter of Gerard de Narbon?

COUNTESS   His sole child, my lord, and bequeathed to my overlooking. I have those hopes of her good that her education promises her dispositions she inherits, which

---

8 hold maintain   virtue benevolence   whose i.e. the Countess and Bertram   stir . . . wanted provoke it even in those who lacked generosity   9 where . . . abundance i.e. in the king   11 amendment recovery   13 practices medical treatments   persecuted time tormented his days/drawn out his suffering   17 passage turn of phrase/transition/event/death   18 honesty honor, integrity   20 Would I wish   24 Narbon Narbonne, southern French city near province of Roussillon   27 still yet/for ever   30 fistula ulcer   32 notorious widely known/evident   35 overlooking guardianship   hopes . . . good i.e. high hopes for her   36 education upbringing   dispositions natural talents

makes fair gifts fairer. For where an unclean mind carries virtuous qualities, there commendations go with pity, they are virtues and traitors too. In her they are the better for
40   their simpleness; she derives her honesty and achieves her goodness.

LAFEW   Your commendations, madam, get from her tears.

COUNTESS   'Tis the best brine a maiden can season her praise in. The remembrance of her father never approaches her
45   heart but the tyranny of her sorrows takes all livelihood from her cheek. No more of this, Helena. Go to, no more, lest it be rather thought you affect a sorrow than to have.

HELEN   I do affect a sorrow indeed, but I have it too.

LAFEW   Moderate lamentation is the right of the dead,
50   excessive grief the enemy to the living.

COUNTESS   If the living be enemy to the grief, the excess makes it soon mortal.

BERTRAM   Madam, I desire your holy wishes.

LAFEW   How understand we that?

55   COUNTESS   Be thou blest, Bertram, and succeed thy father
In manners as in shape. Thy blood and virtue
Contend for empire in thee, and thy goodness
Share with thy birthright. Love all, trust a few,
Do wrong to none. Be able for thine enemy
60   Rather in power than use, and keep thy friend
Under thy own life's key. Be checked for silence,
But never taxed for speech. What heaven more will,

---

37 unclean naturally corrupted   **38 virtuous qualities** fine learned accomplishments   **go with pity** are mingled with regret   **40 simpleness** unaffected simplicity (i.e. not mixed with vice)   **derives** inherits   **43 season** preserve/flavor   **45 livelihood** animation   **46 Go to** expression of dismissal (i.e. "come come")   **47 affect** assume/pretend to have   **than to have** rather than genuinely feel one   **49 of** due to   **51 If . . . mortal** i.e. if resisted, overabundant grief quickly dies   **53 holy** sacred/respected   **54 How . . . that?** What does that mean? (some editors suppose the line is displaced and that it may be a response to Helen or the Countess, not Bertram)   **56 manners** good conduct   **shape** physical appearance   **Thy** may thy   **blood** nobility/parentage   **57 empire** rule   **58 birthright** inherited qualities   **59 able** ready/powerful enough   **60 power** ability, potential   **keep . . . key** value your friend's life as dearly as your own   **61 checked** rebuked   **62 taxed** censured   **What** whatever   **more will** wishes to give you in addition

That thee may furnish and my prayers pluck down,
Fall on thy head! Farewell.— My lord,   *To Lafew*
65   'Tis an unseasoned courtier. Good my lord,
Advise him.

LAFEW   He cannot want the best
That shall attend his love.

COUNTESS   Heaven bless him.— Farewell, Bertram.   [*Exit*]

70   BERTRAM   The best wishes that can be forged in your   *To Helen*
thoughts be servants to you! Be comfortable to my mother,
your mistress, and make much of her.

LAFEW   Farewell, pretty lady. You must hold the credit of
your father.   [*Exeunt Bertram and Lafew*]

75   HELEN   O, were that all! I think not on my father,
And these great tears grace his remembrance more
Than those I shed for him. What was he like?
I have forgot him. My imagination
Carries no favour in't but Bertram's.
80   I am undone. There is no living, none,
If Bertram be away. 'Twere all one
That I should love a bright particular star
And think to wed it, he is so above me.
In his bright radiance and collateral light
85   Must I be comforted, not in his sphere;
Th'ambition in my love thus plagues itself:
The hind that would be mated by the lion
Must die for love. 'Twas pretty, though a plague,
To see him every hour, to sit and draw

63 pluck draw   65 unseasoned inexperienced   67 want lack   best i.e. best advice   68 his
love my love for him   70 forged created, imagined   71 comfortable comforting, supportive
72 make much of be attentive to   73 hold maintain   credit reputation/honor
76 these . . . him i.e. the floods of tears she is shedding because of her unrequited love for
Bertram do more honor to her father's memory than did the (fewer) tears wept at his death
79 favour image, face (puns on the sense of "love token")   80 undone ruined   81 'Twere . . .
That it is the same as if   84 collateral parallel but distant   85 sphere orbit (heavenly bodies
were thought to be surrounded by hollow spheres that produced beautiful music as they
rotated)   87 hind female deer (puns on sense of "servant")   88 pretty pleasing

90   His archèd brows, his hawking eye, his curls
        In our heart's table — heart too capable
        Of every line and trick of his sweet favour:
        But now he's gone, and my idolatrous fancy
        Must sanctify his relics. Who comes here?

        Enter Parolles

95   One that goes with him: I love him for his sake,   *Aside*
        And yet I know him a notorious liar,
        Think him a great way fool, solely a coward.
        Yet these fixed evils sit so fit in him
        That they take place when virtue's steely bones
100   Looks bleak i'th'cold wind. Withal, full oft we see
        Cold wisdom waiting on superfluous folly.

PAROLLES   Save you, fair queen!

HELEN   And you, monarch!

PAROLLES   No.

105 HELEN   And no.

PAROLLES   Are you meditating on virginity?

HELEN   Ay. You have some stain of soldier in you. Let me ask
            you a question. Man is enemy to virginity: how may we
            barricado it against him?

110 PAROLLES   Keep him out.

HELEN   But he assails, and our virginity, though valiant, in
            the defence yet is weak. Unfold to us some warlike resistance.

PAROLLES   There is none. Man setting down before you will
            undermine you and blow you up.

---

90 hawking sharp, keen   **91 table** notebook, drawing tablet   **capable** appreciative, sensitive
92 trick distinguishing feature   **favour** face   **93 fancy** love/infatuation   **94 relics** i.e.
memory   *Parolles* i.e. "words," from French *paroles*   **95 his** i.e. Bertram's   **97 great way**
complete   **solely** wholly   **98 fixed** certain, established   **fit** suitably   **99 take place** take
precedence/are accepted   **steely** i.e. hard, uncompromising   **100 Looks . . . wind** are left out
in the cold/look pale, unappealing   **Withal** therefore   **full oft** very often   **101 waiting on**
attending, deferring to   **superfluous** extravagant, overabundant   **102 Save** God save
queen may play on "quean" (i.e. prostitute)   **107 stain** hint/taint   **109 barricado** barricade
110 Keep ensure he stays (plays on the sense of "build a fortified tower")   **112 Unfold** reveal
113 setting . . . you besieging you (with sexual connotations)   **114 undermine** overthrow/dig
underneath to lay mines/burrow into sexually   **blow you up** cause an explosion/make you
pregnant

115 HELEN   Bless our poor virginity from underminers and blowers up! Is there no military policy how virgins might blow up men?

PAROLLES   Virginity being blown down, man will quicklier be blown up. Marry, in blowing him down again, with the
120 breach yourselves made, you lose your city. It is not politic in the commonwealth of nature to preserve virginity. Loss of virginity is rational increase, and there was never virgin got till virginity was first lost. That you were made of is mettle to make virgins. Virginity by being once lost may be ten times
125 found. By being ever kept, it is ever lost. 'Tis too cold a companion. Away with't!

HELEN   I will stand for't a little, though therefore I die a virgin.

PAROLLES   There's little can be said in't, 'tis against the rule of
130 nature. To speak on the part of virginity is to accuse your mothers, which is most infallible disobedience. He that hangs himself is a virgin: virginity murders itself and should be buried in highways out of all sanctified limit, as a desperate offendress against nature. Virginity breeds mites,
135 much like a cheese, consumes itself to the very paring, and so dies with feeding his own stomach. Besides, virginity is peevish, proud, idle, made of self-love, which is the most inhibited sin in the canon. Keep it not, you cannot choose

---

115 **Bless** (may God) protect   116 **policy** stratagem   118 **be blown up** gain an erection/ have an orgasm   119 **Marry** by the Virgin Mary   **blowing him down** inducing his orgasm, and subsequent loss of erection   120 **breach** vagina/hole in defenses   **city** i.e. virginity   **politic** prudent/strategic   122 **rational increase** logical profit-making/an increase in rational beings through reproduction   **got** begotten, conceived   123 **That** that which   **mettle** substance/coinage (indistinguishable from "metal" in Shakespearean usage)   125 **found** i.e. duplicated in reproduction (by producing ten virgins)   **cold** chaste   127 **stand for't** defend it   129 **in't** in its defense   130 **part** behalf (puns on the sense of "genitals")   131 **infallible** certain   **He . . . virgin** i.e. like a virgin who refuses to reproduce, a crime likened to suicide   133 **highways . . . limit** traditionally suicides were buried at crossroads, in unconsecrated ground   134 **desperate** reckless/dangerous   **offendress** female offender   135 **paring** rind   136 **his** its   **stomach** appetite/pride   137 **peevish** stubborn, perverse   138 **inhibited** prohibited   **canon** list of Church laws

but lose by't. Out with't! Within ten year it will make itself
140 two, which is a goodly increase, and the principal itself not
much the worse. Away with't!

HELEN   How might one do, sir, to lose it to her own liking?

PAROLLES   Let me see. Marry, ill, to like him that ne'er it likes.
'Tis a commodity will lose the gloss with lying: the longer
145 kept, the less worth. Off with't while 'tis vendible. Answer
the time of request. Virginity, like an old courtier, wears her
cap out of fashion: richly suited but unsuitable, just like the
brooch and the toothpick, which wear not now. Your date is
better in your pie and your porridge than in your cheek. And
150 your virginity, your old virginity, is like one of our French
withered pears: it looks ill, it eats dryly. Marry, 'tis a withered
pear: it was formerly better: marry, yet 'tis a withered pear.
Will you anything with it?

HELEN   Not my virginity yet —
155 There shall your master have a thousand loves,
A mother and a mistress and a friend,
A phoenix, captain and an enemy,
A guide, a goddess, and a sovereign,
A counsellor, a traitress, and a dear.
160 His humble ambition, proud humility,
His jarring concord, and his discord dulcet,
His faith, his sweet disaster. With a world

---

139 lose fail to profit (puns on the idea of "losing" one's virginity)   **Out with't!** Away with it!/
put it out to interest   **make itself two** double in value (by increasing at rate of 10 percent per
year)   **140 principal** initial investment   **142 How** what   **143 it** i.e. virginity   **144 gloss**
freshness/shine   **lying** remaining unused (may play on the sense of "lying down")
145 vendible salable, marketable   **Answer . . . request** respond to current consumer demand
147 suited dressed   **unsuitable** unfashionable   **148 toothpick** ornate toothpicks were
fashionable for a period   **wear not** are not in fashion   **date** fruit/age/penis   **149 pie** with
vaginal connotations   **porridge** stew (with vaginal connotations)   **in your cheek** i.e. as sign
of increasing age   **151 pears** with vaginal connotations   **eats dryly** tastes dry   **155 There**
i.e. at court   **156 mother** here begins a list of names and relationships found in love poetry
157 phoenix i.e. paragon, wonder (literally, mythical Arabian bird that was consumed by fire
every five hundred years, then resurrected from the ashes; only one existed at a time)
161 concord harmony   **dulcet** sweet   **162 disaster** unlucky star

Of pretty, fond, adoptious christendoms
That blinking Cupid gossips. Now shall he —
165   I know not what he shall. God send him well!
The court's a learning place, and he is one—

PAROLLES   What one, i'faith?

HELEN   That I wish well. 'Tis pity—

PAROLLES   What's pity?

170   HELEN   That wishing well had not a body in't,
Which might be felt, that we, the poorer born,
Whose baser stars do shut us up in wishes,
Might with effects of them follow our friends,
And show what we alone must think, which never
175   Returns us thanks.

Enter Page

PAGE   Monsieur Parolles, my lord calls for you.   [*Exit*]

PAROLLES   Little Helen, farewell. If I can remember thee, I will
think of thee at court.

HELEN   Monsieur Parolles, you were born under a
charitable star.

180   PAROLLES   Under Mars, ay.

HELEN   I especially think, under Mars.

PAROLLES   Why under Mars?

HELEN   The wars hath so kept you under that you must
needs be born under Mars.

185   PAROLLES   When he was predominant.

HELEN   When he was retrograde, I think rather.

PAROLLES   Why think you so?

HELEN   You go so much backward when you fight.

PAROLLES   That's for advantage.

---

163 fond affectionate/foolish   **adoptious** adopted   **christendoms** baptismal (Christian)
names   **164 blinking** blind   **gossips** is godparent to   **165 well** fortune   **170 body** i.e.
something tangible   **172 baser stars** lesser fortunes   **shut . . . in** confine us to   **173 effects
of them** i.e. fulfilled wishes   **174 alone must think** must only think (not do)   **175 Returns us
thanks** give us gratitude, reward   **180 Mars** Roman god of war   **ay** "I" in Folio, but likely to
be heard by the audience as an ironic "yes" (Mars not being not known for charity)
183 under down/in a lowly position   **185 predominant** in the ascendant, dominant
186 retrograde moving in a contrary direction, backward   **188 backward** i.e. in retreat,
fleeing the enemy   **189 advantage** tactical gain (Helen shifts the sense to "personal interest")

190   HELEN   So is running away, when fear proposes the safety.
              But the composition that your valour and fear makes in you
              is a virtue of a good wing, and I like the wear well.

      PAROLLES   I am so full of businesses, I cannot answer thee
              acutely. I will return perfect courtier in the which, my
195   instruction shall serve to naturalize thee, so thou wilt
              be capable of a courtier's counsel and understand what
              advice shall thrust upon thee. Else thou diest in thine
              unthankfulness, and thine ignorance makes thee away.
              Farewell. When thou hast leisure, say thy prayers. When
200   thou hast none, remember thy friends. Get thee a good
              husband, and use him as he uses thee. So, farewell.   [*Exit*]

      HELEN   Our remedies oft in ourselves do lie,
              Which we ascribe to heaven. The fated sky
              Gives us free scope, only doth backward pull
205   Our slow designs when we ourselves are dull.
              What power is it which mounts my love so high,
              That makes me see, and cannot feed mine eye?
              The mightiest space in fortune nature brings
              To join like likes and kiss like native things.
210   Impossible be strange attempts to those
              That weigh their pains in sense and do suppose
              What hath been cannot be. Who ever strove
              To show her merit that did miss her love?
              The king's disease — my project may deceive me,
215   But my intents are fixed and will not leave me.
              Exit

191 **composition** mixture/constitution (plays on the sense of "truce")   192 **wing** ability to fly
swiftly/jacket's shoulder flap (may pun on the sense of "flank of troops")   **wear** fashion
194 **perfect** (the) complete   **in the which** i.e. in which manner   195 **naturalize** accustom
196 **capable of** receptive to/have (sexual) capacity for   197 **thrust** with sexual connotations
198 **makes thee away** sees you off   199 **leisure** opportunity   201 **use** treat/employ sexually
203 **fated** fateful/with power over destiny   205 **designs** undertakings/plans   **dull** sluggish
207 **feed** satisfy (my longing)   208 **The** across the   **space in fortune** gap in social status/
difference in fortunes   209 **like likes** kindred affections   **native** closely related/of similar
rank/natural   210 **strange attempts** extraordinary endeavors (to be united)   211 **weigh . . .**
sense evaluate their efforts according to common sense   213 **miss** fail to achieve

[Act 1 Scene 2]   *running scene 2*

Flourish cornets. Enter the King of France, with letters, and divers
Attendants

KING   The Florentines and Senoys are by th'ears,
              Have fought with equal fortune and continue
              A braving war.
FIRST LORD   So 'tis reported, sir.
5 KING   Nay, 'tis most credible. We here receive it
              A certainty, vouched from our cousin Austria,
              With caution that the Florentine will move us
              For speedy aid, wherein our dearest friend
              Prejudicates the business and would seem
10   To have us make denial.
FIRST LORD   His love and wisdom,
              Approved so to your majesty, may plead
              For amplest credence.
KING   He hath armed our answer,
15   And Florence is denied before he comes:
              Yet, for our gentlemen that mean to see
              The Tuscan service, freely have they leave
              To stand on either part.
SECOND LORD   It well may serve
20   A nursery to our gentry, who are sick
              For breathing and exploit.
KING   What's he comes here?
Enter Bertram, Lafew and Parolles
FIRST LORD   It is the Count Rossillion, my good lord,
              Young Bertram.

1.2   Location: Paris   *Flourish* fanfare, usually accompanying a person in authority
divers various   **1 Florentines** people from Florence (northern Italian city, capital of Tuscany)
Senoys people from Siena   **by th'ears** at odds, fighting   **3 braving** defiant   **6 cousin** fellow
monarch of   **7 move** urge, appeal to   **8 dearest friend** i.e. Austria   **9 Prejudicates**
prejudges   **10 make denial** i.e. deny aid to the Florentines   **12 Approved** established, proved
13 credence trust   **14 armed** fortified (against entreaties)   **15 Florence** ruler of Florence
16 for as for   **see** i.e. take part in   **17 service** military service   **18 stand** serve, fight   **part**
side   **20 nursery** training ground   **sick** longing   **21 breathing and exploit** active military
employment

25   KING   Youth, thou bear'st thy father's face.   *To Bertram*
           Frank nature, rather curious than in haste,
           Hath well composed thee. Thy father's moral parts
           Mayst thou inherit too! Welcome to Paris.
     BERTRAM   My thanks and duty are your majesty's.
30   KING   I would I had that corporal soundness now,
           As when thy father and myself in friendship
           First tried our soldiership. He did look far
           Into the service of the time and was
           Discipled of the bravest. He lasted long,
35   But on us both did haggish age steal on
           And wore us out of act. It much repairs me
           To talk of your good father; in his youth
           He had the wit which I can well observe
           Today in our young lords. But they may jest
40   Till their own scorn return to them unnoted
           Ere they can hide their levity in honour.
           So like a courtier, contempt nor bitterness
           Were in his pride or sharpness; if they were,
           His equal had awaked them, and his honour,
45   Clock to itself, knew the true minute when
           Exception bid him speak, and at this time
           His tongue obeyed his hand. Who were below him
           He used as creatures of another place
           And bowed his eminent top to their low ranks,
50   Making them proud of his humility,
           In their poor praise he humbled. Such a man

---

26 Frank generous   **rather . . . haste** more fastidious than hasty   **27 parts** qualities
30 corporal soundess good physical health   **32 tried** tested   **did . . . service** had deep
knowledge of military matters   **33 was Discipled of** taught/was taught by   **34 bravest**
boldest/finest/noblest   **35 haggish** haglike, repulsive/frosty   **36 out of act** down beyond
action   **repairs** restores, revives   **40 scorn** mockery   **return . . . unnoted** goes unheeded/is
visited back upon them   **41 Ere** before   **levity in honour** lightheartedness in honorable
action   **42 contempt** neither contempt   **44 equal** i.e. social equal   **awaked** provoked
45 Clock to itself true to itself, reliable, self-governing   **true** exact   **46 Exception** grievance/
disapproval   **47 hand** hand of action/hand of his honor's clock, showing the appropriate
time   **Who** those who   **48 used** treated   **another place** different (higher) rank   **49 top**
head   **51 humbled** humbled himself

Might be a copy to these younger times;
Which, followed well, would demonstrate them now
But goers backward.

55   BERTRAM   His good remembrance, sir,
Lies richer in your thoughts than on his tomb,
So in approof lives not his epitaph
As in your royal speech.

KING   Would I were with him! He would always say —
60   Methinks I hear him now. His plausive words
He scattered not in ears, but grafted them,
To grow there and to bear — 'Let me not live' —
This his good melancholy oft began
On the catastrophe and heel of pastime,
65   When it was out — 'Let me not live,' quoth he,
'After my flame lacks oil, to be the snuff
Of younger spirits, whose apprehensive senses
All but new things disdain; whose judgements are
Mere fathers of their garments, whose constancies
70   Expire before their fashions.' This he wished.
I, after him, do after him wish too,
Since I nor wax nor honey can bring home,
I quickly were dissolvèd from my hive
To give some labourers room.

75   SECOND LORD   You're loved, sir.
They that least lend it you shall lack you first.

KING   I fill a place, I know't. How long is't, count,
Since the physician at your father's died?
He was much famed.

---

52 **copy** example/model   53 **them . . . backward** men of today to be merely inferior
57 **So . . . epitaph** his epitaph is nowhere so profoundly confirmed   **approof** proof,
experience/approbation   60 **plausive** praising   61 **scattered not** did not disperse randomly
grafted cultivated deliberately   62 **bear** i.e. bear fruit   64 **On . . . heel** at the conclusion and
end   **pastime** entertainment, leisure activity   65 **out** over   66 **snuff** burnt-out wick/
hindrance   67 **apprehensive** perceptive/quick-witted   69 **Mere . . . garments** only capable
of inventing new fashions   **constancies** loyalties   71 **I . . . too** I, surviving him, also wish
(plays on idea of following into death)   72 **nor** neither   73 **were** would be   **dissolvèd**
released   74 **labourers** productive worker bees   76 **lend** show, give   **it** i.e. love   **lack** miss

80 BERTRAM   Some six months since, my lord.

KING   If he were living, I would try him yet.

Lend me an arm: the rest have worn me out

With several applications. Nature and sickness

Debate it at their leisure. Welcome, count.

85 My son's no dearer.

BERTRAM   Thank your majesty.   *Exeunt. Flourish*

[Act 1 Scene 3]   *running scene 3*

Enter Countess, Steward [Reynaldo] and Clown [Lavatch]

COUNTESS   I will now hear; what say you of this gentlewoman?

REYNALDO   Madam, the care I have had to even your content, I
wish might be found in the calendar of my past endeavours,
for then we wound our modesty, and make foul the clearness

5 of our deservings, when of ourselves we publish them.

COUNTESS   What does this knave here? Get you gone, sirrah.
The complaints I have heard of you I do not all believe. 'Tis
my slowness that I do not, for I know you lack not folly to
commit them, and have ability enough to make such

10 knaveries yours.

LAVATCH   'Tis not unknown to you, madam, I am a poor
fellow.

COUNTESS   Well, sir.

LAVATCH   No, madam, 'tis not so well that I am poor, though
many of the rich are damned. But if I may have your

15 ladyship's good will to go to the world, Isbel the woman and
I will do as we may.

---

82 **the rest** i.e. other physicians   83 **several** various   **applications** treatments   84 **Debate**
contend over   **it** i.e. his health   **1.3   *Location: Rossillion*   *Lavatch* probably from the
French *la vache* ("the cow")   1 **gentlewoman** i.e. Helen   2 **even your content** please you
3 **calendar** record   4 **clearness** purity   5 **deservings** merits, deserts   **of . . . them** we speak
openly of our own merits   6 **sirrah** sir (used to a social inferior)   11 **poor** wretched, humble
(sense then shifts to "impoverished")   12 **Well** i.e. go on (Lavatch shifts the sense to
"satisfactory")   15 **go . . . world** i.e. get married   **Isbel** typical name for a whore   **woman**
female servant/whore   16 **do** act/have sex

COUNTESS   Wilt thou needs be a beggar?

LAVATCH   I do beg your good will in this case.

COUNTESS   In what case?

20   LAVATCH   In Isbel's case and mine own. Service is no heritage: and I think I shall never have the blessing of God till I have issue o'my body, for they say bairns are blessings.

COUNTESS   Tell me thy reason why thou wilt marry.

LAVATCH   My poor body, madam, requires it. I am driven on by
25   the flesh, and he must needs go that the devil drives.

COUNTESS   Is this all your worship's reason?

LAVATCH   Faith, madam, I have other holy reasons, such as they are.

COUNTESS   May the world know them?

30   LAVATCH   I have been, madam, a wicked creature, as you and all flesh and blood are, and indeed I do marry that I may repent.

COUNTESS   Thy marriage, sooner than thy wickedness.

LAVATCH   I am out o' friends, madam, and I hope to have
35   friends for my wife's sake.

COUNTESS   Such friends are thine enemies, knave.

LAVATCH   You're shallow, madam, in great friends, for the knaves come to do that for me which I am aweary of. He that ears my land spares my team and gives me leave to in the
40   crop. If I be his cuckold, he's my drudge; he that comforts my wife is the cherisher of my flesh and blood; he that cherishes my flesh and blood loves my flesh and blood; he that loves my flesh and blood is my friend: *ergo*, he that kisses my wife is my

---

17 needs of necessity   **20 case** puns on the sense of "vagina"   **Service** employment as a servant (plays on the sense of "sex")   **heritage** inheritance (for children)   **22 issue . . . body** i.e. children   **bairns** children   **25 go** puns on the sense of "have sex"   **26 your worship** title of mock respect   **27 holy** i.e. sanctioned by marriage (puns on "holey," i.e. vaginal)   **29 world** mankind, i.e. secular people   **32 repent** regret marrying/atone for sex out of wedlock   **35 for . . . sake** to keep my wife company (with suggestion of sexual activity)   **37 shallow** lacking in judgment   **in** of   **38 do** with sexual connotations   **39 ears** plows/ has sex with/impregnates   **land** i.e. wife   **spares my team** takes the load off my sexual organs   **gives me leave** allows/enables   **in** harvest/bring in   **40 crop** i.e. of children   **cuckold** man with an unfaithful wife   **drudge** slave/menial worker   **comforts** pleasures (sexually)   **41 cherisher** nourisher/sustainer (in procreative sense)   **43 *ergo*** "therefore" (Latin)

friend. If men could be contented to be what they are, there
45   were no fear in marriage, for young Charbon the Puritan
and old Poysam the Papist, howsome'er their hearts are
severed in religion, their heads are both one. They may jowl
horns together, like any deer i'th'herd.

COUNTESS   Wilt thou ever be a foul-mouthed and calumnious
50   knave?

LAVATCH   A prophet I, madam, and I speak the truth the
next way.

         For I the ballad will repeat,   *Sings*
         Which men full true shall find:
55   Your marriage comes by destiny,
         Your cuckoo sings by kind.

COUNTESS   Get you gone, sir. I'll talk with you more anon.

REYNALDO   May it please you, madam, that he bid Helen come
to you: of her I am to speak.

60   COUNTESS   Sirrah, tell my gentlewoman I would   *To Lavatch*
speak with her — Helen, I mean.

LAVATCH   'Was this fair face the cause,' quoth she,   *Sings*
         'Why the Grecians sackèd Troy?
         Fond done, done fond,
65   Was this King Priam's joy?'
         With that she sighèd as she stood,
         With that she sighèd as she stood,
         And gave this sentence then:
         'Among nine bad if one be good,
70   Among nine bad if one be good,
         There's yet one good in ten.'

---

44 what they are i.e. cuckolds   **45 Charbon the Puritan** meat-eating puritan (from French *chair bonne*: "good flesh," eaten on fast-days)   **46 Poysam the Papist** fish-eating Catholic (from French *poisson*: "fish," eaten on fast-days)   **howsome'er** howsoever/although
47 both one alike (in being cuckolds)   **jowl** dash, knock   **49 ever** always   **calumnious** slanderous   **52 next** nearest/most direct   **56 kind** nature, i.e. to be a cuckold (which sounds like "cuckoo") is natural   **57 anon** at another time   **62 fair face** i.e. of Helen of Troy, the most beautiful woman in the world, whose abduction by Paris caused the Trojan war   **she** perhaps Hecuba, wife of **Priam**   **63 sackèd** plundered   **Troy** ancient city of West Turkey, besieged for ten years during the Trojan war   **64 Fond** foolishly   **65 King Priam** King of Troy, killed during the conflict   **68 sentence** maxim, wise saying   **69 Among** along with

COUNTESS   What, one good in ten? You corrupt the song, sirrah.

LAVATCH   One good woman in ten, madam; which is a
75   purifying o'th'song. Would God would serve the world so all
the year! We'd find no fault with the tithe-woman, if I were
the parson. One in ten, quoth a? An we might have a good
woman born but ere every blazing star, or at an earthquake,
'twould mend the lottery well. A man may draw his heart
80   out ere a pluck one.

COUNTESS   You'll be gone, sir knave, and do as I command you?

LAVATCH   That man should be at woman's command, and yet
no hurt done! Though honesty be no puritan, yet it will do
no hurt. It will wear the surplice of humility over the black
85   gown of a big heart. I am going, forsooth. The business is for
Helen to come hither.   *Exit*

COUNTESS   Well, now.

REYNALDO   I know, madam, you love your gentlewoman entirely.

COUNTESS   Faith, I do. Her father bequeathed her to me, and
90   she herself, without other advantage, may lawfully make
title to as much love as she finds. There is more owing her
than is paid and more shall be paid her than she'll demand.

REYNALDO   Madam, I was very late more near her than I think
she wished me. Alone she was, and did communicate to
95   herself her own words to her own ears. She thought, I dare
vow for her, they touched not any stranger sense. Her matter
was, she loved your son. Fortune, she said, was no goddess,
that had put such difference betwixt their two estates. Love

---

72 **corrupt the song** presumably Lavatch has inverted the words of a well-known song; it may
have originally read "Among nine good if one be bad, / There's yet nine good in ten"
75 **purifying** cleansing, improving   **serve the world** i.e. by consistently providing **one good
woman in ten   76 tithe-woman** tenth woman (i.e. one in ten); the **tithe** was the tenth of one's
farm produce able to be claimed by the **parson   77 An** if   **78 but . . . earthquake** i.e. rarely
blazing star comet   **79 mend . . . well** improve the odds   **draw** pull   **80 one** i.e. a good
woman   **82 That** to think that   **83 honesty** truth/virtue   **84 wear . . . heart** i.e. conform by
hiding pride beneath an outward appearance of obedience, just as Puritans wore the
prescribed Anglican **surplice** over the more extreme Calvinist **black gown   85 forsooth** in
truth   **89 bequeathed** left (by will)/entrusted   **90 advantage** financial interest/additional
personal benefits   **make title** lay claim   **93 late** recently   **96 stranger sense** other person's
or stranger's hearing   **matter** subject, theme   **98 estates** stations in life

no god, that would not extend his might only where qualities
100 were level. Dian no queen of virgins, that would suffer her
poor knight surprised without rescue in the first assault or
ransom afterward. This she delivered in the most bitter touch
of sorrow that e'er I heard virgin exclaim in, which I held my
duty speedily to acquaint you withal, sithence, in the loss
105 that may happen, it concerns you something to know it.

COUNTESS   You have discharged this honestly. Keep it to
yourself. Many likelihoods informed me of this before, which
hung so tott'ring in the balance that I could neither believe
nor misdoubt. Pray you leave me. Stall this in your bosom,
110 and I thank you for your honest care. I will speak with you
further anon.   *Exit Steward [Reynaldo]*

Enter Helen

Even so it was with me when I was young.   *Aside*
If ever we are nature's, these are ours. This thorn
Doth to our rose of youth rightly belong.
115 Our blood to us, this to our blood is born:
It is the show and seal of nature's truth,
Where love's strong passion is impressed in youth.
By our remembrances of days foregone,
Such were our faults, or then we thought them none.
120 Her eye is sick on't. I observe her now.

HELEN   What is your pleasure, madam?

COUNTESS   You know, Helen, I am a mother to you.

HELEN   Mine honourable mistress.

COUNTESS   Nay, a mother. Why not a mother? When I said
      'a mother',
125 Methought you saw a serpent. What's in 'mother'
That you start at it? I say I am your mother,

---

99 no i.e. unworthy of being a   only where qualities except where ranks   100 Dian Diana,
Roman goddess of chastity, the moon, and hunting   suffer allow   101 surprised to be
captured/attacked   102 touch feeling/expression/note   104 withal with   sithence since
loss harm   105 something somewhat   106 discharged performed   107 likelihoods
indications   109 misdoubt disbelieve   Stall confine, lodge, hide   113 these difficulties/
pangs of love   115 blood passion   116 show appearance/display   seal sign/confirmation
117 impressed imprinted, stamped   119 or or rather/but   120 observe see through/note
125 Methought it seemed to me   126 start flinch

And put you in the catalogue of those
That were enwombèd mine. 'Tis often seen
Adoption strives with nature, and choice breeds
130   A native slip to us from foreign seeds.
You ne'er oppressed me with a mother's groan,
Yet I express to you a mother's care.
God's mercy, maiden! Does it curd thy blood
To say I am thy mother? What's the matter,
135   That this distempered messenger of wet,
The many-coloured Iris, rounds thine eye?
— Why? That you are my daughter?

HELEN   That I am not.

COUNTESS   I say I am your mother.

140 **HELEN**   Pardon, madam.
The Count Rossillion cannot be my brother:
I am from humble, he from honoured name,
No note upon my parents, his all noble.
My master, my dear lord he is, and I
145   His servant live, and will his vassal die.
He must not be my brother.

COUNTESS   Nor I your mother.

HELEN   You are my mother, madam, would you were —
So that my lord your son were not my brother —
150   Indeed my mother! Or were you both our mothers,
I care no more for than I do for heaven,
So I were not his sister. Can't no other
But, I your daughter, he must be my brother?

COUNTESS   Yes, Helen, you might be my daughter-in-law.
155   God shield you mean it not! Daughter and mother
So strive upon your pulse. What, pale again?

---

128 enwombèd mine carried in my womb   129 Adoption i.e. (love for) adopted children
strives competes   nature i.e. (love for) one's own children   choice . . . seeds we choose to
graft a cutting from another plant onto our stock, and thus make it into our own
131 mother's groan i.e. in labor   133 curd curdle   135 distempered distressed/unseasonal,
inclement   136 Iris Greek goddess of the rainbow   rounds encircles   138 not i.e. not your
daughter-in-law   143 note mark of distinction   parents ancestors   145 vassal subject/
servant   149 So provided that   150 both our mothers mother of us both   151 no . . . than
as much as   152 Can't no other can it be no other way   155 shield ensure/forbid

My fear hath catched your fondness. Now I see
The mystery of your loveliness, and find
Your salt tears' head. Now to all sense 'tis gross:
160   You love my son. Invention is ashamed
Against the proclamation of thy passion
To say thou dost not: therefore tell me true.
But tell me then 'tis so, for look, thy cheeks
Confess it, t'one to th'other, and thine eyes
165   See it so grossly shown in thy behaviours
That in their kind they speak it. Only sin
And hellish obstinacy tie thy tongue,
That truth should be suspected. Speak, is't so?
If it be so, you have wound a goodly clew.
170   If it be not, forswear't: howe'er, I charge thee,
As heaven shall work in me for thine avail,
To tell me truly.

HELEN   Good madam, pardon me.

COUNTESS   Do you love my son?

175 **HELEN**   Your pardon, noble mistress.

COUNTESS   Love you my son?

HELEN   Do not you love him, madam?

COUNTESS   Go not about; my love hath in't a bond
Whereof the world takes note. Come, come, disclose
180   The state of your affection, for your passions
Have to the full appeached.

HELEN   Then I confess,   ↑*Kneels*↑
Here on my knee, before high heaven and you,
That before you, and next unto high heaven,
185   I love your son.
My friends were poor but honest, so's my love.

---

157 catched caught   **fondness** foolishness/affection   **158 loveliness** many editors emend to
"loneliness" (solitary melancholy)   **159 head** source   **sense** perception   **gross** obvious
160 Invention (your) devising of excuse   **161 Against** in the face of   **166 kind** natural way (i.e.
by weeping)   **168 That . . . suspected** for fear that truth will be regarded with suspicion/to
ensure that truth will not be guessed at   **169 clew** ball (of thread)   **170 forswear't** deny it
(under oath)   **howe'er** in any case   **charge** command   **171 avail** benefit   **178 Go not about**
don't be roundabout (in answering)   **bond** i.e. maternal bond   **179 takes note** recognizes
181 appeached informed against (you)   **184 before** more than   **186 friends** relatives

Be not offended, for it hurts not him
That he is loved of me; I follow him not
By any token of presumptuous suit,
190   Nor would I have him till I do deserve him,
Yet never know how that desert should be.
I know I love in vain, strive against hope.
Yet in this captious and intenible sieve
I still pour in the waters of my love
195   And lack not to lose still; thus, Indian-like,
Religious in mine error, I adore
The sun that looks upon his worshipper
But knows of him no more. My dearest madam,
Let not your hate encounter with my love,
200   For loving where you do; but if yourself,
Whose agèd honour cites a virtuous youth,
Did ever in so true a flame of liking
Wish chastely and love dearly, that your Dian
Was both herself and love — O, then, give pity
205   To her whose state is such that cannot choose
But lend and give where she is sure to lose;
That seeks not to find that her search implies,
But riddle-like lives sweetly where she dies.

COUNTESS   Had you not lately an intent — speak truly —
210   To go to Paris?
HELEN   Madam, I had.
COUNTESS   Wherefore? Tell true.
HELEN   I will tell truth, by grace itself I swear.
You know my father left me some prescriptions

---

189 token sign, evidence, indication (plays on the sense of "love token")   **presumptuous suit**
unwarranted aim/expectant courtship   **193 captious** capacious/eager to take in/deceptive
intenible incapable of holding   **194 still** continually   **195 lack . . . still** yet do not run out
of more to pour in and waste/do not run out of more to keep continuously pouring in and
losing   **196 Religious** ardent/worshipful   **198 no more** nothing other (than to look on him)
199 encounter with contest, fight   **201 cites** confirms, acknowledges   **204 herself** i.e.
chastity   **206 lend . . . lose** i.e. bestow affection where it is sure of no success   **207 that** what
implies involves, seeks   **208 lives . . . dies** i.e. in loving Bertram, Helen is doomed to eternal
disappointment   **212 Wherefore?** Why?   **213 grace** God's grace   **214 prescriptions**
ancient customs/instructions/doctor's prescriptions

215   Of rare and proved effects, such as his reading
And manifest experience had collected
For general sovereignty, and that he willed me
In heedfull'st reservation to bestow them,
As notes whose faculties inclusive were
220   More than they were in note. Amongst the rest,
There is a remedy, approved, set down,
To cure the desp'rate languishings whereof
The king is rendered lost.

COUNTESS   This was your motive for Paris, was it? Speak.

225 HELEN   My lord your son made me to think of this;
Else Paris and the medicine and the king
Had from the conversation of my thoughts
Haply been absent then.

COUNTESS   But think you, Helen,
230   If you should tender your supposèd aid,
He would receive it? He and his physicians
Are of a mind. He, that they cannot help him,
They, that they cannot help. How shall they credit
A poor unlearnèd virgin, when the schools,
235   Embowelled of their doctrine, have left off
The danger to itself?

HELEN   There's something in't
More than my father's skill, which was the great'st
Of his profession, that his good receipt
240   Shall for my legacy be sanctified
By th'luckiest stars in heaven, and would your honour
But give me leave to try success, I'd venture

---

216 manifest evident   **217 sovereignty** efficacy/healing   **218 In . . . them** to reserve them
for use with the greatest care   **219 notes** instructions/doctor's prescriptions   **faculties
inclusive** comprehensive capabilities   **220 in note** recognized to be   **221 approved** tested,
proven   **222 desp'rate** despairing, hopeless   **223 rendered lost** deemed incurable
227 conversation processes, reflections   **228 Haply** perhaps   **230 tender** offer   **232 a mind**
the same opinion   **233 credit** believe/trust   **234 schools** universities, medical faculties
235 Embowelled disemboweled, emptied   **doctrine** learning, science   **left off** abandoned
239 receipt prescription/remedy   **240 sanctified** blessed   **242 try success** find out what
happens   **venture** risk

The well-lost life of mine on his grace's cure
By such a day and hour.

245   COUNTESS   Dost thou believe't?

HELEN   Ay, madam, knowingly.

COUNTESS   Why, Helen, thou shalt have my leave and love,
Means and attendants and my loving greetings
To those of mine in court. I'll stay at home

250   And pray God's blessing into thy attempt.
Be gone tomorrow. And be sure of this:
What I can help thee to thou shalt not miss.   *Exeunt*

Act 2 [Scene 1]

running scene 4

*Enter the King [carried in a chair] with divers young Lords taking
leave for the Florentine war, Count Rossillion [Bertram] and Parolles.
Flourish cornets*

KING   Farewell, young lords. These warlike principles
Do not throw from you. And you, my lords, farewell.
Share the advice betwixt you. If both gain, all
The gift doth stretch itself as 'tis received,

5   And is enough for both.

FIRST LORD   'Tis our hope, sir,
After well-entered soldiers, to return
And find your grace in health.

KING   No, no, it cannot be; and yet my heart

10   Will not confess he owes the malady
That doth my life besiege. Farewell, young lords.
Whether I live or die, be you the sons
Of worthy Frenchmen. Let higher Italy —
Those bated that inherit but the fall

---

243 **well-lost** i.e. lost for a good cause   244 **such a** a specific   246 **knowingly** i.e. securely, with confidence   247 **leave** permission   250 **into** unto/upon   252 **miss** lack
2.1   *Location: Paris*   1 **principles** i.e. advice   2 **throw from you** forget   4 **gift** i.e. of advice   7 **well-entered** (becoming) experienced   10 **owes** owns   13 **higher Italy** high-ranking Italians/northern Italy (Tuscany)   14 **Those . . . monarchy** except those who merely inherit their places from what is left of the Holy Roman Empire/they that are cast down by having merely the remains of the Holy Roman Empire

15   Of the last monarchy — see that you come
        Not to woo honour, but to wed it, when
        The bravest questant shrinks. Find what you seek,
        That fame may cry you loud. I say, farewell.

SECOND LORD   Health at your bidding serve your majesty!

20 KING   Those girls of Italy, take heed of them:
        They say our French lack language to deny
        If they demand. Beware of being captives
        Before you serve.

BOTH   Our hearts receive your warnings.

25 KING   Farewell.— Come hither to me.   *King steps aside with*

FIRST LORD   O, my sweet lord, that you will   *some lords/To Bertram*
        stay behind us!

PAROLLES   'Tis not his fault, the spark.

SECOND LORD   O, 'tis brave wars!

PAROLLES   Most admirable. I have seen those wars.

30 BERTRAM   I am commanded here, and kept a coil with
        'Too young' and 'the next year' and ''tis too early'.

PAROLLES   An thy mind stand to't, boy, steal away bravely.

BERTRAM   I shall stay here the forehorse to a smock,
        Creaking my shoes on the plain masonry,

35   Till honour be bought up and no sword worn
        But one to dance with. By heaven, I'll steal away.

FIRST LORD   There's honour in the theft.

PAROLLES   Commit it, count.

SECOND LORD   I am your accessary, and so farewell.

40 BERTRAM   I grow to you, and our parting is a tortured body.

FIRST LORD   Farewell, captain.

SECOND LORD   Sweet Monsieur Parolles!

---

16 woo court, flirt with   **wed** i.e. own, be bound to   **17 questant** seeker, one on a quest
shrinks recoils (plays on the sense of "loses his erection")   **18 cry** proclaim   **21 lack . . .
deny** i.e. cannot say no   **22 captives** i.e. to the girls' charms   **23 serve** fight (plays on the
sense of "have sex")   **27 spark** young man about town   **28 brave** splendid   **30 here** to stay
here   **kept a coil** fussed over   **32 bravely** boldly/worthily   **33 forehorse . . . smock** lead
horse in a team led by a woman   **34 masonry** stonework floor (i.e. not a battlefield)
35 bought up won by others   **36 one . . . with** i.e. an ornamental weapon   **steal** sneak (the
First Lord plays on the sense of "rob")   **40 grow to** become attached to   **a tortured body** like
a body being torn apart

PAROLLES   Noble heroes, my sword and yours are kin. Good
sparks and lustrous, a word, good metals. You shall find in
45   the regiment of the Spinii one Captain Spurio, with his
cicatrice, an emblem of war, here on his sinister cheek; it was
this very sword entrenched it. Say to him I live, and observe
his reports for me.

FIRST LORD   We shall, noble captain.

50   PAROLLES   Mars dote on you for his novices!—   *[Exeunt Lords]*
What will ye do?   *To Bertram*

BERTRAM   Stay the king.   *Bertram and Parolles stand aside*

PAROLLES   Use a more spacious ceremony to the   *To Bertram*
noble lords. You have restrained yourself within the list of
55   too cold an adieu. Be more expressive to them, for they wear
themselves in the cap of the time, there do muster true
gait, eat, speak, and move under the influence of the most
received star. And though the devil lead the measure, such
are to be followed. After them, and take a more dilated
60   farewell.

BERTRAM   And I will do so.

PAROLLES   Worthy fellows, and like to prove   *The King comes forward*
most sinewy sword-men.

Exeunt [Bertram and Parolles]

Enter Lafew

LAFEW   Pardon, my lord, for me and for my tidings.   *Kneels*

65   KING   I'll fee thee to stand up.

LAFEW   Then here's a man stands that has brought   *Rises*
his pardon.
I would you had kneeled, my lord, to ask me mercy,
And that at my bidding you could so stand up.

---

44 a word in a word   **metals** blades/spirits ("mettles")   **45 Spurio** "counterfeit" (Italian)
46 cicatrice scar   **sinister** left   **47 entrenched** gashed, grooved   **48 reports** response
50 Mars may Mars   **novices** recruits   **52 Stay** wait on/obey (Second Folio repunctuates
"Stay:" which changes the sense to "Wait: the king is coming")   **53 spacious ceremony**
ample courtesy   **54 list** boundary   **55 wear . . . time** i.e. are fashionable/notable
56 muster true gait display correct bearing/behavior   **58 received** fashionable   **measure**
stately dance   **59 dilated** extended   **62 like** likely   **63 sinewy** muscular, energetic
64 tidings news   **65 fee** pay   **66 brought his pardon** i.e. something to earn it

KING   I would I had, so I had broke thy pate,
70   And asked thee mercy for't.

LAFEW   Good faith, across. But, my good lord, 'tis thus:
Will you be cured of your infirmity?

KING   No.

LAFEW   O, will you eat no grapes, my royal fox?
75   Yes, but you will my noble grapes, an if
My royal fox could reach them. I have seen a medicine
That's able to breathe life into a stone,
Quicken a rock, and make you dance canary
With sprightly fire and motion, whose simple touch,
80   Is powerful to araise King Pippin, nay,
To give great Charlemain a pen in's hand
And write to her a love-line.

KING   What 'her' is this?

LAFEW   Why, Doctor She: my lord, there's one arrived,
85   If you will see her. Now, by my faith and honour,
If seriously I may convey my thoughts
In this my light deliverance, I have spoke
With one that, in her sex, her years, profession,
Wisdom and constancy, hath amazed me more
90   Than I dare blame my weakness. Will you see her,
For that is her demand, and know her business?
That done, laugh well at me.

KING   Now, good Lafew,
Bring in the admiration that we with thee
95   May spend our wonder too, or take off thine
By wondering how thou took'st it.

---

69 broke thy pate given you a blow to the skull   **71 across** i.e. a clumsy hit (in jousting, to
break a lance **across** rather than striking directly with the point showed poor skill)
74 will . . . fox in Aesop's fable the fox declared the grapes were sour because he couldn't reach
them; the king dismisses the idea of recovery because he thinks it impossible   **75 will** will eat/
want   **an if** if   **76 medicine** doctor   **78 Quicken** give life to   **canary** a lively Spanish dance
79 simple minimal/herbal/medicinal   **80 araise** raise from the dead/sexually arouse   **King
Pippin** eighth-century French king, father of **Charlemain** (Charlemagne)   **81 pen** plays on
the sense of "penis"   **87 light** lighthearted/sexually suggestive   **deliverance** delivery,
reporting   **88 profession** claims of skill   **90 blame** attribute to   **weakness** partiality,
susceptibility   **94 admiration** object of wonder   **95 spend** expend   **take off** reduce, remove
96 took'st conceived of, caught

LAFEW   Nay, I'll fit you,
And not be all day neither.

KING   Thus he his special nothing ever   *Lafew goes to the door*
prologues.   *or exits and re-enters*

Enter Helen

100   LAFEW   Nay, come your ways.   *To Helen*

KING   This haste hath wings indeed.

LAFEW   Nay, come your ways.
This is his majesty, say your mind to him.
A traitor you do look like, but such traitors
105   His majesty seldom fears. I am Cressid's uncle,
That dare leave two together. Fare you well.   *Exit*

KING   Now, fair one, does your business follow us?

HELEN   Ay, my good lord.
Gerard de Narbon was my father,
110   In what he did profess, well found.

KING   I knew him.

HELEN   The rather will I spare my praises towards him.
Knowing him is enough. On's bed of death
Many receipts he gave me, chiefly one
115   Which, as the dearest issue of his practice,
And of his old experience th'only darling,
He bade me store up, as a triple eye,
Safer than mine own two. More dear I have so,
And hearing your high majesty is touched
120   With that malignant cause wherein the honour
Of my dear father's gift stands chief in power,
I come to tender it and my appliance
With all bound humbleness.

---

97 fit satisfy   **99 special nothing** particular trifles   **ever prologues** always introduces
Enter Helen some editors suppose that she is disguised, since in Act 2 Scene 3 Lafew appears
surprised at her identity, despite having met her in Act 1 Scene 1; this is possible, but it seems
more likely that he is complicit with her plan (hence **Cressid's uncle**) and that the later surprise
is feigned   **100 come your ways** come along   **105 Cressid's uncle** Pandarus, go-between for
the lovers Troilus and Cressida   **107 follow** relate to   **110 profess** practice, make a
profession of   **well found** of established skill   **114 receipts** recipes for medical cures
115 issue product   **116 th'only** the foremost/peerless   **117 triple** third   **118 Safer** more
safely   **120 cause . . . power** disease (**cause**) for which the worth of my father's gift is most
effective   **122 tender** offer   **appliance** remedy/treatment   **123 bound** prepared/dutiful

KING   We thank you, maiden,
125   But may not be so credulous of cure,
       When our most learnèd doctors leave us, and
       The congregated college have concluded
       That labouring art can never ransom nature
       From her inaidible estate. I say we must not
130   So stain our judgement, or corrupt our hope,
       To prostitute our past-cure malady
       To empirics, or to dissever so
       Our great self and our credit, to esteem
       A senseless help when help past sense we deem.
135 HELEN   My duty then shall pay me for my pains:
       I will no more enforce mine office on you,
       Humbly entreating from your royal thoughts
       A modest one to bear me back again.
      KING   I cannot give thee less, to be called grateful.
140   Thou thought'st to help me, and such thanks I give
       As one near death to those that wish him live.
       But what at full I know, thou know'st no part,
       I knowing all my peril, thou no art.
       HELEN   What I can do can do no hurt to try,
145   Since you set up your rest gainst remedy.
       He that of greatest works is finisher
       Oft does them by the weakest minister:
       So holy writ in babes hath judgement shown,
       When judges have been babes; great floods have flown

125 credulous readily believing   127 congregated college i.e. of doctors   128 art skill/
scholarship/science   129 inaidible unable to be assisted   131 prostitute submit (basely)
132 empirics quack doctors   dissever divide   133 great self kingly person   credit
reputation   esteem give merit to, believe in   134 senseless foolish   sense rational hope
deem judge (it to be)   135 duty i.e. as a subject (having tried to help you)   pains efforts
136 office services, duty   138 modest one slight thought/thought that confirms my modest,
seeemly behavior   to . . . again for me to return with/to conduct me home   139 to than to
142 at full in detail   no part not at all   143 art (sufficient) medical skill   145 set . . . rest
stake everything (derived from the card game primero)   146 He i.e. God   148 holy writ the
Bible, which contains several examples of the young being wiser than their elders   babes
foolish/inexperienced   149 great . . . sources Moses struck rock from which water flowed for
the thirsty Israelites (Exodus 17)

150 From simple sources, and great seas have dried
When miracles have by the great'st been denied.
Oft expectation fails, and most oft there
Where most it promises, and oft it hits
Where hope is coldest and despair most shifts.

155 KING   I must not hear thee. Fare thee well, kind maid.
Thy pains not used must by thyself be paid:
Proffers not took reap thanks for their reward.

HELEN   Inspirèd merit so by breath is barred.
It is not so with him that all things knows
160 As 'tis with us that square our guess by shows.
But most it is presumption in us when
The help of heaven we count the act of men.
Dear sir, to my endeavours give consent.
Of heaven, not me, make an experiment.
165 I am not an impostor that proclaim
Myself against the level of mine aim,
But know I think, and think I know most sure,
My art is not past power, nor you past cure.

KING   Art thou so confident? Within what space
170 Hop'st thou my cure?

HELEN   The greatest grace lending grace
Ere twice the horses of the sun shall bring
Their fiery torcher his diurnal ring,
Ere twice in murk and occidental damp
175 Moist Hesperus hath quenched her sleepy lamp,
Or four and twenty times the pilot's glass

---

150 simple small   **great . . . dried** Moses led the Israelites through the Red Sea, which parted,
allowing them to pass on dry ground (Exodus 14)   **151 great'st** great persons, such as
Pharaoh, who complained about God's power   **153 hits** succeeds   **154 shifts** operates
156 by . . . paid be their own reward   **157 Proffers** offers   **for** as   **158 Inspirèd** divinely
inspired (plays on the sense of "inhaled")   **breath** words   **160 square** shape   **shows**
appearances   **162 count** consider   **164 experiment** trial   **165 impostor** swindler
proclaim . . . aim declare my success before attempting to hit the target/claim skill that is
greater than my ability   **169 space** period of time   **171 greatest** i.e. God's   **173 torcher**
torchbearer, the sun god, who was carried across the sky in a horse-drawn chariot   **diurnal**
ring daily circuit   **174 occidental** western (i.e. sunset)   **175 Hesperus** the evening star
(Venus)   **176 pilot's glass** nautical hourglass

Hath told the thievish minutes how they pass,
What is infirm from your sound parts shall fly,
Health shall live free and sickness freely die.

180 KING   Upon thy certainty and confidence
What dar'st thou venture?

HELEN   Tax of impudence,
A strumpet's boldness, a divulgèd shame
Traduced by odious ballads: my maiden's name
185 Seared otherwise, nay, worse of worst, extended
With vilest torture, let my life be ended.

KING   Methinks in thee some blessèd spirit doth speak
His powerful sound within an organ weak:
And what impossibility would slay
190 In common sense, sense saves another way.
Thy life is dear, for all that life can rate
Worth name of life in thee hath estimate:
Youth, beauty, wisdom, courage, all
That happiness and prime can happy call.
195 Thou this to hazard needs must intimate
Skill infinite or monstrous desperate.
Sweet practicer, thy physic I will try,
That ministers thine own death if I die.

HELEN   If I break time, or flinch in property
200 Of what I spoke, unpitied let me die,
And well deserved. Not helping, death's my fee.
But if I help, what do you promise me?

KING   Make thy demand.

HELEN   But will you make it even?

205 KING   Ay, by my sceptre and my hopes of heaven.

---

181 venture risk/wager   182 Tax accusation   183 strumpet's harlot's/whore's
184 Traduced slandered   185 Seared branded   extended stretched on a rack   189 slay
deny, extinguish   190 sense higher wisdom/natural feeling, instinct   191 rate value
192 estimate value   194 prime youth   195 Thou . . . hazard your willingness to risk this
needs necessarily   196 monstrous desperate unnaturally reckless   197 practicer
practitioner   physic medical advice/medicine   198 ministers delivers (plays on the sense of
"dispenses healing")   199 break time miss my deadline   property any particular respect
201 Not in not   204 make it even fulfill it

HELEN   Then shalt thou give me with thy kingly hand
               What husband in thy power I will command:
               Exempted be from me the arrogance
               To choose from forth the royal blood of France,
210   My low and humble name to propagate
               With any branch or image of thy state.
               But such a one, thy vassal, whom I know
               Is free for me to ask, thee to bestow.
KING   Here is my hand. The premises observed,
215   Thy will by my performance shall be served.
               So make the choice of thy own time, for I,
               Thy resolved patient, on thee still rely.
               More should I question thee, and more I must —
               Though more to know could not be more to trust —
220   From whence thou cam'st, how tended on. But rest
               Unquestioned welcome and undoubted blest.—
               Give me some help here, ho!— If thou proceed
               As high as word, my deed shall match thy deed.

                              Flourish. Exeunt [the King is carried out]

[Act 2 Scene 2]   *running scene 5*

Enter Countess and Clown [Lavatch]

COUNTESS   Come on, sir, I shall now put you to the height of
               your breeding.
LAVATCH   I will show myself highly fed and lowly taught. I
               know my business is but to the court.
5 COUNTESS   To the court! Why, what place make you special,
               when you put off that with such contempt? But to the court!
LAVATCH   Truly, madam, if God have lent a man any
               manners, he may easily put it off at court: he that cannot

---

207 What whatever   **208 Exempted** far removed   **214 premises observed** conditions
noted/fulfilled   **215 performance** carrying out (of the request)   **216 of** in   **217 resolved**
determined   **still** always   **220 tended on** attended   **221 Unquestioned** unquestionably
223 high as word amply as promised   **2.2** *Location: Rossillion*   **1 put . . . height**
thoroughly test   **2 breeding** education/upbringing   **3 highly fed** overfed   **lowly**
inadequately   **5 make you** do you think   **6 put off** dismiss   **8 put** pass

make a leg, put off's cap, kiss his hand and say nothing, has
10   neither leg, hands, lip, nor cap; and indeed such a fellow, to
say precisely, were not for the court. But for me, I have an
answer will serve all men.

COUNTESS   Marry, that's a bountiful answer that fits all
questions.

15 LAVATCH   It is like a barber's chair that fits all buttocks: the
pin-buttock, the quatch-buttock, the brawn-buttock, or any
buttock.

COUNTESS   Will your answer serve fit to all questions?

LAVATCH   As fit as ten groats is for the hand of an attorney, as
20   your French crown for your taffety punk, as Tib's rush for
Tom's forefinger, as a pancake for Shrove Tuesday, a morris
for May Day, as the nail to his hole, the cuckold to his horn,
as a scolding quean to a wrangling knave, as the nun's lip to
the friar's mouth, nay, as the pudding to his skin.

25 COUNTESS   Have you, I say, an answer of such fitness for all
questions?

LAVATCH   From below your duke to beneath your constable, it
will fit any question.

COUNTESS   It must be an answer of most monstrous size that
30   must fit all demands.

LAVATCH   But a trifle neither, in good faith, if the learned
should speak truth of it. Here it is, and all that belongs to't.
Ask me if I am a courtier, it shall do you no harm to learn.

9 make a leg bow   **12 answer** throughout the exchange this word seems to have phallic
connotations (**question** thus suggests "vagina")   **16 pin** narrow/sharp   **quatch** probably
squat/fat   **brawn** meaty/well-rounded   **18 fit** suitably   **19 groats** fourpenny coins
20 French crown gold coin/bald head (symptom of syphilis)   **taffety punk** finely dressed
whore   **Tib** typical name for lower-class girl/whore (diminutive of "Isabel")   **rush** ring made
of reeds/vagina   **21 Tom** typical name for a rogue   **forefinger** with phallic connotations
pancake traditionally eaten on Shrove Tuesday, the feasting day before Lent   **morris** morris
dance   **22 nail** with phallic connotations   **his** its   **hole** with vaginal connotations
cuckold man with an unfaithful wife   **horn** traditionally cuckolds were supposed to sprout
horns   **23 quean** prostitute (puns on "queen")   **wrangling knave** quarrelsome servant/
rogue   **24 pudding** sausage (perhaps with phallic connotations)   **his** its   **31 neither** on the
contrary

COUNTESS   To be young again, if we could. I will be a fool in
35   question, hoping to be the wiser by your answer. I pray you,
sir, are you a courtier?

LAVATCH   O lord, sir! There's a simple putting off. More, more,
a hundred of them.

COUNTESS   Sir, I am a poor friend of yours that loves you.

40   LAVATCH   O lord, sir! Thick, thick, spare not me.

COUNTESS   I think, sir, you can eat none of this homely meat.

LAVATCH   O lord, sir! Nay, put me to't, I warrant you.

COUNTESS   You were lately whipped, sir, as I think.

LAVATCH   O lord, sir! Spare not me.

45   COUNTESS   Do you cry, 'O lord, sir!' at your whipping, and
'Spare not me'? Indeed your 'O lord, sir!' is very sequent to
your whipping: you would answer very well to a whipping, if
you were but bound to't.

LAVATCH   I ne'er had worse luck in my life in my 'O lord, sir!' I
50   see things may serve long, but not serve ever.

COUNTESS   I play the noble housewife with the time
To entertain it so merrily with a fool.

LAVATCH   O lord, sir! Why, there't serves well again.

COUNTESS   An end, sir. To your business. Give Helen   *Gives a letter*
this,
55   And urge her to a present answer back. Commend
me to my kinsmen and my son. This is not much.

LAVATCH   Not much commendation to them.

COUNTESS   Not much employment for you. You understand me?

LAVATCH   Most fruitfully. I am there before my legs.

60   COUNTESS   Haste you again.   *Exeunt [separately]*

---

34 fool in question ignorant/inexperienced in questioning (you)   **37 putting off** evasion
40 O lord, sir! a fashionable phrase amongst affected courtiers   **Thick** quickly   **41 homely
meat** plain food   **46 is very sequent** follows logically   **47 answer** reply cleverly/respond well
48 bound to't obliged to reply/tied up for it   **51 noble** used ironically, as she is wasting time
55 present immediate   **Commend me** convey my regards   **59 fruitfully** abundantly   **before
my legs** i.e. very quickly   **60 again** back again

[Act 2 Scene 3]   *running scene 6*

Enter Count [Bertram], Lafew and Parolles

LAFEW	They say miracles are past, and we have our philosophical persons to make modern and familiar, things supernatural and causeless. Hence is it that we make trifles of terrors, ensconcing ourselves into seeming knowledge
5	when we should submit ourselves to an unknown fear.
PAROLLES	Why, 'tis the rarest argument of wonder that hath shot out in our latter times.
BERTRAM	And so 'tis.
LAFEW	To be relinquished of the artists—
10 PAROLLES	So I say, both of Galen and Paracelsus.
LAFEW	Of all the learnèd and authentic fellows—
PAROLLES	Right, so I say.
LAFEW	That gave him out incurable—
PAROLLES	Why, there 'tis. So say I too.
15 LAFEW	Not to be helped —
PAROLLES	Right. As 'twere a man assured of a—
LAFEW	Uncertain life and sure death.
PAROLLES	Just, you say well. So would I have said.
LAFEW	I may truly say, it is a novelty to the world.
20 PAROLLES	It is, indeed: if you will have it in showing, you shall read it in— what-do-ye-call there?

Points to the ballad Lafew holds

LAFEW	'A showing of a heavenly effect in an	*Reads*
	earthly actor.'	
PAROLLES	That's it. I would have said the very same.	

2.3 *Location: Paris*   **2 philosophical persons** scholars of "natural philosophy"
modern everyday   **things** things that seem   **3 causeless** inexplicable by natural causes
4 ensconcing ourselves into fortifying ourselves with   **5 unknown fear** fear of the unknown
6 rarest most extraordinary   **argument** topic, issue   **7 shot out** suddenly appeared   **latter**
most recent   **9 relinquished of** abandoned by   **artists** scholars, medical practitioners
10 Galen famous second-century Greek physician   **Paracelsus** famous sixteenth-century
Swiss physician   **11 authentic fellows** accredited members of the medical profession
13 gave him out proclaimed him to be   **18 Just** exactly   **20 showing** visible/printed form

25 LAFEW   Why, your dolphin is not lustier. 'Fore me, I speak in
            respect—

    PAROLLES   Nay, 'tis strange, 'tis very strange. That is the brief
            and the tedious of it, and he's of a most facinerious spirit
            that will not acknowledge it to be the—

30 LAFEW   Very hand of heaven.

    PAROLLES   Ay, so I say.

    LAFEW   In a most weak—

    PAROLLES   And debile minister, great power, great transcen-
            dence, which should indeed give us a further use to be made
35   than alone the recovery of the king, as to be—

    LAFEW   Generally thankful.

Enter King, Helen and Attendants

    PAROLLES   I would have said it; you say well. Here comes the
            king.   *Lafew and Parolles stand aside*

    LAFEW   *Lustigue*, as the Dutchman says. I'll like a maid the
40   better whilst I have a tooth in my head. Why, he's able to lead
            her a coranto.

    PAROLLES   *Mor du vinager!* Is not this Helen?

    LAFEW   'Fore God, I think so.

    KING   Go, call before me all the lords in court.

                                          [Exit Attendant]

45   Sit, my preserver, by thy patient's side,   *Helen sits*
            And with this healthful hand, whose banished sense
            Thou hast repealed, a second time receive
            The confirmation of my promised gift,
            Which but attends thy naming.

Enter three or four Lords

50   Fair maid, send forth thine eye: this youthful parcel
            Of noble bachelors stand at my bestowing,

---

25 dolphin puns on "dauphin" (i.e. heir to the French throne)   **'Fore me** before me; mild
oath, like "upon my soul"   **27 brief . . . tedious** short and the long   **28 facinerious** extremely
wicked   **33 debile minister** feeble agent   **36 Generally** universally   **39 *Lustigue*** lusty,
vigorous (from the German *lustig*)   **Dutchman** German   **40 tooth** sweet tooth, i.e. appetite
for pleasure   **41 coranto** lively dance   **42 *Mor du vinager!*** pseudo-French oath, literally,
"death of/by vinegar"   **46 banished sense** loss of feeling   **47 repealed** recalled, given a
second chance   **49 attends** awaits   **50 parcel** group   **51 my bestowing** my power to give in
marriage

O'er whom both sovereign power and father's voice
I have to use. Thy frank election make.
Thou hast power to choose, and they none to forsake.

55 HELEN   To each of you one fair and virtuous mistress
Fall, when love please! Marry, to each, but one!

LAFEW   I'd give bay curtal and his furniture
My mouth no more were broken than these boys',
And writ as little beard.

60 KING   Peruse them well:
Not one of those but had a noble father.

HELEN   Gentlemen, heaven hath through me restored the
king to health.

She addresses her to a Lord

ALL   We understand it, and thank heaven for you.

65 HELEN   I am a simple maid, and therein wealthiest
That I protest I simply am a maid.
Please it your majesty, I have done already.
The blushes in my cheeks thus whisper me,
'We blush that thou shouldst choose. But be refused,

70 Let the white death sit on thy cheek for ever,
We'll ne'er come there again.'

KING   Make choice and see,
Who shuns thy love shuns all his love in me.

HELEN   Now, Dian, from thy altar do I fly,

75 And to imperial Love, that god most high,
Do my sighs stream.— Sir, will you hear my suit?   *To First Lord*

FIRST LORD   And grant it.

HELEN   Thanks, sir. All the rest is mute.

LAFEW   I had rather be in this choice than throw   *Aside*

80 ames-ace for my life.

---

53 frank election free choice   **54 forsake** refuse   **57 bay . . . furniture** my bay horse with a
docked tail (**curtal**), and all his trappings   **58 My . . . boys'** to have as many teeth/to be as
little broken to the bit (i.e. youthful) as these boys   **59 writ** to be able to claim/exhibit
She . . . Lord some editors suppose that this direction is misplaced and belongs with the later
line spoken to First Lord   **66 protest** declare   **68 whisper** whisper to   **70 white death** pallor
of death   **73 Who** he who   **his . . . me** my love for him   **74 Dian** Diana, Roman goddess of
chastity   **75 Love** i.e. Cupid, **god** of love   **78 All . . . mute** there is no more to be said
80 ames-ace double ace, lowest throw in dice   **for my life** were my life at stake

HELEN   The honour, sir, that flames in your   *To Second Lord*
     fair eyes
     Before I speak, too threat'ningly replies.
     Love make your fortunes twenty times above
     Her that so wishes, and her humble love.
85 SECOND LORD   No better, if you please.
     HELEN   My wish receive,
     Which great love grant! And so I take my leave.
     LAFEW   Do all they deny her? An they were sons   *Aside*
     of mine, I'd have them whipped, or I would send them to
90 th'Turk to make eunuchs of.
     HELEN   Be not afraid that I your hand should   *To Third Lord*
     take.
     I'll never do you wrong for your own sake.
     Blessing upon your vows, and in your bed
     Find fairer fortune, if you ever wed!
95 LAFEW   These boys are boys of ice, they'll none have   *Aside*
     her. Sure they are bastards to the English, the French ne'er
     got 'em.
     HELEN   You are too young, too happy, and too   *To Fourth Lord*
     good,
     To make yourself a son out of my blood.
100 FOURTH LORD   Fair one, I think not so.
     LAFEW   There's one grape yet. I am sure thy father   *Aside*
     drunk wine. But if thou be'st not an ass, I am a youth of
     fourteen. I have known thee already.
     HELEN   I dare not say I take you, but I give   *To Bertram*
105 Me and my service, ever whilst I live,
     Into your guiding power. This is the man.
     KING   Why, then, young Bertram, take her: she's thy wife.

---

81 **honour** high status/willingness to marry/admiration   83 **Love** may Love   84 **Her . . .**
wishes i.e. myself, Helen   85 **No better** i.e. I wish for nothing better than your **humble love**
90 **th'Turk** i.e. non-Christian barbarian   96 **Sure** surely   97 **got** conceived   98 **happy**
fortunate   101 **grape** i.e. fruit of good lineage   102 **drunk wine** i.e. to give you good blood
103 **known** seen through

BERTRAM   My wife, my liege? I shall beseech your highness,
In such a business give me leave to use
110   The help of mine own eyes.

KING   Know'st thou not, Bertram, what she has done
for me?

BERTRAM   Yes, my good lord,
But never hope to know why I should marry her.

KING   Thou know'st she has raised me from my sickly bed.

115   BERTRAM   But follows it, my lord, to bring me down
Must answer for your raising? I know her well:
She had her breeding at my father's charge.
A poor physician's daughter my wife? Disdain
Rather corrupt me ever!

120   KING   'Tis only title thou disdain'st in her, the which
I can build up. Strange is it that our bloods,
Of colour, weight and heat, poured all together,
Would quite confound distinction, yet stands off
In differences so mighty. If she be
125   All that is virtuous, save what thou dislik'st,
A poor physician's daughter, thou dislik'st
Of virtue for the name. But do not so.
From lowest place whence virtuous things proceed,
The place is dignified by th'doer's deed.
130   Where great additions swell's, and virtue none,
It is a dropsied honour. Good alone
Is good without a name. Vileness is so:
The property by what it is should go,
Not by the title. She is young, wise, fair.
135   In these to nature she's immediate heir,

---

115 bring me down i.e. by making me marry a social inferior (with associations of bringing into the marriage bed, and, possibly, of losing one's erection)   **117 breeding** upbringing **charge** order/expense   **119 corrupt** debase/contaminate   **ever** forever   **120 title** lack of title   **123 confound distinction** be indistinguishable   **stands off** separate   **128 proceed** come forth   **130 great . . . none** titles puff us up rather than virtue (**swell's**: "swell is," elided for meter)   **131 dropsied** swollen/proud/diseased   **133 property** inherent quality   **go** i.e. be known   **135 heir** because the qualities are inherited from nature

And these breed honour. That is honour's scorn,
Which challenges itself as honour's born
And is not like the sire. Honours thrive,
When rather from our acts we them derive
140 Than our foregoers. The mere word's a slave,
Deboshed on every tomb, on every grave
A lying trophy, and as oft is dumb,
Where dust and damned oblivion is the tomb
Of honoured bones indeed. What should be said?
145 If thou canst like this creature as a maid,
I can create the rest: virtue and she
Is her own dower, honour and wealth from me.

BERTRAM   I cannot love her, nor will strive to do't.

KING   Thou wrong'st thyself if thou shouldst strive to
choose.

150 HELEN   That you are well restored, my lord, I'm glad.
Let the rest go.

KING   My honour's at the stake, which to defeat,
I must produce my power. Here, take her hand,
Proud scornful boy, unworthy this good gift,
155 That dost in vile misprision shackle up
My love and her desert. That canst not dream,
We, poising us in her defective scale,
Shall weigh thee to the beam. That wilt not know,
It is in us to plant thine honour where
160 We please to have it grow. Check thy contempt:
Obey our will, which travails in thy good.
Believe not thy disdain, but presently

136 That . . . sire true honor is scornful of inherited title when accompanying behavior not
worthy of it   140 foregoers ancestors   141 Deboshed debauched, corrupted   142 trophy
memorial   144 honoured bones indeed i.e. the remains of those who were truly honorable
147 dower dowry   148 strive attempt   149 choose assert your own choice   150 restored
cured   152 at the stake tied up like a bear to be baited, under attack   which which threat
154 this of this   155 misprision scorn   156 desert right/recompense   That you who
157 We the royal plural   poising weighing   defective i.e. lighter (as she is humble)
158 weigh . . . beam outweigh you and tip your scale up to the crossbar   159 in us within my
royal power   160 Check restrain   161 travails in labors for   162 Believe not deny
presently immediately

Do thine own fortunes that obedient right
Which both thy duty owes and our power claims,
165 Or I will throw thee from my care forever
Into the staggers and the careless lapse
Of youth and ignorance, both my revenge and hate
Loosing upon thee, in the name of justice,
Without all terms of pity. Speak. Thine answer.

170 BERTRAM   Pardon, my gracious lord, for I submit
My fancy to your eyes. When I consider
What great creation and what dole of honour
Flies where you bid it, I find that she, which late
Was in my nobler thoughts most base, is now
175 The praisèd of the king, who, so ennobled,
Is as 'twere born so.

KING   Take her by the hand,
And tell her she is thine, to whom I promise
A counterpoise, if not to thy estate,
180 A balance more replete.

BERTRAM   I take her hand.

KING   Good fortune and the favour of the king
Smile upon this contract, whose ceremony
Shall seem expedient on the now-born brief,
185 And be performed tonight. The solemn feast
Shall more attend upon the coming space,
Expecting absent friends. As thou lov'st her,
Thy love's to me religious, else, does err.

Exeunt. Parolles and Lafew stay
behind commenting of this wedding

LAFEW   Do you hear, monsieur? A word with you.

190 PAROLLES   Your pleasure, sir.

---

166 the staggers giddiness, unsteadiness (also, a horse disease affecting balance)   **careless**
untended/reckless/irresponsible   **lapse** decline   **168 Loosing** being loosed, inflicted
169 all terms any form   **171 fancy** desire   **172 great creation** creation of greatness   **dole**
portion   **173 which late** who recently   **175 who** i.e. Helen   **179 counterpoise** equal weight
(i.e. in dowry)   **not** not equal   **180 replete** complete/perfect/abundant   **183 whose . . .**
brief the formal accomplishment of which (i.e. marriage) shall quite properly follow the
present agreement   **186 more . . . space** have to wait for a time   **187 Expecting** waiting for
(the arrival of)   **As** as long as   **188 religious** sacred/true/dutiful   **err** go astray

LAFEW   Your lord and master did well to make his
recantation.

PAROLLES   Recantation? My lord? My master?

LAFEW   Ay. Is it not a language I speak?

195 PAROLLES   A most harsh one, and not to be understood
without bloody succeeding. My master?

LAFEW   Are you companion to the Count Rossillion?

PAROLLES   To any count, to all counts, to what is man.

LAFEW   To what is count's man. Count's master is of
200 another style.

PAROLLES   You are too old, sir. Let it satisfy you, you are too old.

LAFEW   I must tell thee, sirrah, I write man, to which title
age cannot bring thee.

PAROLLES   What I dare too well do, I dare not do.

205 LAFEW   I did think thee, for two ordinaries, to be a pretty
wise fellow. Thou didst make tolerable vent of thy travel, it
might pass. Yet the scarfs and the bannerets about thee did
manifoldly dissuade me from believing thee a vessel of too
great a burden. I have now found thee. When I lose thee
210 again, I care not. Yet art thou good for nothing but taking up,
and that thou'rt scarce worth.

PAROLLES   Hadst thou not the privilege of antiquity upon
thee—

LAFEW   Do not plunge thyself too far in anger, lest thou
215 hasten thy trial, which if— lord have mercy on thee for a hen!
So, my good window of lattice, fare thee well. Thy casement I
need not open, for I look through thee. Give me thy hand.

PAROLLES   My lord, you give me most egregious indignity.

---

196 **succeeding** consequences (i.e. a fight)   197 **companion** comrade/rascal   198 **man**
manly/mankind (Lafew shifts the sense to "servant")   201 **too old** i.e. for a duel   **satisfy**
appease (in place of a duel)   202 **write** claim to be   204 **dare . . . do** have the courage to
accomplish only too well, I dare not because of your old age   205 **ordinaries** standard meals
206 **vent** utterance   207 **scarfs** military sashes   **bannerets** small banners   208 **vessel**
ship, adorned with flags   209 **burden** cargo   **found** seen through   **thee** i.e. your company
210 **taking up** arresting/calling to account   212 **antiquity** old age   215 **trial** testing of
supposed courage   **hen** i.e. not a bold cock; perhaps also refers to Parolles' "plumage"
216 **window of lattice** ale-house (whose red lattice windows signified its function)   **casement**
window   218 **egregious** outrageous

LAFEW Ay, with all my heart, and thou art worthy of it.

220 PAROLLES I have not, my lord, deserved it.

LAFEW Yes, good faith, every dram of it, and I will not bate thee a scruple.

PAROLLES Well, I shall be wiser.

LAFEW Even as soon as thou canst, for thou hast to pull at a
225 smack o'th'contrary. If ever thou be'st bound in thy scarf and beaten, thou shall find what it is to be proud of thy bondage. I have a desire to hold my acquaintance with thee, or rather my knowledge, that I may say in the default, he is a man I know.

230 PAROLLES My lord, you do me most insupportable vexation.

LAFEW I would it were hell-pains for thy sake, and my poor doing eternal. For doing I am past, as I will by thee, in what motion age will give me leave.   *Exit*

PAROLLES Well, thou hast a son shall take this disgrace off me;
235 scurvy, old, filthy, scurvy lord! Well, I must be patient. There is no fettering of authority. I'll beat him, by my life, if I can meet him with any convenience, an he were double and double a lord. I'll have no more pity of his age than I would have of— I'll beat him, an if I could but meet him again.

Enter Lafew

240 LAFEW Sirrah, your lord and master's married. There's news for you: you have a new mistress.

PAROLLES I most unfeignedly beseech your lordship to make some reservation of your wrongs. He is my good lord. Whom I serve above is my master.

245 LAFEW Who? God?

---

221 **dram** small amount   **bate** lessen   222 **scruple** tiny amount   223 **wiser** i.e. in future
224 **pull . . . contrary** swallow a good quantity of your foolishness   227 **bondage** what binds
you (i.e. the scarves of which he is **proud**)   **hold** maintain   228 **in the default** when you fail
229 **know** understand/see through   231 **poor doing** inadequate ability to inflict **vexation**
232 **doing** action (plays on the sense of "having sex")   **will** will pass (puns on **past** as
"passed")   **in . . . leave** with what movement age will allow me   234 **shall . . . me** upon
whom I will vent my anger for these insults   235 **scurvy** contemptible   236 **fettering**
imprisoning   237 **with any convenience** on a suitable occasion   **an** even if
243 **reservation** concealment   **wrongs** insults   **good lord** i.e. patron (rather than employer)
Whom he whom

PAROLLES   Ay, sir.

LAFEW   The devil it is that's thy master. Why dost thou garter up thy arms o' this fashion? Dost make hose of thy sleeves? Do other servants so? Thou wert best set thy lower
250   part where thy nose stands. By mine honour, if I were but two hours younger, I'd beat thee. Methink'st thou art a general offence, and every man should beat thee. I think thou wast created for men to breathe themselves upon thee.

PAROLLES   This is hard and undeserved measure, my lord.

255   LAFEW   Go to, sir. You were beaten in Italy for picking a kernel out of a pomegranate. You are a vagabond and no true traveller. You are more saucy with lords and honourable personages than the commission of your birth and virtue gives you heraldry. You are not worth another word, else I'd
260   call you knave. I leave you.   *Exit*

PAROLLES   Good, very good, it is so then. Good, very good, let it be concealed awhile.

Enter Count Rossillion [Bertram]

BERTRAM   Undone, and forfeited to cares forever!

PAROLLES   What's the matter, sweet heart?

265   BERTRAM   Although before the solemn priest I have sworn, I will not bed her.

PAROLLES   What, what, sweetheart?

BERTRAM   O my Parolles, they have married me! I'll to the Tuscan wars and never bed her.

270   PAROLLES   France is a dog-hole, and it no more merits The tread of a man's foot: to th'wars!

BERTRAM   There's letters from my mother. What th'import is, I know not yet.

PAROLLES   Ay, that would be known. To th'wars, my boy, to th'wars!

---

248 **garter** tie (with scarves)   **hose** stockings, usually tied up with garters   249 **set . . . stands** put your penis where your nose should be/smell your bottom   253 **breathe** exercise (through fighting)   254 **measure** treatment/judgment   255 **Go to** expression of dismissive impatience   **picking . . . pomegranate** i.e. a small offense, as an excuse   256 **vagabond** itinerant vagrant, traveling without license   257 **true** honest/licensed   **saucy** insolent   258 **commission** warrant, allowance   259 **heraldry** i.e. authority, entitlement   263 **Undone** ruined   **cares** troubles, sorrows   272 **import** content, sense

275 He wears his honour in a box unseen
That hugs his kicky-wicky here at home,
Spending his manly marrow in her arms,
Which should sustain the bound and high curvet
Of Mars' fiery steed. To other regions,
280 France is a stable, we that dwell in't jades:
Therefore, to th'war!

BERTRAM   It shall be so. I'll send her to my house,
Acquaint my mother with my hate to her,
And wherefore I am fled, write to the king
285 That which I durst not speak. His present gift
Shall furnish me to those Italian fields
Where noble fellows strike. War is no strife
To the dark house and the detested wife.

PAROLLES   Will this *capriccio* hold in thee? Art sure?

290 BERTRAM   Go with me to my chamber, and advise me.
I'll send her straight away. Tomorrow
I'll to the wars, she to her single sorrow.

PAROLLES   Why, these balls bound, there's noise in it. 'Tis hard.
A young man married is a man that's marred:
295 Therefore away, and leave her bravely, go.
The king has done you wrong, but hush, 'tis so.   *Exeunt*

[Act 2 Scene 4]   *running scene 6 continues*

Enter Helena and Clown [Lavatch]   *Helen reading a letter*

HELEN   My mother greets me kindly. Is she well?

LAVATCH   She is not well, but yet she has her health: she's very
merry, but yet she is not well: but thanks be given, she's very
well and wants nothing i'th'world; but yet she is not well.

---

275 **box** container/vagina   276 **kicky-wicky** woman   277 **Spending** expending/wasting/
ejaculating   **marrow** vitality/sexual energy/semen   278 **curvet** horse's leap   280 **jades**
worn-out horses   286 **furnish me to** equip me for   **fields** battlefields   288 **To** compared to
dark house gloomy house/lunatic asylum   289 *capriccio* "whim" (Italian)   **Art** are you
291 **straight** immediately   293 **balls bound** tennis balls bounce (i.e. are spirited, to be
reckoned with; plays on the sense of "testicles")   294 **marred** ruined (plays on **married**)
2.4   1 **kindly** affectionately/as a mother   2 **well** i.e. at rest, dead   4 **wants** lacks

5 HELEN   If she be very well, what does she ail, that she's not
           very well?

   LAVATCH   Truly, she's very well indeed, but for two things.

   HELEN   What two things?

   LAVATCH   One, that she's not in heaven, whither God send her
           quickly. The other, that she's in earth, from whence God send
10   her quickly.

   Enter Parolles

   PAROLLES   Bless you, my fortunate lady.

   HELEN   I hope, sir, I have your good will to have mine own
           good fortune.

   PAROLLES   You had my prayers to lead them on, and to keep
15   them on, have them still. O, my knave, how does my old lady?

   LAVATCH   So that you had her wrinkles and I her money, I
           would she did as you say.

   PAROLLES   Why, I say nothing.

   LAVATCH   Marry, you are the wiser man, for many a man's
20   tongue shakes out his master's undoing: to say nothing, to
           do nothing, to know nothing, and to have nothing, is to be a
           great part of your title, which is within a very little of
           nothing.

   PAROLLES   Away! Thou'rt a knave.

25 LAVATCH   You should have said, sir, 'Before a knave thou'rt a
           knave.' That's, 'Before me thou'rt a knave.' This had been
           truth, sir.

   PAROLLES   Go to, thou art a witty fool. I have found thee.

   LAVATCH   Did you find me in yourself, sir? Or were you taught
30   to find me? The search, sir, was profitable. And much fool
           may you find in you, even to the world's pleasure and the
           increase of laughter.

---

14 them i.e. your good fortune   15 them i.e. my prayers   16 So provided that   17 did may
pun on "died"   19 man's servant's   20 shakes out brings about   22 title status as man or
servant/name ("Parolles," or "words"; also puns on "tittle"—i.e. "tiny amount")   25 Before
in the presence of   26 Before me i.e. upon my soul   28 Go to i.e. enough of that   found
thee found you out, found you to be a fool   29 me i.e. folly   31 even to i.e. enough for

PAROLLES   A good knave, i'faith, and well fed.—
        Madam, my lord will go away tonight.
35   A very serious business calls on him.
        The great prerogative and rite of love,
        Which, as your due, time claims, he does acknowledge,
        But puts it off to a compelled restraint,
        Whose want, and whose delay, is strewed with sweets,
40   Which they distil now in the curbèd time,
        To make the coming hour o'erflow with joy
        And pleasure drown the brim.
HELEN   What's his will else?
PAROLLES   That you will take your instant leave o'th'king
45   And make this haste as your own good proceeding,
        Strength'ned with what apology you think
        May make it probable need.
HELEN   What more commands he?
PAROLLES   That, having this obtained, you presently
50   Attend his further pleasure.
HELEN   In everything I wait upon his will.
PAROLLES   I shall report it so.   *Exit*
HELEN   I pray you.— Come, sirrah.   *Exeunt*

                             To Parolles/ To Lavatch

[Act 2 Scene 5]   *running scene 6 continues*

Enter Lafew and Bertram

LAFEW   But I hope your lordship thinks not him a soldier.
BERTRAM   Yes, my lord, and of very valiant approof.
LAFEW   You have it from his own deliverance.

---

33 well fed probably refers to "better fed than taught" (proverbial); possibly "energetic,
spirited"   **36 rite of love** i.e. sexual consummation of marriage   **38 to** owing to
39 Whose . . . delay the delay and absence of which   **sweets** sweet-scented flowers   **40 they**
i.e. **want** and **delay**   **curbèd** restrained   **42 drown** overflow   **43 else** besides   **45 make**
represent   **as** as if it were   **proceeding** course of action/idea   **46 apology** excuse
47 probable need plausible necessity   **50 Attend** await   **pleasure** command, will
2.5   **2 approof** proven quality/testimony   **3 deliverance** utterance

BERTRAM   And by other warranted testimony.

5 LAFEW   Then my dial goes not true. I took this lark for a
bunting.

BERTRAM   I do assure you, my lord, he is very great in
knowledge and accordingly valiant.

LAFEW   I have then sinned against his experience and
10 transgressed against his valour, and my state that way is
dangerous, since I cannot yet find in my heart to repent.
Here he comes. I pray you make us friends. I will pursue the
amity.

Enter Parolles

PAROLLES   These things shall be done, sir.   *To Bertram*

15 LAFEW   Pray you, sir, who's his tailor?   *To Bertram*

PAROLLES   Sir?

LAFEW   O, I know him well. Ay, 'sir', he. 'Sir' 's a good
workman, a very good tailor.

BERTRAM   Is she gone to the king?   *Aside to Parolles*

20 PAROLLES   She is.

BERTRAM   Will she away tonight?

PAROLLES   As you'll have her.

BERTRAM   I have writ my letters, casketed my treasure,
Given order for our horses, and tonight,
25 When I should take possession of the bride,
End ere I do begin.

LAFEW   A good traveller is something at the latter   *Aside*
end of a dinner, but one that lies three thirds and uses a
known truth to pass a thousand nothings with, should be
30 once heard and thrice beaten.— God save you, captain.

BERTRAM   Is there any unkindness between my lord   *To Parolles*
and you, monsieur?

PAROLLES   I know not how I have deserved to run into my
lord's displeasure.

---

5 **dial** timepiece/compass   **I . . . bunting** i.e. I underestimated him; reversal of "to take a
bunting for a lark" (proverbial; the **lark** was the superior bird)   8 **accordingly** suitably
10 **state** i.e. condition of my soul   11 **find** find it   15 **tailor** refers to Parolles' garments; "the
tailor makes the man" is proverbial   22 **you'll have** you wanted   27 **something** i.e. an asset,
with plenty of stories to tell the guests   28 **three thirds** i.e. all the time   31 **unkindness** ill will

35 LAFEW   You have made shift to run into't, boots and spurs
            and all, like him that leapt into the custard. And out of it
            you'll run again, rather than suffer question for your
            residence.

    BERTRAM   It may be you have mistaken him, my lord.

40 LAFEW   And shall do so ever, though I took him at's prayers.
            Fare you well, my lord, and believe this of me: there can be
            no kernel in this light nut. The soul of this man is his clothes.
            Trust him not in matter of heavy consequence. I have kept of
            them tame, and know their natures.— Farewell, monsieur. I
45   have spoken better of you than you have or will to deserve at
            my hand, but we must do good against evil.   [*Exit*]

    PAROLLES   An idle lord, I swear.

    BERTRAM   I think so.

    PAROLLES   Why, do you not know him?

50 BERTRAM   Yes, I do know him well, and common speech
    Gives him a worthy pass. Here comes my clog.

    Enter Helena [with an attendant]

    HELEN   I have, sir, as I was commanded from you,
            Spoke with the king and have procured his leave
            For present parting, only he desires
55   Some private speech with you.

    BERTRAM   I shall obey his will.
            You must not marvel, Helen, at my course,
            Which holds not colour with the time, nor does
            The ministration and requirèd office
60   On my particular. Prepared I was not
            For such a business: therefore am I found
            So much unsettled. This drives me to entreat you

---

35 made shift contrived   **36 him . . . custard** the jester who traditionally jumped into **custard**
at the Lord Mayor's annual feast in London   **37 suffer question** endure questioning
38 residence i.e. why you are there   **39 mistaken** misjudged/misidentified (Lafew shifts the
sense to "been offended by him")   **43 heavy** serious/not **light**   **44 them tame** such creatures
as pets   **45 to deserve** deserve   **47 idle** foolish   **49 know** i.e. rather than merely **think**
51 pass reputation   **clog** hindrance (block of wood tied to man or animal to prevent escape)
54 present parting immediate departure   **58 colour** appropriate character   **time** i.e. the
immediate aftermath of marriage   **59 ministration . . . particular** duty and obligation of me
as husband

That presently you take your way for home,
And rather muse than ask why I entreat you,
65   For my respects are better than they seem
And my appointments have in them a need
Greater than shows itself at the first view
To you that know them not. This to my mother.   *Gives a letter*
'Twill be two days ere I shall see you, so
70   I leave you to your wisdom.

HELEN   Sir, I can nothing say,
But that I am your most obedient servant.

BERTRAM   Come, come, no more of that.

HELEN   And ever shall
75   With true observance seek to eke out that
Wherein toward me my homely stars have failed
To equal my great fortune.

BERTRAM   Let that go.
My haste is very great. Farewell. Hie home.

80   HELEN   Pray, sir, your pardon.

BERTRAM   Well, what would you say?

HELEN   I am not worthy of the wealth I owe,
Nor dare I say 'tis mine, and yet it is.
But, like a timorous thief, most fain would steal
85   What law does vouch mine own.

BERTRAM   What would you have?

HELEN   Something, and scarce so much: nothing, indeed.
I would not tell you what I would, my lord.
Faith yes:
90   Strangers and foes do sunder, and not kiss.

BERTRAM   I pray you stay not, but in haste to horse.

HELEN   I shall not break your bidding, good my lord.—
Where are my other men?—   *To Attendant*

Monsieur, farewell.   *Exit*

---

64 **muse** wonder   65 **respects** reasons   66 **appointments** purposes, affairs
75 **observance** dutiful service   **eke out** supplement, increase   76 **homely stars** humble
origins   77 **great fortune** i.e. as your wife   79 **Hie** hurry   82 **owe** own   84 **fain** willingly
85 **vouch** affirm to be   88 **would** want   90 **sunder** part   91 **stay** delay

95   BERTRAM   Go thou toward home, where I will never come
Whilst I can shake my sword or hear the drum.
Away, and for our flight.

PAROLLES   Bravely, *corragio*!   [*Exeunt*]

Act 3 [Scene 1]   *running scene 7*

*Flourish. Enter the Duke of Florence, the two Frenchmen [First and
Second Lords Dumaine] with a troop of Soldiers*

DUKE   So that from point to point now have you heard
The fundamental reasons of this war,
Whose great decision hath much blood let forth
And more thirsts after.

5   FIRST LORD   Holy seems the quarrel
Upon your grace's part, black and fearful
On the opposer.

DUKE   Therefore we marvel much our cousin France
Would in so just a business shut his bosom

10   Against our borrowing prayers.

SECOND LORD   Good my lord,
The reasons of our state I cannot yield,
But like a common and an outward man
That the great figure of a council frames

15   By self-unable motion: therefore dare not
Say what I think of it, since I have found
Myself in my incertain grounds to fail
As often as I guessed.

DUKE   Be it his pleasure.

20   FIRST LORD   But I am sure the younger of our nature,
     That surfeit on their ease, will day by day
     Come here for physic.

    DUKE   Welcome shall they be,
     And all the honours that can fly from us
25   Shall on them settle. You know your places well.
     When better fall, for your avails they fell.
     Tomorrow to th'field.   *Flourish* [*Exeunt*]

[Act 3 Scene 2]   *running scene 8*

Enter Countess and Clown [*Lavatch*]

COUNTESS   It hath happened all as I would have had it, save
that he comes not along with her.

LAVATCH   By my troth, I take my young lord to be a very
melancholy man.

5   COUNTESS   By what observance, I pray you?

LAVATCH   Why, he will look upon his boot and sing: mend the
ruff and sing: ask questions and sing: pick his teeth and sing.
I know a man that had this trick of melancholy sold a goodly
manor for a song.

10   COUNTESS   Let me see what he writes, and when   *Opens a letter*
he means to come.

LAVATCH   I have no mind to Isbel since I was at court. Our old
lings and our Isbels o'th'country are nothing like your old
ling and your Isbels o'th'court. The brains of my Cupid's
15   knocked out, and I begin to love, as an old man loves money,
with no stomach.

COUNTESS   What have we here?

---

20 **younger . . . nature** young men of our temperament, outlook (some editors emend "nature"
to "nation")   21 **surfeit . . . ease** grow sick of overindulgence in leisure   22 **physic** cure,
perhaps by letting blood through war   24 **fly from** be bestowed by   26 **better fall** better
places fall vacant   **avails** advantages (as you may fill them)   **3.2** *Location: Rossillion*
3 **troth** faith   5 **observance** observation, signs   6 **mend** adjust   8 **sold** who sold   12 **mind
to** inclination for   13 **lings** salt cod, slang for "vaginas/whores" (similar play possible in
country)   14 **brains** plays on the sense of "semen" (thus making **Cupid** a personified penis
and giving **knocked out** sexual connotations)   16 **stomach** appetite

LAVATCH   E'en that you have there.   *Exit*

COUNTESS   [*Reads*] *a letter*

'I have sent you a daughter-in-law. She hath recovered the
20   king, and undone me. I have wedded her, not bedded her,
and sworn to make the "not" eternal. You shall hear I am
run away: know it before the report come. If there be
breadth enough in the world, I will hold a long distance. My
duty to you. Your unfortunate son, Bertram.'
25   This is not well, rash and unbridled boy.
To fly the favours of so good a king,
To pluck his indignation on thy head
By the misprizing of a maid too virtuous
For the contempt of empire.

Enter Clown [Lavatch]

30   LAVATCH   O, madam, yonder is heavy news within, between
two soldiers and my young lady!

COUNTESS   What is the matter?

LAVATCH   Nay, there is some comfort in the news, some
comfort. Your son will not be killed so soon as I thought he
35   would.

COUNTESS   Why should he be killed?

LAVATCH   So say I, madam, if he run away, as I hear he does.
The danger is in standing to't. That's the loss of men, though
it be the getting of children. Here they come will tell you
40   more. For my part, I only hear your son was run away.

[*He may exit*]

Enter Helen and two Gentlemen [First and Second Lords Dumaine]

SECOND LORD   Save you, good madam.

HELEN   Madam, my lord is gone, forever gone.

FIRST LORD   Do not say so.

COUNTESS   Think upon patience. Pray you, gentlemen,
45   I have felt so many quirks of joy and grief

---

18 **E'en** just, the same as   19 **recovered** cured   21 **"not"** with a pun on the marital knot
23 **hold** remain at   26 **fly** flee   28 **misprizing** despising/undervaluing   29 **of empire** even of
an emperor   30 **heavy** sad/serious   **within** inside   38 **standing to't** standing one's ground/
having an erection (both courses of action may lead to death—literally and in the sense of
"orgasm")   39 **getting** begetting, conception   41 **Save** God save   45 **quirks** turns

That the first face of neither, on the start
Can woman me unto't. Where is my son, I pray you?

FIRST LORD   Madam, he's gone to serve the Duke of Florence:
We met him thitherward, for thence we came,
50   And after some dispatch in hand at court,
Thither we bend again.

HELEN   Look on his letter, madam, here's my   *Shows a letter*
passport.

'When thou canst get the ring upon my finger,   *Reads*
which never shall come off, and show me a child begotten of
55   thy body that I am father to, then call me husband. But in
such a "then" I write a "never".' This is a dreadful sentence.

COUNTESS   Brought you this letter, gentlemen?

FIRST LORD   Ay, madam, and for the contents' sake are sorry for
our pains.

60   COUNTESS   I prithee, lady, have a better cheer.
If thou engrossest all the griefs are thine,
Thou robb'st me of a moiety: he was my son,
But I do wash his name out of my blood,
And thou art all my child. Towards Florence is he?

65   FIRST LORD   Ay, madam.

COUNTESS   And to be a soldier?

FIRST LORD   Such is his noble purpose, and believe't,
The duke will lay upon him all the honour
That good convenience claims.

70   COUNTESS   Return you thither?

SECOND LORD   Ay, madam, with the swiftest wing of speed.

HELEN   'Till I have no wife I have nothing in France.'   *Reads*
'Tis bitter.

COUNTESS   Find you that there?

---

46 **face** appearance   **on the start** at its sudden arrival   47 **woman** make behave like a
woman, i.e. weep   49 **thitherward** on his way there   **thence** from there   50 **dispatch in
hand** settlement of business   51 **bend** direct our steps   52 **passport** license to travel
56 **sentence** statement/judgment   60 **have . . . cheer** bear a happier countenance/be
encouraged   61 **engrossest** monopolize   **are** that are   62 **moiety** share/half   64 **all my**
my only   69 **convenience** propriety

75 HELEN   Ay, madam.

SECOND LORD   'Tis but the boldness of his hand, haply, which his
heart was not consenting to.

COUNTESS   Nothing in France, until he have no wife!
There's nothing here that is too good for him

80   But only she, and she deserves a lord
That twenty such rude boys might tend upon
And call her hourly mistress. Who was with him?

SECOND LORD   A servant only, and a gentleman
Which I have sometime known.

85 COUNTESS   Parolles, was it not?

SECOND LORD   Ay, my good lady, he.

COUNTESS   A very tainted fellow, and full of wickedness.
My son corrupts a well-derivèd nature
With his inducement.

90 SECOND LORD   Indeed, good lady,
The fellow has a deal of that too much,
Which holds him much to have.

COUNTESS   You're welcome, gentlemen.
I will entreat you, when you see my son,

95   To tell him that his sword can never win
The honour that he loses: more I'll entreat you
Written to bear along.

FIRST LORD   We serve you, madam,
In that and all your worthiest affairs.

100 COUNTESS   Not so, but as we change our courtesies.
Will you draw near?   *Exeunt [all but Helen]*

HELEN   'Till I have no wife, I have nothing in France.'
Nothing in France, until he has no wife!
Thou shalt have none, Rossillion, none in France.

105   Then hast thou all again. Poor lord, is't I

---

76 **haply** perhaps   81 **rude** ignorant/unkind/rough   88 **a well-derivèd** his own well-
descended   89 **his inducement** Parolles' bad influence   91 **deal** quantity   **that** influence
92 **holds . . . have** maintains and benefits him considerably   97 **Written** in writing
100 **but . . . courtesies** only insofar as I am able to repay your courtesy   **change** exchange
101 **draw near** come along (with me)   104 **Rossillion** i.e. Bertram

That chase thee from thy country and expose
Those tender limbs of thine to the event
Of the none-sparing war? And is it I
That drive thee from the sportive court, where thou
110   Wast shot at with fair eyes, to be the mark
Of smoky muskets? O you leaden messengers
That ride upon the violent speed of fire,
Fly with false aim, move the still-peering air
That sings with piercing. Do not touch my lord.
115   Whoever shoots at him, I set him there.
Whoever charges on his forward breast,
I am the caitiff that do hold him to't,
And though I kill him not, I am the cause
His death was so effected. Better 'twere
120   I met the ravin lion when he roared
With sharp constraint of hunger: better 'twere
That all the miseries which nature owes
Were mine at once. No, come thou home, Rossillion,
Whence honour but of danger wins a scar,
125   As oft it loses all. I will be gone:
My being here it is that holds thee hence.
Shall I stay here to do't? No, no, although
The air of paradise did fan the house
And angels officed all. I will be gone,
130   That pitiful rumour may report my flight,
To consolate thine ear. Come night, end day!
For with the dark, poor thief, I'll steal away.   *Exit*

---

107 **event** outcome   109 **sportive** playful/lighthearted/amorous   110 **mark** target
111 **leaden messengers** i.e. bullets   113 **move** part/stir (to pity) (sometimes emended to
"cleave" or "wound")   **still-peering** ever watchful (some editors emend to "still-piecing")
114 **sings** i.e. whistles as a bullet pierces it/cries in pain/sings in indifference   115 **set
him there** put him in the position   116 **forward** in the front line/facing the enemy
117 **caitiff** wretch   120 **ravin** ravenous   121 **constraint** compulsion   122 **owes** owns
124 **Whence . . . scar** from where honor merely earns a scar by undergoing danger   125 **oft**
often as   **all** i.e. life   127 **do't** i.e. keep you away   **although** even if   129 **officed all** carried
out all household duties   130 **pitiful** compassionate   131 **consolate** console   132 **steal**
creep (plays on the sense of "rob")

[Act 3 Scene 3]

*Flourish. Enter the Duke of Florence, Rossillion [Bertram], Drum and
Trumpets, soldiers, Parolles*

DUKE   The general of our horse thou art, and we,
              Great in our hope, lay our best love and credence
              Upon thy promising fortune.

BERTRAM   Sir, it is

5   A charge too heavy for my strength, but yet
              We'll strive to bear it for your worthy sake
              To th'extreme edge of hazard.

DUKE   Then go thou forth,
              And fortune play upon thy prosperous helm

10   As thy auspicious mistress!

BERTRAM   This very day,
              Great Mars, I put myself into thy file.
              Make me but like my thoughts, and I shall prove
              A lover of thy drum, hater of love.   *Exeunt*

[Act 3 Scene 4]

Enter Countess and Steward [Reynaldo]

COUNTESS   Alas! And would you take the letter of her?
              Might you not know she would do as she has done,
              By sending me a letter? Read it again.

REYNALDO   [*Reads the*] *letter*
              'I am Saint Jaques' pilgrim, thither gone.

5   Ambitious love hath so in me offended,
              That barefoot plod I the cold ground upon,
              With sainted vow my faults to have amended.

3.3 *Location: Florence   Drum and Trumpets* i.e. a drummer and a trumpeter
2 Great pregnant/swelling   **lay** wager   **credence** trust, faith   **7 th'extreme edge** the
utmost limit   **9 helm** helmet   **12 file** rank of soldiers   **13 like my thoughts** i.e. valiant
3.4 *Location: Rossillion*   **1 of** from   **4 "I . . . free"** this letter is cast in the form of a
sonnet   **Saint Jaques** Saint James, whose shrine was at Compostella, in northwest Spain
7 sainted holy/dedicated to a saint

Write, write, that from the bloody course of war
My dearest master, your dear son, may hie.
10   Bless him at home in peace, whilst I from far
His name with zealous fervour sanctify.
His taken labours bid him me forgive.
I, his despiteful Juno, sent him forth
From courtly friends, with camping foes to live
15   Where death and danger dogs the heels of worth.
He is too good and fair for death and me,
Whom I myself embrace, to set him free.'

COUNTESS   Ah, what sharp stings are in her mildest words!
Reynaldo, you did never lack advice so much,
20   As letting her pass so: had I spoke with her,
I could have well diverted her intents,
Which thus she hath prevented.

REYNALDO   Pardon me, madam.
If I had given you this at overnight,
25   She might have been o'erta'en, and yet she writes
Pursuit would be but vain.

COUNTESS   What angel shall
Bless this unworthy husband? He cannot thrive,
Unless her prayers, whom heaven delights to hear
30   And loves to grant, reprieve him from the wrath
Of greatest justice. Write, write, Reynaldo,
To this unworthy husband of his wife.
Let every word weigh heavy of her worth
That he does weigh too light. My greatest grief,
35   Though little he do feel it, set down sharply.
Dispatch the most convenient messenger.
When haply he shall hear that she is gone,
He will return, and hope I may that she,
Hearing so much, will speed her foot again,

---

9 hie hasten   12 taken undertaken   13 despiteful cruel, malicious   Juno supreme
goddess, who imposed twelve labors on Hercules   14 camping tent-dwelling (i.e. army)
17 Whom i.e. death   19 advice judgment   22 prevented forestalled   24 at overnight last
night   29 whom i.e. both Helen and her prayers   32 unworthy husband husband unworthy
33 weigh heavy of emphasize   37 When haply perhaps when

40 Led hither by pure love. Which of them both
Is dearest to me, I have no skill in sense
To make distinction. Provide this messenger.
My heart is heavy and mine age is weak.
Grief would have tears, and sorrow bids me speak.   *Exeunt*

[Act 3 Scene 5]

running scene 11

*A tucket afar off. Enter old Widow of Florence, her daughter [Diana],
and Mariana with other Citizens*

WIDOW   Nay, come, for if they do approach the city, we shall
lose all the sight.

DIANA   They say the French count has done most
honourable service.

5 WIDOW   It is reported that he has taken their greatest
commander, and that with his own hand he slew the duke's
brother.   *Tucket*
We have lost our labour. They are gone a contrary way.
Hark! You may know by their trumpets.

10 MARIANA   Come, let's return again, and suffice ourselves with
the report of it. Well, Diana, take heed of this French earl.
The honour of a maid is her name, and no legacy is so rich as
honesty.

WIDOW   I have told my neighbour how you have been
15 solicited by a gentleman his companion.

MARIANA   I know that knave, hang him! One Parolles: a filthy
officer he is in those suggestions for the young earl. Beware
of them, Diana; their promises, enticements, oaths, tokens
and all these engines of lust, are not the things they go
20 under. Many a maid hath been seduced by them, and the

---

41 **sense** perception   42 **Provide** equip   **3.5** *Location: Florence   tucket* trumpet
fanfare   *Diana* significantly, given her role, the name of the goddess of chastity and hunting;
the Folio entry direction calls her "Violenta," which was perhaps Shakespeare's first thought
for the name   2 **lose all** entirely miss   5 **their** i.e. Siena's   10 **suffice** satisfy   11 **earl** i.e.
Bertram   12 **name** reputation   13 **honesty** chastity   15 **solicited** entreated, courted
17 **officer** agent   **suggestions** promptings toward evil/entreaties   **for** on behalf of
19 **engines** devices/plots   **go under** appear to be

misery is example that so terrible shows in the wreck of
maidenhood, cannot for all that dissuade succession, but
that they are limed with the twigs that threatens them. I
hope I need not to advise you further, but I hope your own
25   grace will keep you where you are, though there were no
further danger known but the modesty which is so lost.

DIANA   You shall not need to fear me.

Enter Helen [disguised as a pilgrim]

WIDOW   I hope so. Look, here comes a pilgrim. I know she will
lie at my house: thither they send one another. I'll question
30   her.— God save you, pilgrim! Whither are you bound?

HELEN   To Saint Jaques le Grand.
Where do the palmers lodge, I do beseech you?

WIDOW   At the Saint Francis here beside the port.

HELEN   Is this the way?   *A march afar*

35   WIDOW   Ay, marry, is't. Hark you!
They come this way. If you will tarry,
Holy pilgrim, but till the troops come by,
I will conduct you where you shall be lodged,
The rather for I think I know your hostess
40   As ample as myself.

HELEN   Is it yourself?

WIDOW   If you shall please so, pilgrim.

HELEN   I thank you, and will stay upon your leisure.

WIDOW   You came, I think, from France?

45   HELEN   I did so.

WIDOW   Here you shall see a countryman of yours
That has done worthy service.

HELEN   His name, I pray you.

DIANA   The Count Rossillion. Know you such a one?

---

21 **wreck of maidenhood** loss of virginity   22 **succession** (others from) doing the same
23 **that** for all that   **limed** trapped (like birds caught in lime, a sticky substance smeared on
twigs)   25 **grace** virtue   **though** even if   26 **further . . . lost** worse risk than the loss of
virginity (i.e. pregnancy)   27 **fear** fear for   29 **lie** lodge   32 **palmers** pilgrims   33 **Saint
Francis** inn with the sign of Saint Francis   **port** city gate   36 **tarry** wait   39 **for** because
40 **ample** well, fully   43 **stay upon** await   **leisure** convenience

50 HELEN   But by the ear, that hears most nobly of him:
            His face I know not.

    DIANA   Whatsome'er he is,
            He's bravely taken here. He stole from France,
            As 'tis reported, for the king had married him
55   Against his liking. Think you it is so?

    HELEN   Ay, surely, mere the truth. I know his lady.

    DIANA   There is a gentleman that serves the count
            Reports but coarsely of her.

    HELEN   What's his name?

60 DIANA   Monsieur Parolles.

    HELEN   O, I believe with him,
            In argument of praise, or to the worth
            Of the great count himself, she is too mean
            To have her name repeated. All her deserving
65   Is a reservèd honesty, and that
            I have not heard examined.

    DIANA   Alas, poor lady!
            'Tis a hard bondage to become the wife
            Of a detesting lord.

70 WIDOW   I write good creature: wheresoe'er she is,
            Her heart weighs sadly. This young maid might do her
            A shrewd turn if she pleased.

    HELEN   How do you mean?
            Maybe the amorous count solicits her
75   In the unlawful purpose?

    WIDOW   He does indeed,
            And brokes with all that can in such a suit
            Corrupt the tender honour of a maid.
            But she is armed for him and keeps her guard
80   In honestest defence.

---

52 Whatsome'er whoever   **53 bravely taken** highly regarded   **54 for** because   **56 mere** absolutely   **61 believe** agree   **62 argument** any issue   **to** in comparison with   **63 mean** lowly/unworthy   **64 All her deserving** her only merit   **65 reservèd honesty** well-guarded chastity   **66 examined** called into question   **70 write** style her (some editors emend to "warrant")   **72 shrewd** malicious   **77 brokes** bargains, negotiates   **suit** endeavor, request   **80 honestest** most chaste

Drum and colours. Enter Count Rossillion [Bertram], Parolles and the
whole army

MARIANA	The gods forbid else!
WIDOW	So, now they come:

That is Antonio, the duke's eldest son.
That, Escalus.

85 HELEN   Which is the Frenchman?

DIANA   He,

That with the plume. 'Tis a most gallant fellow.
I would he loved his wife: if he were honester
He were much goodlier. Is't not a handsome gentleman?

90 HELEN   I like him well.

DIANA   'Tis pity he is not honest. Yond's that same knave
That leads him to these places. Were I his lady,
I would poison that vile rascal.

HELEN   Which is he?

95 DIANA   That jackanapes with scarves. Why is he melancholy?

HELEN   Perchance he's hurt i'th'battle.

PAROLLES   Lose our drum! Well.

MARIANA   He's shrewdly vexed at something. Look, he has
spied us.

100 WIDOW   Marry, hang you!

MARIANA   And your courtesy, for a ring-carrier!

Exeunt [Bertram, Parolles and army]

WIDOW   The troop is past. Come, pilgrim, I will bring you
Where you shall host. Of enjoined penitents
There's four or five, to great Saint Jaques bound,
105 Already at my house.

HELEN   I humbly thank you:
Please it this matron and this gentle maid
To eat with us tonight, the charge and thanking
Shall be for me. And, to requite you further,

---

colours battle flags   **81 else** (that it should be) otherwise   **88 honester** more honorable
95 jackanapes monkey   **98 shrewdly** sorely   **101 courtesy** curtsy (i.e. bow)   **ring-carrier**
pimp   **103 host** lodge   **enjoined penitents** those bound by oath to undertake pilgrimage as
penance for sin   **107 Please it** if it please   **108 charge** expense   **109 for me** mine

110   I will bestow some precepts of this virgin
        Worthy the note.

BOTH   We'll take your offer kindly.   *Exeunt*

[Act 3 Scene 6]   *running scene 12*

Enter Count Rossillion [Bertram] and the [two] Frenchmen, as at first

SECOND LORD   Nay, good my lord, put him to't, let him have his
        way.

FIRST LORD   If your lordship find him not a hilding, hold me no
        more in your respect.

5   SECOND LORD   On my life, my lord, a bubble.

    BERTRAM   Do you think I am so far deceived in him?

    SECOND LORD   Believe it, my lord, in mine own direct knowledge,
        without any malice, but to speak of him as my kinsman, he's
        a most notable coward, an infinite and endless liar, an hourly
10   promise-breaker, the owner of no one good quality worthy
        your lordship's entertainment.

    FIRST LORD   It were fit you knew him, lest reposing too far in his
        virtue, which he hath not, he might at some great and trusty
        business in a main danger fail you.

15 BERTRAM   I would I knew in what particular action to try him.

    FIRST LORD   None better than to let him fetch off his drum,
        which you hear him so confidently undertake to do.

    SECOND LORD   I, with a troop of Florentines, will suddenly
        surprise him; such I will have whom I am sure he knows not
20   from the enemy: we will bind and hoodwink him so, that he
        shall suppose no other but that he is carried into the leaguer
        of the adversaries, when we bring him to our own tents. Be
        but your lordship present at his examination. If he do not,
        for the promise of his life and in the highest compulsion of

---

110 **precepts of** advice on   112 **kindly** gratefully   **3.6** *Location: battlefield*   1 **to't** to
the test   3 **hilding** good-for-nothing   5 **bubble** i.e. nothing/showy/easily destroyed   8 **as** as
if he were   11 **entertainment** patronage   12 **reposing** trusting, relying   13 **trusty** requiring
trustworthiness   15 **try** test   16 **fetch off** rescue/retrieve   19 **surprise** ambush, attack
knows not cannot distinguish   20 **hoodwink** blindfold/deceive   21 **leaguer** military camp

25   base fear, offer to betray you and deliver all the intelligence in
his power against you, and that with the divine forfeit of his
soul upon oath, never trust my judgement in anything.

FIRST LORD   O, for the love of laughter, let him fetch his drum.
He says he has a stratagem for't. When your lordship sees
30   the bottom of his success in't, and to what metal this
counterfeit lump of ore will be melted, if you give him not
John Drum's entertainment, your inclining cannot be
removed. Here he comes.

Enter Parolles

SECOND LORD   O, for the love of laughter, hinder not   *Aside to*
35   the honour of his design. Let him fetch off his drum   *Bertram*
in any hand.

BERTRAM   How now, monsieur? This drum sticks sorely in
your disposition.

FIRST LORD   A pox on't! Let it go, 'tis but a drum.

40   PAROLLES   'But a drum'? Is't 'but a drum'? A drum so lost?
There was excellent command: to charge in with our horse
upon our own wings, and to rend our own soldiers!

FIRST LORD   That was not to be blamed in the command of the
service: it was a disaster of war that Caesar himself could
45   not have prevented if he had been there to command.

BERTRAM   Well, we cannot greatly condemn our success.
Some dishonour we had in the loss of that drum, but it is not
to be recovered.

PAROLLES   It might have been recovered.

50   BERTRAM   It might, but it is not now.

PAROLLES   It is to be recovered. But that the merit of service is
seldom attributed to the true and exact performer, I would
have that drum or another, or *hic jacet*.

---

25 intelligence secret information   **27 oath** i.e. the vow he took never to divulge the
intelligence   30 bottom extent   **31 ore** precious metal   **give . . . entertainment** i.e. beat
him/cast him out (proverbial)   **32 inclining** partiality, liking (for Parolles)   **36 in any hand** in
any case   **37 sticks . . . disposition** is really upsetting you   **sticks** stabs   **39 pox** plague
42 wings flanks, on either side of the main body of troops   **rend** tear apart, devastate   **43 in**
upon   **command . . . service** military orders   **51 But** were it not   **53 *hic jacet*** i.e. I shall
die—literally "here lies" (Latin), phrase found on tombstones

BERTRAM   Why, if you have a stomach, to't, monsieur: if you
55   think your mystery in stratagem can bring this instrument
of honour again into his native quarter, be magnanimous in
the enterprise and go on. I will grace the attempt for a
worthy exploit. If you speed well in it, the duke shall both
speak of it and extend to you what further becomes his
60   greatness, even to the utmost syllable of your worthiness.

PAROLLES   By the hand of a soldier, I will undertake it.

BERTRAM   But you must not now slumber in it.

PAROLLES   I'll about it this evening, and I will presently pen
down my dilemmas, encourage myself in my certainty, put
65   myself into my mortal preparation, and by midnight look to
hear further from me.

BERTRAM   May I be bold to acquaint his grace you are gone
about it?

PAROLLES   I know not what the success will be, my lord, but the
70   attempt I vow.

BERTRAM   I know thou'rt valiant, and to the possibility of thy
soldiership will subscribe for thee. Farewell.

PAROLLES   I love not many words.   *Exit*

SECOND LORD   No more than a fish loves water. Is not this a
75   strange fellow, my lord, that so confidently seems to undertake
this business, which he knows is not to be done, damns
himself to do and dares better be damned than to do't?

FIRST LORD   You do not know him, my lord, as we do. Certain it
is that he will steal himself into a man's favour and for a
80   week escape a great deal of discoveries, but when you find
him out, you have him ever after.

BERTRAM   Why, do you think he will make no deed at all of this
that so seriously he does address himself unto?

---

54 **stomach** appetite/courage   55 **mystery** skill   56 **his** its   57 **grace** honor   58 **speed**
fare/succeed   59 **becomes** befits   62 **slumber in it** i.e. delay   63 **presently** immediately
pen write   64 **dilemmas** choices of action   65 **mortal preparation** spiritual readiness either
for my death or those of the men I kill   71 **possibility** competence, capacity   72 **subscribe**
vouch   76 **damns himself** i.e. by swearing falsely   81 **have** have a true understanding of
82 **make no deed** perform no part/make no attempt

SECOND LORD   None in the world. But return with an invention
85   and clap upon you two or three probable lies. But we have
almost embossed him. You shall see his fall tonight; for
indeed he is not for your lordship's respect.

FIRST LORD   We'll make you some sport with the fox ere we case
him. He was first smoked by the old lord Lafew. When his
90   disguise and he is parted, tell me what a sprat you shall find
him, which you shall see this very night.

SECOND LORD   I must go look my twigs. He shall be caught.

BERTRAM   Your brother he shall go along with me.   *To First Lord*

FIRST LORD   As't please your lordship. I'll leave you.   [*Exit*]

95   BERTRAM   Now will I lead you to the house, and show you
The lass I spoke of.

SECOND LORD   But you say she's honest.

BERTRAM   That's all the fault. I spoke with her but once
And found her wondrous cold, but I sent to her
100   By this same coxcomb that we have i'th'wind
Tokens and letters which she did re-send.
And this is all I have done. She's a fair creature.
Will you go see her?

SECOND LORD   With all my heart, my lord.   *Exeunt*

[Act 3 Scene 7]   *running scene 13*

Enter Helen and Widow

HELEN   If you misdoubt me that I am not she,
I know not how I shall assure you further,
But I shall lose the grounds I work upon.

WIDOW   Though my estate be fall'n, I was well born,
5   Nothing acquainted with these businesses,

---

85 probable plausible   **86 embossed** hunted down/driven to exhaustion   **87 for** worthy of
88 case skin, unmask   **89 smoked** smoked out, exposed   **90 sprat** small fish (i.e.
contemptible person)   **92 look my twigs** see to my bird-trap   **93 Your . . . me** i.e. Bertram
pulls rank and orders the Second Lord to accompany him in his pursuit of Diana, leaving the
First Lord to undertake the ambush on Parolles   **100 coxcomb** fool (literally, fool's cap)
have i'th'wind have scented, are tracking   **3.7   *Location: Florence*   1 misdoubt**
disbelieve, suspect   **3 But . . . upon** without losing the foundations my plans rely on
4 estate worldly fortune

And would not put my reputation now
In any staining act.

HELEN   Nor would I wish you.
First, give me trust, the count he is my husband,
10   And what to your sworn counsel I have spoken
Is so from word to word. And then you cannot,
By the good aid that I of you shall borrow,
Err in bestowing it.

WIDOW   I should believe you,
15   For you have showed me that which well approves
You're great in fortune.

HELEN   Take this purse of gold,   *Gives a purse*
And let me buy your friendly help thus far,
Which I will over-pay and pay again
20   When I have found it. The count he woos your daughter,
Lays down his wanton siege before her beauty,
Resolves to carry her: let her in fine consent,
As we'll direct her how 'tis best to bear it.
Now his important blood will naught deny
25   That she'll demand: a ring the county wears,
That downward hath succeeded in his house
From son to son, some four or five descents
Since the first father wore it. This ring he holds
In most rich choice, yet in his idle fire,
30   To buy his will, it would not seem too dear,
Howe'er repented after.

WIDOW   Now I see
The bottom of your purpose.

HELEN   You see it lawful, then: it is no more,
35   But that your daughter, ere she seems as won,
Desires this ring; appoints him an encounter;

---

10 **sworn counsel** private hearing that you have vowed to keep secret   11 **so . . . word** true in
every word   12 **By** with respect to   15 **approves** proves, demonstrates   20 **found it** received
your **help**   21 **wanton** lascivious   22 **carry** win   **in fine** in the end/to sum up   23 **bear**
manage   24 **important blood** urgent sexual passion   25 **county** count   29 **rich choice**
high esteem   **idle fire** foolish ardor   30 **will** sexual desire   33 **bottom** essence   34 **lawful** to
be lawful   36 **appoints . . . encounter** arranges a meeting with him

In fine, delivers me to fill the time,
Herself most chastely absent. After,
To marry her, I'll add three thousand crowns
40   To what is passed already.

WIDOW   I have yielded:
Instruct my daughter how she shall persever,
That time and place with this deceit so lawful
May prove coherent. Every night he comes
45   With musics of all sorts and songs composed
To her unworthiness. It nothing steads us
To chide him from our eaves, for he persists
As if his life lay on't.

HELEN   Why then tonight
50   Let us assay our plot, which, if it speed,
Is wicked meaning in a lawful deed,
And lawful meaning in a lawful act,
Where both not sin, and yet a sinful fact.
But let's about it.   [*Exeunt*]

Act 4 [Scene 1]   *running scene 14*

*Enter one of the Frenchmen [the First Lord Dumaine], with five or six
other Soldiers in ambush*

FIRST LORD   He can come no other way but by this hedge-corner.
When you sally upon him, speak what terrible language you
will: though you understand it not yourselves, no matter, for
we must not seem to understand him, unless some one
5   among us, whom we must produce for an interpreter.

FIRST SOLDIER   Good captain, let me be th'interpreter.

---

39 **marry her** enable her to marry   40 **is passed** has been given   42 **persever** proceed
44 **coherent** fitting   45 **musics** musicians/instruments/music   46 **unworthiness** humble
status/because convincing her to do an unworthy deed   **steads** profits   47 **chide** scold, drive
away   48 **lay** depended   50 **assay** try   **speed** succeed   51 **meaning** intention (on
Bertram's part)   **lawful deed** i.e. marital sex   53 **fact** i.e. Bertram's belief that he is having
sex with another woman   4.1 ***Location: battlefield***   2 **sally** burst out   **terrible**
terrifying   4 **unless** except for

FIRST LORD   Art not acquainted with him? Knows he not thy
voice?

FIRST SOLDIER   No, sir, I warrant you.

10   FIRST LORD   But what linsey-woolsey hast thou to speak to us
again?

FIRST SOLDIER   E'en such as you speak to me.

FIRST LORD   He must think us some band of strangers
i'th'adversary's entertainment. Now he hath a smack of all

15   neighbouring languages: therefore we must every one be a
man of his own fancy, not to know what we speak one to
another, so we seem to know, is to know straight our purpose:
choughs' language, gabble enough and good enough. As for
you, interpreter, you must seem very politic. But couch, ho!

20   Here he comes, to beguile two hours in a sleep, and then to
return and swear the lies he forges.   *They hide*

Enter Parolles

PAROLLES   Ten o'clock. Within these three hours 'twill be time
enough to go home. What shall I say I have done? It must be
a very plausive invention that carries it. They begin to smoke

25   me, and disgraces have of late knocked too often at my door.
I find my tongue is too foolhardy, but my heart hath the fear
of Mars before it and of his creatures, not daring the reports
of my tongue.

FIRST LORD   This is the first truth that e'er   *Speaks aside to the*

30   thine own tongue was guilty of.   *others throughout*

PAROLLES   What the devil should move me to undertake the
recovery of this drum, being not ignorant of the
impossibility, and knowing I had no such purpose? I must
give myself some hurts, and say I got them in exploit: yet

35   slight ones will not carry it. They will say, 'Came you off with

---

10 linsey-woolsey cloth made of flax and wool (i.e. verbal mixture, nonsense)   **11 again** in
response   **13 strangers** foreigners   **14 entertainment** employment   **smack** taste,
smattering   **16 fancy** creativity   **to know** knowing   **17 so** so long as   **know straight**
directly achieve   **18 choughs** jackdaws, plays on "chuff," meaning "rustic, clown"
19 politic cunning   **couch** lie down, hide   **20 beguile** while away   **24 plausive** plausible
it it off   **smoke** smoke out, suspect   **27 creatures** i.e. soldiers   **not . . . tongue** and I am
afraid to carry out my boasts   **34 hurts** wounds

so little?' And great ones I dare not give. Wherefore, what's
the instance? Tongue, I must put you into a butter-woman's
mouth and buy myself another of Bajazet's mule, if you
prattle me into these perils.

40   **FIRST LORD**   Is it possible he should know what he is, and be that
he is?

  PAROLLES   I would the cutting of my garments would serve the
turn, or the breaking of my Spanish sword.

  FIRST LORD   We cannot afford you so.

45   **PAROLLES**   Or the baring of my beard, and to say it was in
stratagem.

  FIRST LORD   'Twould not do.

  PAROLLES   Or to drown my clothes, and say I was stripped.

  FIRST LORD   Hardly serve.

50   **PAROLLES**   Though I swore I leaped from the window of the
citadel.

  FIRST LORD   How deep?

  PAROLLES   Thirty fathom.

  FIRST LORD   Three great oaths would scarce make that be
55   believed.

  PAROLLES   I would I had any drum of the enemy's. I would
swear I recovered it.

  FIRST LORD   You shall hear one anon.

  PAROLLES   A drum now of the enemy's—

Alarum within   *The Lord and Soldiers come out of hiding*

60   **FIRST LORD**   *Throca movousus, cargo, cargo, cargo.*   *First Soldier will act as*

  ALL   *Cargo, cargo, cargo, villianda par corbo, cargo.*   *Interpreter*

  PAROLLES   O, ransom, ransom! Do not hide mine eyes.   *They seize*

  INTERPRETER   *Boskos thromuldo boskos.*   *and blindfold Parolles*

---

37 instance motive (for doing this)/proof (of my supposed exploits)   **Tongue . . . mouth** with
sexual connotations   **butter-woman** dairywoman/whore (i.e. chatty/lecherous)   **38 of** from
Bajazet's mule mules were proverbially silent and sometimes associated with Turks, but
emperors such as Bajazet had "mute" slaves, so some editors emend accordingly; or there may
be a garbled allusion to Balaam's ass in the Bible, which only spoke at God's command
42 serve the turn suffice   **44 afford** allow/let (you) off   **45 baring** shaving   **in stratagem** an
act of cunning, for disguise   **51 citadel** presumably the enemy fortress   **53 Thirty fathom**
180 feet   *Alarum* call to arms

PAROLLES   I know you are the Muskos' regiment,
65   And I shall lose my life for want of language.
        If there be here German, or Dane, low Dutch,
        Italian, or French, let him speak to me,
        I'll discover that which shall undo the Florentine.

INTERPRETER   *Boskos vauvado.* I understand thee, and can speak
70   thy tongue. *Kerelybonto.* Sir, betake thee to thy faith, for
        seventeen poniards are at thy bosom.

PAROLLES   O!

INTERPRETER   O, pray, pray, pray! *Manka revania dulche.*

FIRST LORD   *Oscorbidulchos volivorco.*

75   INTERPRETER   The general is content to spare thee yet,
        And, hoodwinked as thou art, will lead thee on
        To gather from thee. Haply thou mayst inform
        Something to save thy life.

PAROLLES   O, let me live,
80   And all the secrets of our camp I'll show,
        Their force, their purposes. Nay, I'll speak that
        Which you will wonder at.

INTERPRETER   But wilt thou faithfully?

PAROLLES   If I do not, damn me.

85   INTERPRETER   *Acordo linta.*
        Come on, thou art granted space.

                    Exeunt [*with Parolles guarded*]

A short alarum within

FIRST LORD   Go tell the Count Rossillion and my brother
        We have caught the woodcock, and will keep him muffled
        Till we do hear from them.

90   SECOND SOLDIER   Captain, I will.

FIRST LORD   A will betray us all unto ourselves:
        Inform on that.

---

64 Muskos probably Muscovites   **66 low Dutch** Dutch; **German** was known as "high Dutch"
68 discover reveal   **70 betake thee** entrust thyself   **71 poniards** daggers   **76 hoodwinked**
blindfolded   **lead thee on** take you elsewhere/direct the conversation   **77 gather** gain
information   **86 space** time/a temporary reprieve   **88 woodcock** proverbially stupid bird
muffled blindfolded   **91 A** he   **92 Inform on** report

SECOND SOLDIER   So I will, sir.

FIRST LORD   Till then I'll keep him dark and safely locked.

Exeunt

[Act 4 Scene 2]

Enter Bertram and the maid called Diana

BERTRAM   They told me that your name was Fontybell.

DIANA   No, my good lord, Diana.

BERTRAM   Titled goddess,
And worth it, with addition! But, fair soul,

5   In your fine frame hath love no quality?
If the quick fire of youth light not your mind,
You are no maiden, but a monument.
When you are dead, you should be such a one
As you are now, for you are cold and stern,

10   And now you should be as your mother was
When your sweet self was got.

DIANA   She then was honest.

BERTRAM   So should you be.

DIANA   No:

15   My mother did but duty, such, my lord,
As you owe to your wife.

BERTRAM   No more o'that.
I prithee do not strive against my vows:
I was compelled to her, but I love thee

20   By love's own sweet constraint, and will forever
Do thee all rights of service.

DIANA   Ay, so you serve us
Till we serve you, but when you have our roses,

4.2   *Location: Florence*   **1 Fontybell** i.e. "beautiful fountain"   **3 goddess** Diana was the
goddess of chastity and hunting   **4 worth** worthy of   **addition** additional distinction
5 frame being, shape   **quality** part   **6 quick** lively   **7 monument** statue   **11 got** conceived
12 honest chaste (i.e. married; Bertram shifts the sense to "frank, open")   **18 vows** i.e. of love
for Diana/to have nothing to do with Helen   **20 constraint** compulsion   **21 rights** duties
23 serve gratify sexually   **roses** virginities/vaginas

You barely leave our thorns to prick ourselves

25   And mock us with our bareness.

BERTRAM   How have I sworn!

DIANA   'Tis not the many oaths that makes the truth,

But the plain single vow that is vowed true.

What is not holy, that we swear not by,

30   But take the high'st to witness. Then, pray you tell me:

If I should swear by Jove's great attributes,

I loved you dearly, would you believe my oaths

When I did love you ill? This has no holding,

To swear by him whom I protest to love

35   That I will work against him: therefore your oaths

Are words and poor conditions but unsealed,

At least in my opinion.

BERTRAM   Change it, change it.

Be not so holy-cruel: love is holy,

40   And my integrity ne'er knew the crafts

That you do charge men with. Stand no more off,

But give thyself unto my sick desires,

Who then recovers. Say thou art mine, and ever

My love as it begins shall so persèver.

45   DIANA   I see that men make ropes in such a scar

That we'll forsake ourselves. Give me that ring.

BERTRAM   I'll lend it thee, my dear, but have no power

To give it from me.

DIANA   Will you not, my lord?

50   BERTRAM   It is an honour 'longing to our house,

Bequeathèd down from many ancestors,

---

24 **barely** in a naked state/only just   **thorns . . . ourselves** i.e. with shame (quibbles on the idea that this is in place of a man's **prick**)   25 **bareness** loss of the rose of virginity/ defenselessness   30 **high'st** i.e. God   **to** as our   31 **Jove** supreme Roman god   33 **ill** imperfectly/immorally   **holding** consistency (i.e. is untenable)   34 **protest** profess 36 **words** mere words   **conditions** contracts   **unsealed** i.e. not valid legally   38 **it** i.e. your opinion   39 **holy-cruel** cruel by being holy   40 **crafts** skills/deceits   42 **sick** i.e. needing cure   43 **Who** which will   **recovers** recover   45 **scar** perhaps in the sense of "precipice," i.e. dangerous place or "sore/fault, blemish" or "fear/panic" (modern "scare"); the general sense is that men create dangerous situations for women in which they may lose their sense of propriety and behave recklessly; some editors emend to "snare"   50 **honour** object of distinction

Which were the greatest obloquy i'th'world
In me to lose.

DIANA   Mine honour's such a ring:

55   My chastity's the jewel of our house,
Bequeathèd down from many ancestors,
Which were the greatest obloquy i'th'world
In me to lose. Thus your own proper wisdom
Brings in the champion honour on my part

60   Against your vain assault.

BERTRAM   Here, take my ring.   *Gives her a ring*
My house, mine honour, yea, my life, be thine,
And I'll be bid by thee.

DIANA   When midnight comes, knock at my chamber-
window:

65   I'll order take my mother shall not hear.
Now will I charge you in the band of truth,
When you have conquered my yet maiden bed,
Remain there but an hour, nor speak to me.
My reasons are most strong and you shall know them

70   When back again this ring shall be delivered:
And on your finger in the night I'll put
Another ring, that what in time proceeds
May token to the future our past deeds.
Adieu, till then. Then, fail not. You have won

75   A wife of me, though there my hope be done.

BERTRAM   A heaven on earth I have won by wooing thee.

[*Exit*]

DIANA   For which live long to thank both heaven and me.
You may so in the end.
My mother told me just how he would woo,

80   As if she sat in's heart. She says all men
Have the like oaths. He had sworn to marry me

---

52 **obloquy** disgrace   54 **honour's** virginity's   **ring** with vaginal connotations   58 **proper**
personal   63 **bid** commanded   65 **order take** make arrangements   66 **band** bond   67 **yet**
maiden still virgin   72 **proceeds** comes to pass   73 **token** betoken, signify   75 **wife** i.e. by
having sex   **hope** i.e. of marrying Bertram   **be done** ends   81 **like** same

When his wife's dead: therefore I'll lie with him
When I am buried. Since Frenchmen are so braid,
Marry that will, I live and die a maid.
85   Only in this disguise I think't no sin
To cozen him that would unjustly win.   *Exit*

[Act 4 Scene 3]   *running scene 16*

Enter the two French Captains [the Lords Dumaine] and some two or three Soldiers

FIRST LORD   You have not given him his mother's letter?

SECOND LORD   I have delivered it an hour since: there is something in't that stings his nature, for on the reading it he changed almost into another man.

5   FIRST LORD   He has much worthy blame laid upon him for shaking off so good a wife and so sweet a lady.

SECOND LORD   Especially he hath incurred the everlasting displeasure of the king, who had even tuned his bounty to sing happiness to him. I will tell you a thing, but you shall let
10   it dwell darkly with you.

FIRST LORD   When you have spoken it, 'tis dead, and I am the grave of it.

SECOND LORD   He hath perverted a young gentlewoman here in Florence, of a most chaste renown, and this night he fleshes
15   his will in the spoil of her honour. He hath given her his monumental ring, and thinks himself made in the unchaste composition.

FIRST LORD   Now, God delay our rebellion! As we are ourselves, what things are we!

---

83 braid i.e. twisted, deceitful   **84 Marry** let those marry   **85 disguise** deceptive role
86 cozen trick   **4.3** *Location: battlefield*   **2 since** ago   **5 worthy** deserved   **8 his bounty** (the instrument of) his generosity   **10 darkly** secretly   **13 perverted** seduced/ corrupted   **14 fleshes** rewards with meat (as hounds were given a piece of the kill; sexual connotations)   **15 will** sexual desire/penis   **spoil** plundered loot/despoiling/meat given to hounds   **16 monumental** i.e. serving as a reminder of his ancestry   **made** successful **17 composition** bargain (plays on the sense of "something made")   **18 delay** subdue **rebellion** rebellious, lustful appetites   **ourselves** i.e. human

20 SECOND LORD   Merely our own traitors. And as in the common course of all treasons, we still see them reveal themselves, till they attain to their abhorred ends, so he that in this action contrives against his own nobility, in his proper stream o'erflows himself.

25 FIRST LORD   Is it not meant damnable in us, to be trumpeters of our unlawful intents? We shall not then have his company tonight?

SECOND LORD   Not till after midnight, for he is dieted to his hour.

FIRST LORD   That approaches apace. I would gladly have him
30 see his company anatomized, that he might take a measure of his own judgements, wherein so curiously he had set this counterfeit.

SECOND LORD   We will not meddle with him till he come, for his presence must be the whip of the other.

35 FIRST LORD   In the meantime, what hear you of these wars?

SECOND LORD   I hear there is an overture of peace.

FIRST LORD   Nay, I assure you, a peace concluded.

SECOND LORD   What will Count Rossillion do then? Will he travel higher, or return again into France?

40 FIRST LORD   I perceive by this demand, you are not altogether of his council.

SECOND LORD   Let it be forbid, sir! So should I be a great deal of his act.

FIRST LORD   Sir, his wife some two months since fled from his
45 house. Her pretence is a pilgrimage to Saint Jaques le Grand; which holy undertaking with most austere sanctimony she accomplished. And there residing, the tenderness of her

---

20 **Merely** entirely   21 **still** always   **themselves** i.e. their true, treacherous natures
22 **attain to** reach   **ends** objectives/deaths   **he** i.e. Bertram   23 **contrives** conspires
proper stream own current of desire   25 **Is . . . meant** does it not show (as)   28 **dieted . . .**
hour restricted to his appointed time   29 **apace** quickly   30 **company** companion
anatomized dissected, revealed   31 **curiously . . . counterfeit** elaborately he has displayed this
false jewel (Parolles)   33 **him** i.e. Parolles   **he . . . his** i.e. Bertram   34 **the other** i.e. Parolles
36 **overture** opening, move toward   39 **higher** further   40 **demand** question   **of his council**
in his confidence   42 **deal . . . act** partaker in his affairs   45 **pretence** purpose
46 **sanctimony** holiness

nature became as a prey to her grief; in fine, made a groan of her last breath, and now she sings in heaven.

50   SECOND LORD   How is this justified?

FIRST LORD   The stronger part of it by her own letters, which makes her story true, even to the point of her death. Her death itself, which could not be her office to say is come, was faithfully confirmed by the rector of the place.

55   SECOND LORD   Hath the count all this intelligence?

FIRST LORD   Ay, and the particular confirmations, point from point, to the full arming of the verity.

SECOND LORD   I am heartily sorry that he'll be glad of this.

FIRST LORD   How mightily sometimes we make us comforts of
60   our losses!

SECOND LORD   And how mightily some other times we drown our gain in tears! The great dignity that his valour hath here acquired for him shall at home be encountered with a shame as ample.

65   FIRST LORD   The web of our life is of a mingled yarn, good and ill together: our virtues would be proud if our faults whipped them not; and our crimes would despair if they were not cherished by our virtues.

Enter a [Servant as a] Messenger

How now! Where's your master?

70   SERVANT   He met the duke in the street, sir, of whom he hath taken a solemn leave: his lordship will next morning for France. The duke hath offered him letters of commendations to the king.

SECOND LORD   They shall be no more than needful there, if they
75   were more than they can commend.

Enter Count Rossillion [Bertram]

---

50 **justified** proved   53 **office** role   54 **rector** priest/ruler   57 **arming** establishment, strengthening   **verity** truth   59 **make . . . of** take comfort in   63 **encountered** met
68 **cherished** comforted, pitied   71 **solemn** formal   **for** leave for   72 **offered** given
74 **needful** necessary   **if** even if   75 **more . . . commend** stronger commendations than Bertram deserves

FIRST LORD   They cannot be too sweet for the king's tartness. Here's his lordship now.— How now, my lord! Is't not after midnight?

BERTRAM   I have tonight dispatched sixteen businesses, a
80   month's length apiece, by an abstract of success: I have congied with the duke, done my adieu with his nearest, buried a wife, mourned for her, writ to my lady mother I am returning, entertained my convoy and between these main parcels of dispatch effected many nicer needs. The last was
85   the greatest, but that I have not ended yet.

SECOND LORD   If the business be of any difficulty, and this morning your departure hence, it requires haste of your lordship.

BERTRAM   I mean, the business is not ended, as fearing to hear
90   of it hereafter. But shall we have this dialogue between the fool and the soldier? Come, bring forth this counterfeit module, h'as deceived me like a double-meaning prophesier.

SECOND LORD   Bring him forth.   *To Soldiers*
H'as sat i'th'stocks all night, poor gallant knave.

                                                    [*Exit some Soldiers*]

95   BERTRAM   No matter. His heels have deserved it in usurping his spurs so long. How does he carry himself?

SECOND LORD   I have told your lordship already, the stocks carry him. But to answer you as you would be understood: he weeps like a wench that had shed her milk, he hath confessed
100   himself to Morgan, whom he supposes to be a friar, from the time of his remembrance to this very instant disaster of his setting i'th'stocks. And what think you he hath confessed?

---

79 dispatched settled   **80 by . . . success** quickly and successfully/here follows a summary of my success   **81 congied with** taken ceremonious leave of   **nearest** closest company   **83 entertained my convoy** hired my means of transport   **84 parcels of dispatch** major items of business   **nicer** more delicate/lascivious   **89 hear of it** i.e. because Diana may be pregnant and/or may claim him as her husband   **92 module** model (of a soldier)   **double-meaning prophesier** ambiguous, equivocal oracle   **94 stocks** instrument of public punishment in which the arms, head, or legs were confined   **gallant** showy, ostentatious
95 usurping laying false claim to   **96 spurs** symbols of knightly valor   **carry** bear, conduct (the Second Lord puns on the sense of "transport")   **99 shed** spilled   **101 time . . . remembrance** beginning of his memory   **instant disaster** current misfortune

BERTRAM   Nothing of me, has a?

SECOND LORD   His confession is taken, and it shall be read to his
105   face: if your lordship be in't, as I believe you are, you must
have the patience to hear it.

Enter Parolles [blindfolded] with his Interpreter

BERTRAM   A plague upon him! Muffled? He can say nothing of
me. Hush, hush.

FIRST LORD   Hoodman comes! *Portotartarossa*.

110   INTERPRETER   He calls for the tortures. What will you say
without 'em?

PAROLLES   I will confess what I know without constraint. If ye
pinch me like a pasty, I can say no more.

INTERPRETER   *Bosko chimurcho*.

115   FIRST LORD   *Boblibindo chicurmurco*.

INTERPRETER   You are a merciful general. Our general bids you
answer to what I shall ask you out of a note.

PAROLLES   And truly, as I hope to live.

INTERPRETER   'First demand of him how many horse   *Pretends to*
120   the duke is strong.' What say you to that?   *read*

PAROLLES   Five or six thousand, but very weak and
unserviceable. The troops are all scattered, and the
commanders very poor rogues, upon my reputation and
credit and as I hope to live.

125   INTERPRETER   Shall I set down your answer so?

PAROLLES   Do. I'll take the sacrament on't, how and which way
you will.   *Bertram and the Lords speak aside throughout*

BERTRAM   All's one to him. What a past-saving slave is this?

FIRST LORD   You're deceived, my lord: this is Monsieur Parolles,
130   the gallant militarist — that was his own phrase — that had
the whole theoric of war in the knot of his scarf, and the
practice in the chape of his dagger.

---

103 a he   109 Hoodman term for the blindfolded player in the game Blind Man's Bluff
112 constraint force   113 pasty meat pie with pinched crusts   117 note memorandum/list
119 horse cavalry   120 is strong i.e. has   126 take the sacrament i.e. swear most
religiously   how and which however and whichever   128 All's one it's all the same   past-
saving beyond redemption   131 theoric theory   132 chape metal plate covering the point of
the sheath

SECOND LORD   I will never trust a man again for keeping his
sword clean, nor believe he can have everything in him by
135   wearing his apparel neatly.

INTERPRETER   Well, that's set down.   *To Parolles*

PAROLLES   'Five or six thousand horse,' I said — I will say true
— 'or thereabouts', set down, for I'll speak truth.

FIRST LORD   He's very near the truth in this.

140   **BERTRAM**   But I con him no thanks for't, in the nature he
delivers it.

PAROLLES   'Poor rogues', I pray you say.

INTERPRETER   Well, that's set down.

PAROLLES   I humbly thank you, sir. A truth's a truth, the
145   rogues are marvellous poor.

INTERPRETER   'Demand of him, of what strength   *Pretends to*
they are a-foot.' What say you to that?   *read*

PAROLLES   By my troth, sir, if I were to live this present hour,
I will tell true. Let me see: Spurio, a hundred and fifty:
150   Sebastian, so many: Corambus, so many: Jaques, so many:
Guiltian, Cosmo, Lodowick and Gratii, two hundred fifty
each: mine own company, Chitopher, Vaumond, Bentii, two
hundred fifty each. So that the muster-file, rotten and sound,
upon my life, amounts not to fifteen thousand poll, half of
155   the which dare not shake the snow from off their cassocks,
lest they shake themselves to pieces.

BERTRAM   What shall be done to him?

FIRST LORD   Nothing, but let him have thanks. Demand of him
my condition, and what credit I have with the duke.

160   **INTERPRETER**   Well, that's set down. 'You shall   *Pretends to*
demand of him, whether one Captain Dumaine be   *read*
i'th'camp, a Frenchman, what his reputation is with the
duke, what his valour, honesty, and expertness in wars, or
whether he thinks it were not possible, with well-weighing

---

134 clean free from blood/polished   **140 con** i.e. give   **in the nature** considering the way in
which   **145 marvellous** extremely   **147 a-foot** in terms of foot soldiers   **148 live** i.e. live
only for   **150 so** as   **153 muster-file** official list of soldiers   **rotten and sound** (of those
both) sick and healthy   **154 poll** heads, i.e. soldiers   **155 cassocks** soldier's cloaks/coats
159 condition (military) character   **164 well-weighing** heavy/persuasive

165 sums of gold, to corrupt him to a revolt.' What say you to this? What do you know of it?

PAROLLES   I beseech you let me answer to the particular of the inter'gatories: demand them singly.

INTERPRETER   Do you know this Captain Dumaine?

170 PAROLLES   I know him: a was a botcher's 'prentice in Paris, from whence he was whipped for getting the shrieve's fool with child — a dumb innocent that could   *First Lord attempts* not say him nay.   *to hit Parolles*

BERTRAM   Nay, by your leave, hold your hands, though I know

175 his brains are forfeit to the next tile that falls.

INTERPRETER   Well, is this captain in the Duke of Florence's camp?

PAROLLES   Upon my knowledge he is, and lousy.

FIRST LORD   Nay look not so upon me. We shall hear of your

180 lord anon.

INTERPRETER   What is his reputation with the duke?

PAROLLES   The duke knows him for no other but a poor officer of mine, and writ to me this other day to turn him out o'th'band. I think I have his letter in my pocket.

185 INTERPRETER   Marry, we'll search.   *They search his pockets*

PAROLLES   In good sadness, I do not know. Either it is there, or it is upon a file with the duke's other letters in my tent.

INTERPRETER   Here 'tis. Here's a paper. Shall I read it to you?

PAROLLES   I do not know if it be it or no.

190 BERTRAM   Our interpreter does it well.

FIRST LORD   Excellently.

INTERPRETER   'Dian, the count's a fool, and full of gold'—   *Reads*

PAROLLES   That is not the duke's letter, sir. That is an advertisement to a proper maid in Florence, one Diana, to

195 take heed of the allurement of one Count Rossillion, a foolish

---

167 particular individual points   **168 inter'gatories** questions   **170 botcher** mender (of clothes and shoes)   **'prentice** apprentice   **171 shrieve's fool** idiot girl in the sheriff's care
172 innocent fool   **173 him nay** no to him   **175 his . . . falls** i.e. he is in danger of a sudden death   **178 lousy** lice-infested/contemptible   **184 o'th'band** of the military company
186 good sadness all seriousness   **194 advertisement** advice, warning   **proper** respectable

idle boy, but for all that very ruttish. I pray you, sir, put it up
again.

INTERPRETER   Nay, I'll read it first, by your favour.

PAROLLES   My meaning in't, I protest, was very honest in the
200   behalf of the maid, for I knew the young count to be a
dangerous and lascivious boy, who is a whale to virginity
and devours up all the fry it finds.

BERTRAM   Damnable both-sides rogue!

INTERPRETER   [*Reads the*] letter
'When he swears oaths, bid him drop gold, and take it.
205   After he scores, he never pays the score.
Half won is match well made, match and well make it;
He ne'er pays after-debts, take it before.
And say a soldier, Dian, told thee this:
Men are to mell with, boys are not to kiss.
210   For count of this, the count's a fool, I know it,
Who pays before, but not when he does owe it.
Thine, as he vowed to thee in thine ear, Parolles.'

BERTRAM   He shall be whipped through the army with this
rhyme in's forehead.

215   SECOND LORD   This is your devoted friend, sir, the manifold
linguist and the armipotent soldier.

BERTRAM   I could endure anything before but a cat, and now
he's a cat to me.

INTERPRETER   I perceive, sir, by the general's looks, we shall be
220   fain to hang you.

PAROLLES   My life, sir, in any case. Not that I am afraid to die,
but that, my offences being many, I would repent out the
remainder of nature. Let me live, sir, in a dungeon, i'th'stocks,
or anywhere, so I may live.

---

196 **ruttish** lustful   **up** back   198 **favour** permission   202 **fry** young fish   203 **both-sides**
two-faced   204 **drop** offer, pay with   205 **scores** incurs a bill   206 **Half . . . it** one is halfway
there if the bargain is well-made, so set out your terms clearly (or "be even") and succeed
207 **after-debts** outstanding bills   **it** i.e. payment   209 **mell** mingle/have sex   210 **For**
count on account/so be sure   211 **before** in advance   214 **in's** on his   215 **manifold**
linguist speaker of many languages   216 **armipotent** powerful in arms   220 **fain** obliged
223 **nature** my natural life

225 INTERPRETER   We'll see what may be done, so you confess freely:
therefore, once more to this Captain Dumaine. You have
answered to his reputation with the duke and to his valour.
What is his honesty?

PAROLLES   He will steal, sir, an egg out of a cloister, for rapes
230 and ravishments he parallels Nessus. He professes not
keeping of oaths, in breaking 'em he is stronger than
Hercules. He will lie, sir, with such volubility that you would
think truth were a fool. Drunkenness is his best virtue, for he
will be swine-drunk, and in his sleep he does little harm, save
235 to his bed-clothes about him. But they know his conditions
and lay him in straw. I have but little more to say, sir, of his
honesty: he has everything that an honest man should not
have; what an honest man should have, he has nothing.

FIRST LORD   I begin to love him for this.

240 BERTRAM   For this description of thine honesty? A pox upon
him for me. He's more and more a cat.

INTERPRETER   What say you to his expertness in war?

PAROLLES   Faith, sir, h'as led the drum before the English
tragedians — to belie him, I will not — and more of his
245 soldiership I know not, except, in that country he had the
honour to be the officer at a place there called Mile-end, to
instruct for the doubling of files. I would do the man what
honour I can, but of this I am not certain.

FIRST LORD   He hath out-villained villainy so far that the rarity
250 redeems him.

BERTRAM   A pox on him, he's a cat still.

INTERPRETER   His qualities being at this poor price, I need not to
ask you if gold will corrupt him to revolt.

---

229 egg . . . cloister i.e. trifling thing, even from a holy place   230 Nessus centaur who tried
to rape Hercules' wife   professes not does not make a practice of   232 Hercules Greek hero
famed for feats of strength   234 swine-drunk drunk as a pig (i.e. excessively drunk—and thus
likely to wet his bed-clothes)   235 they i.e. the servants who put him to bed   conditions
habits   243 led . . . tragedians drums announced a performance by actors   244 belie tell
lies about   246 Mile-end field outside the city of London where citizen militia were trained
247 doubling of files simple military marching maneuver

PAROLLES   Sir, for a cardecue he will sell the fee-simple of his
255   salvation, the inheritance of it, and cut th'entail from all
       remainders, and a perpetual succession for it perpetually.

INTERPRETER   What's his brother, the other Captain Dumaine?

SECOND LORD   Why does he ask him of me?

INTERPRETER   What's he?

260   PAROLLES   E'en a crow o'th'same nest: not altogether so great
       as the first in goodness, but greater a great deal in evil. He
       excels his brother for a coward, yet his brother is reputed one
       of the best that is. In a retreat he outruns any lackey; marry,
       in coming on he has the cramp.

265   INTERPRETER   If your life be saved, will you undertake to betray
       the Florentine?

PAROLLES   Ay, and the captain of his horse, Count Rossillion.

INTERPRETER   I'll whisper with the general, and know his
       pleasure.

270   PAROLLES   I'll no more drumming. A plague of all   *Aside*
       drums! Only to seem to deserve well, and to beguile the
       supposition of that lascivious young boy, the count, have I
       run into this danger. Yet who would have suspected an
       ambush where I was taken?

275   INTERPRETER   There is no remedy, sir, but you must die. The
       general says, you that have so traitorously discovered the
       secrets of your army and made such pestiferous reports of
       men very nobly held, can serve the world for no honest use:
       therefore you must die. Come, headsman, off with his head.

280   PAROLLES   O lord, sir, let me live, or let me see my death!

FIRST LORD   That shall you, and take your leave of all your
       friends. So, look about you: know you any here?   *Unblindfolds him*

BERTRAM   Good morrow, noble captain.

SECOND LORD   God bless you, Captain Parolles.

---

254 **cardecue** *quart d'écu,* small French silver coin   **fee-simple** absolute possession (legal term
used of land or property)   255 **cut . . . perpetually** prevent inheritance to all subsequent heirs
forever   262 **for** as   263 **lackey** errand-running servant   264 **coming on** advancing
267 **captain . . . horse** cavalry commander   270 **no more** have nothing more to do with
271 **beguile the supposition** deceive the opinion   276 **discovered** revealed   277 **pestiferous**
malicious, pestilent   278 **held** regarded

285 FIRST LORD   God save you, noble captain.

SECOND LORD   Captain, what greeting will you to my Lord Lafew?
I am for France.

FIRST LORD   Good captain, will you give me a copy of the sonnet
you writ to Diana in behalf of the Count Rossillion? An I
290 were not a very coward, I'd compel it of you. But fare you
well.   *Exeunt [Bertram and Lords]*

INTERPRETER   You are undone, captain — all your scarf that has
a knot on't yet.

PAROLLES   Who cannot be crushed with a plot?

295 INTERPRETER   If you could find out a country where but women
were that had received so much shame, you might begin an
impudent nation. Fare ye well, sir. I am for France too. We
shall speak of you there.   *Exeunt [Interpreter and Soldiers]*

PAROLLES   Yet am I thankful. If my heart were great
300 'Twould burst at this. Captain I'll be no more,
But I will eat and drink, and sleep as soft
As captain shall. Simply the thing I am
Shall make me live. Who knows himself a braggart,
Let him fear this; for it will come to pass
305 That every braggart shall be found an ass.
Rust, sword. Cool, blushes. And, Parolles, live
Safest in shame. Being fooled, by fool'ry thrive;
There's place and means for every man alive.
I'll after them.   *Exit*

[Act 4 Scene 4]   *running scene 17*

Enter Helen, Widow and Diana

HELEN   That you may well perceive I have not wronged you,
One of the greatest in the Christian world
Shall be my surety, 'fore whose throne 'tis needful,

---

286 **you** you send   287 **for** bound for   289 **in** on   290 **a very** an absolute   292 **undone**
ruined/undressed   295 **but** only   297 **impudent** shameless, immodest   299 **great** big/noble
303 **Who** he who   307 **fooled** made a fool of/tricked   **4.4** *Location: Florence*
2 **One . . . world** i.e. the French king   3 **surety** guarantor

Ere I can perfect mine intents, to kneel.
5   Time was, I did him a desirèd office,
Dear almost as his life, which gratitude
Through flinty Tartar's bosom would peep forth,
And answer thanks. I duly am informed
His grace is at Marseilles, to which place
10   We have convenient convoy. You must know
I am supposèd dead. The army breaking,
My husband hies him home, where, heaven aiding,
And by the leave of my good lord the king,
We'll be before our welcome.

15   WIDOW   Gentle madam,
You never had a servant to whose trust
Your business was more welcome.

HELEN   Nor you, mistress,
Ever a friend whose thoughts more truly labour
20   To recompense your love. Doubt not but heaven
Hath brought me up to be your daughter's dower,
As it hath fated her to be my motive
And helper to a husband. But, O strange men,
That can such sweet use make of what they hate,
25   When saucy trusting of the cozened thoughts
Defiles the pitchy night, so lust doth play
With what it loathes for that which is away.
But more of this hereafter. You, Diana,
Under my poor instructions yet must suffer
30   Something in my behalf.

DIANA   Let death and honesty
Go with your impositions, I am yours,
Upon your will to suffer.

---

6 **which gratitude** gratitude for which   7 **Through** even through   **Tartar** inhabitant of
Central Asia, considered pitiless and savage   10 **convenient convoy** suitable means of
transport   11 **breaking** disbanding   12 **hies him** hastens   14 **our welcome** i.e. we are
expected   21 **be** i.e. provide   **dower** dowry   22 **motive** agent/means   25 **saucy trusting**
lecherous acceptance   **cozened** deluded   26 **Defiles** blackens/pollutes   **pitchy** dark (pitch
is a tar-like substance)   27 **loathes** i.e. Helen   **for . . . away** i.e. in place of Diana   29 **yet**
further   31 **death and honesty** i.e. a chaste death   32 **Go with** i.e. result from   **impositions**
commands   33 **Upon** at

HELEN   Yet, I pray you:

35   But with the word the time will bring on summer,
When briars shall have leaves as well as thorns,
And be as sweet as sharp. We must away.
Our wagon is prepared, and time revives us:
All's well that ends well, still the fine's the crown;
40   Whate'er the course, the end is the renown.   *Exeunt*

[Act 4 Scene 5]   *running scene 18*

Enter Clown [Lavatch], Old Lady [Countess] and Lafew

LAFEW   No, no, no, your son was misled with a snipt-taffeta
fellow there, whose villainous saffron would have made all
the unbaked and doughy youth of a nation in his colour.
Your daughter-in-law had been alive at this hour, and your
5   son here at home, more advanced by the king than by that
red-tailed humble-bee I speak of.

COUNTESS   I would I had not known him. It was the death of
the most virtuous gentlewoman that ever nature had praise
for creating. If she had partaken of my flesh, and cost me the
10   dearest groans of a mother, I could not have owed her a
more rooted love.

LAFEW   'Twas a good lady, 'twas a good lady. We may pick a
thousand salads ere we light on such another herb.

LAVATCH   Indeed, sir, she was the sweet marjoram of the
15   salad, or rather, the herb of grace.

LAFEW   They are not herbs, you knave, they are nose-herbs.

---

34 Yet for a while   35 But . . . word through the power of word alone: either a metaphysical
reference to the "word of God" or a meta-theatrical reference to the power of theater
38 revives will reinvigorate   39 fine's end's   40 renown i.e. important thing
4.5   *Location: Rossillion*   1 with by   snipt-taffeta in slashed silk, indicative of showiness
2 saffron orange-red dye used to color ruffs and food   3 unbaked uncooked/immature/
impressionable   doughy dough-like/malleable   4 Your i.e. had it not been for Parolles, your
6 humble-bee bumble-bee   10 dearest direst/most precious   groans . . . mother i.e. in labor
11 rooted established/planted (Lafew develops this sense)   13 light on come across
14 sweet marjoram type of herb   15 herb of grace rue, herb associated with repentance
(suggests Helen's spiritual grace)   16 herbs edible salad plants   nose-herbs scented plants
for smelling

	LAVATCH	I am no great Nebuchadnezzar, sir. I have not much skill in grace.
	LAFEW	Whether dost thou profess thyself, a knave or a fool?
20	LAVATCH	A fool, sir, at a woman's service, and a knave at a man's.
	LAFEW	Your distinction?
	LAVATCH	I would cozen the man of his wife and do his service.
	LAFEW	So you were a knave at his service, indeed.
25	LAVATCH	And I would give his wife my bauble, sir, to do her service.
	LAFEW	I will subscribe for thee, thou art both knave and fool.
	LAVATCH	At your service.
30	LAFEW	No, no, no.
	LAVATCH	Why, sir, if I cannot serve you, I can serve as great a prince as you are.
	LAFEW	Who's that? A Frenchman?
35	LAVATCH	Faith, sir, a has an English maine, but his fisnomy is more hotter in France than there.
	LAFEW	What prince is that?
	LAVATCH	The black prince, sir, alias the prince of darkness, alias the devil.
	LAFEW	Hold thee, there's my purse: I give thee *Gives a purse*
40		not this to suggest thee from thy master thou talkest of. Serve him still.
	LAVATCH	I am a woodland fellow, sir, that always loved a great fire, and the master I speak of ever keeps a good fire. But sure he is the prince of the world. Let his nobility remain
45		in's court. I am for the house with the narrow gate, which I

---

17 Nebuchadnezzar Babylonian king, forced from his kingdom and made to eat grass
18 grace puns on "grass"   **19 Whether** which of the two   **20 fool** supposedly fools had big penises   **service** employment/sexual service   **23 cozen** cheat   **service** duty, i.e. sex
25 bauble fool's baton with a carved head on one end/penis   **do** with sexual connotations
27 subscribe vouch/answer   **34 maine** mane, like that of a royal English lion/meinie, family, retinue   **fisnomy** physiognomy, facial features   **35 hotter in France** choleric, angry, warlike (to the French)/susceptible to the "French disease" (syphilis)   **37 black prince** Edward the Black Prince of England, son of Edward III   **39 Hold thee** be quiet   **40 suggest** tempt
42 woodland rustic, i.e. simple   **43 fire** also "hellfire"   **44 prince . . . world** another title for the **devil**   **45 narrow gate** according to the Bible, the route to salvation (Matthew 7:13)

take to be too little for pomp to enter. Some that humble themselves may, but the many will be too chill and tender, and they'll be for the flowery way that leads to the broad gate and the great fire.

50 LAFEW   Go thy ways, I begin to be aweary of thee, and I tell thee so before, because I would not fall out with thee. Go thy ways. Let my horses be well looked to, without any tricks.

LAVATCH   If I put any tricks upon 'em, sir, they shall be jades' tricks, which are their own right by the law of nature.   *Exit*

55 LAFEW   A shrewd knave and an unhappy.

COUNTESS   So a is. My lord that's gone made himself much sport out of him. By his authority he remains here, which he thinks is a patent for his sauciness, and indeed he has no pace, but runs where he will.

60 LAFEW   I like him well, 'tis not amiss. And I was about to tell you, since I heard of the good lady's death and that my lord your son was upon his return home, I moved the king my master to speak in the behalf of my daughter, which, in the minority of them both, his majesty, out of a self-gracious 65 remembrance did first propose. His highness hath promised me to do it, and to stop up the displeasure he hath conceived against your son, there is no fitter matter. How does your ladyship like it?

COUNTESS   With very much content, my lord, and I wish it 70 happily effected.

LAFEW   His highness comes post from Marseilles, of as able body as when he numbered thirty. A will be here tomorrow, or I am deceived by him that in such intelligence hath seldom failed.

---

46 pomp proud, showy people   **47 many** majority   **chill** faint-hearted/sensitive to cold (thus preferring the warmth of hellfire)   **tender** fond of comfort   **50 Go thy ways** be off   **51 before** now, before I grow truly fed up with you   **52 tricks** i.e. tampering with the horses' feed to save hay   **53 jades' tricks** mischief caused by badly behaved horses   **55 shrewd** cunning, mischievous   **unhappy** unlucky/discontented/mischievous   **56 gone** dead (i.e. her husband the count)   **59 pace** restraint, obedient movement (horse-training term)   **61 lady's** i.e. Helen's   **62 moved** urged, persuaded   **64 minority** youth, when they were minors   **self-gracious remembrance** his own thoughtfulness, without prompting   **65 propose** i.e. for marriage to Bertram   **71 post** rapidly   **72 numbered** was aged   **73 him** i.e. a messenger   **intelligence** information

75   COUNTESS   It rejoices me that I hope I shall see him ere I die. I
have letters that my son will be here tonight. I shall beseech
your lordship to remain with me till they meet together.

LAFEW   Madam, I was thinking with what manners I might
safely be admitted.

80   COUNTESS   You need but plead your honourable privilege.

LAFEW   Lady, of that I have made a bold charter, but I thank
my God it holds yet.

Enter Clown [Lavatch]

LAVATCH   O madam, yonder's my lord your son with a patch
of velvet on's face. Whether there be a scar under't or no, the
85   velvet knows, but 'tis a goodly patch of velvet: his left cheek
is a cheek of two pile and a half, but his right cheek is worn
bare.

LAFEW   A scar nobly got, or a noble scar, is a good liv'ry of
honour, so belike is that.

90   LAVATCH   But it is your carbonadoed face.

LAFEW   Let us go see your son, I pray you. I long to talk with
the young noble soldier.

LAVATCH   Faith, there's a dozen of 'em, with delicate fine hats
and most courteous feathers, which bow the head and nod
95   at every man.   *Exeunt*

Act 5 [Scene 1]   *running scene 19*

Enter Helen, Widow and Diana, with two Attendants

HELEN   But this exceeding posting day and night
Must wear your spirits low. We cannot help it:
But since you have made the days and nights as one,
To wear your gentle limbs in my affairs,

---

78 with . . . admitted how I might with propriety be allowed to be present (at the meeting of
Bertram and the king)   **80 but** only   **your honourable privilege** the privilege due your
honored self   **81 charter** claim   **83 patch of velvet** used to cover either battle scars or those
resulting from syphilis treatment   **85 knows** plays on no   **86 two . . . half** i.e. covered with
thick velvet   **worn bare** without a velvet patch/hairless (from syphilis)   **88 liv'ry** badge
89 belike probably   **90 carbonadoed** slashed (like meat for cooking)/cut in the manner of
incisions made for syphilis treatment   **5.1**   *Location: Marseilles*   **1 exceeding posting**
exceptional haste   **2 wear** wear out

5   Be bold you do so grow in my requital
       As nothing can unroot you. In happy time.

Enter a Gentle Astringer   *Perhaps with a hawk*

       This man may help me to his majesty's ear,
       If he would spend his power. God save you, sir.

GENTLEMAN   And you.

10   HELEN   Sir, I have seen you in the court of France.

GENTLEMAN   I have been sometimes there.

HELEN   I do presume, sir, that you are not fall'n
       From the report that goes upon your goodness,
       And therefore, goaded with most sharp occasions
15   Which lay nice manners by, I put you to
       The use of your own virtues, for the which
       I shall continue thankful.

GENTLEMAN   What's your will?

HELEN   That it will please you
20   To give this poor petition to the king,   *Shows a petition*
       And aid me with that store of power you have
       To come into his presence.

GENTLEMAN   The king's not here.

HELEN   Not here, sir?

25   GENTLEMAN   Not, indeed.
       He hence removed last night, and with more haste
       Than is his use.

WIDOW   Lord, how we lose our pains!

HELEN   All's well that ends well yet,
30   Though time seem so adverse and means unfit.
       I do beseech you, whither is he gone?

GENTLEMAN   Marry, as I take it, to Rossillion,
       Whither I am going.

HELEN   I do beseech you, sir,
35   Since you are like to see the king before me,

---

5 bold confident   **my requital** the reward I shall give you   **6 In happy time** fortunately met
Gentle Astringer gentleman keeper of hawks   **8 spend** exert   **12 fall'n** less than/altered
14 sharp urgent   **occasions** needs   **15 nice** overscrupulous   **put** urge/compel
20 petition request   **26 hence removed** departed from here   **27 use** custom   **28 pains**
efforts   **35 like** likely

Commend the paper to his gracious hand,   *Gives petition*
Which I presume shall render you no blame,
But rather make you thank your pains for it.
I will come after you with what good speed
40   Our means will make us means.

GENTLEMAN   This I'll do for you.

HELEN   And you shall find yourself to be well thanked,
Whate'er falls more. We must to horse again.
Go, go, provide.   [*Exeunt, separately*]

[Act 5 Scene 2]   *running scene 20*

Enter Clown [Lavatch] and Parolles

PAROLLES   Good Monsieur Lavache, give my lord   *Gives Lavatch*
Lafew this letter. I have ere now, sir, been better   *a letter*
known to you, when I have held familiarity with fresher
clothes. But I am now, sir, muddied in Fortune's mood, and
5   smell somewhat strong of her strong displeasure.

LAVATCH   Truly, Fortune's displeasure is but sluttish if it smell
so strongly as thou speakest of. I will henceforth eat no fish of
Fortune's butt'ring. Prithee allow the wind.

PAROLLES   Nay, you need not to stop your nose, sir. I spake but
10   by a metaphor.

LAVATCH   Indeed, sir, if your metaphor stink, I will stop my
nose, or against any man's metaphor. Prithee get thee
further.

PAROLLES   Pray you, sir, deliver me this paper.

15   LAVATCH   Foh! Prithee stand away. A paper from Fortune's
close-stool to give to a nobleman! Look, here he comes
himself.

---

36 **Commend** commit   37 **presume** assure (you)   40 **means . . . means** resources will
enable us   43 **falls more** else happens   44 **provide** prepare   **5.2**   *Location: Rossillion*
1 **Lavache** Parolles clarifies the name's probable derivation (*vache* is French for "cow")
4 **mood** anger/temper (puns on "mud")   6 **sluttish** a whore/dirty   8 **butt'ring** preparation/
cooking   **allow the wind** i.e. stand downwind of me, so I don't have to smell you   9 **stop**
block   14 **me** for me   15 **paper** i.e. soiled with excrement   16 **close-stool** toilet/chamber-
pot enclosed in a stool

Enter Lafew

Here is a purr of Fortune's, sir, or of Fortune's cat — but not a musk-cat — that has fallen into the unclean fishpond of her displeasure, and as he says, is muddied withal. Pray you, sir, use the carp as you may, for he looks like a poor, decayed, ingenious, foolish, rascally knave. I do pity his distress in my smiles of comfort and leave him to your lordship.   [*Exit*]

PAROLLES   My lord, I am a man whom Fortune hath cruelly scratched.

LAFEW   And what would you have me to do? 'Tis too late to pare her nails now. Wherein have you played the knave with Fortune that she should scratch you, who of herself is a good lady and would not have knaves thrive long under her? There's a cardecue for you. Let the justices make you and   *Gives coin* Fortune friends; I am for other business.   *Starts to leave*

PAROLLES   I beseech your honour to hear me one single word.

LAFEW   You beg a single penny more. Come, you shall ha't, save your word.   *Gives another coin*

PAROLLES   My name, my good lord, is Parolles.

LAFEW   You beg more than 'word' then. Cox my passion! Give me your hand. How does your drum?

PAROLLES   O my good lord, you were the first that found me.

LAFEW   Was I, in sooth? And I was the first that lost thee.

PAROLLES   It lies in you, my lord, to bring me in some grace, for you did bring me out.

LAFEW   Out upon thee, knave! Dost thou put upon me at once both the office of God and the devil? One brings thee in grace and the other brings thee out. The   *Trumpets sound*

18 **purr** knave, jack in a card game/cat noise/animal dung   19 **musk-cat** i.e. perfume, the musky substance obtained from the anal glands of the civet cat   20 **withal** with it   21 **carp** fish bred in ponds/chatterer   22 **ingenious** wily/un-genious, i.e. stupid   23 **smiles of comfort** gloating (ironic usage)   27 **pare** trim   30 **cardecue** small silver coin   **justices** magistrates, responsible for dealing with beggars under Elizabethan law   36 **"word"** a single word, as Parolles' name means "words"   **Cox my passion!** By God's passion! (i.e. Christ's suffering)   **Cox** cock's (i.e. God's)   38 **me** me out   39 **sooth** truth   **lost** parted with/ abandoned   40 **in** into   **grace** favor   41 **out** of favor   42 **Out upon thee** expression of frustration and condemnation

45   king's coming. I know by his trumpets. Sirrah, inquire
further after me. I had talk of you last night. Though you are
a fool and a knave, you shall eat. Go to, follow.

PAROLLES   I praise God for you.   [*Exeunt*]

[Act 5 Scene 3]   *running scene 20 continues*

Flourish. Enter King, Old Lady [Countess], Lafew, the two French
Lords, with Attendants

KING   We lost a jewel of her, and our esteem
Was made much poorer by it: but your son,
As mad in folly, lacked the sense to know
Her estimation home.

5   COUNTESS   'Tis past, my liege,
And I beseech your majesty to make it
Natural rebellion, done i'th'blade of youth,
When oil and fire, too strong for reason's force,
O'erbears it and burns on.

10   KING   My honoured lady,
I have forgiven and forgotten all,
Though my revenges were high bent upon him,
And watched the time to shoot.

LAFEW   This I must say,

15   But first I beg my pardon, the young lord
Did to his majesty, his mother and his lady
Offence of mighty note; but to himself
The greatest wrong of all. He lost a wife
Whose beauty did astonish the survey

20   Of richest eyes, whose words all ears took captive,
Whose dear perfection hearts that scorned to serve
Humbly called mistress.

---

45 inquire . . . me ask for me later   **5.3   1 of** in   **our esteem** my worth   **4 home** fully,
truly   **6 make** consider   **7 Natural** i.e. of the passions   **i'th'blade** in the greenness,
immaturity (sometimes emended to "blaze" for consistency with subsequent fire imagery)
12 high bent pulled fully taut for action (like a bow)   **13 watched** awaited   **15 my pardon**
i.e. you to pardon me   **19 astonish** stun/dazzle   **survey** sight, gaze   **20 richest** most noble/
most experienced

KING   Praising what is lost
Makes the remembrance dear. Well, call him hither.
25   We are reconciled, and the first view shall kill
All repetition. Let him not ask our pardon.
The nature of his great offence is dead,
And deeper than oblivion we do bury
Th'incensing relics of it. Let him approach
30   A stranger, no offender; and inform him
So 'tis our will he should.

GENTLEMAN   I shall, my liege.   [*Exit*]

KING   What says he to your daughter? Have you   *To Lafew*
spoke?

35   LAFEW   All that he is hath reference to your highness.

KING   Then shall we have a match. I have letters sent me
That sets him high in fame.

Enter Count Bertram   *With a patch of velvet on his left cheek*

LAFEW   He looks well on't.

KING   I am not a day of season,
40   For thou mayst see a sunshine and a hail
In me at once. But to the brightest beams
Distracted clouds give way, so stand thou forth.
The time is fair again.

BERTRAM   My high-repented blames,
45   Dear sovereign, pardon to me.

KING   All is whole.
Not one word more of the consumèd time.
Let's take the instant by the forward top,
For we are old, and on our quick'st decrees
50   Th'inaudible and noiseless foot of time

---

25 view sight (of him)   **kill All repetition** put an end to going over past wrongs   **27 dead** forgotten (also a reminder that Helen is supposed dead)   **29 incensing relics** anger-rousing memories   **30 stranger** i.e. person whose story is unknown   **32 GENTLEMAN** i.e. an attendant   **35 hath reference to** is at the disposal of   **39 day of season** i.e. inclined to one unchanging disposition   **season** time of year/weather   **42 Distracted** breaking/agitated   **44 high-repented blames** bitterly regretted faults   **45 to** in   **46 whole** mended/well   **47 consumèd** used up/passed   **48 take . . . top** tug occasion by the forelock (hair at the front of the head)   **49 quick'st** most lively/urgent

Steals ere we can effect them. You remember
The daughter of this lord?

BERTRAM   Admiringly, my liege. At first
I stuck my choice upon her, ere my heart
55   Durst make too bold a herald of my tongue,
Where the impression of mine eye infixing,
Contempt his scornful perspective did lend me,
Which warped the line of every other favour,
Scorned a fair colour, or expressed it stol'n,
60   Extended or contracted all proportions
To a most hideous object. Thence it came
That she whom all men praised and whom myself,
Since I have lost, have loved, was in mine eye
The dust that did offend it.

65   KING   Well excused.
That thou didst love her, strikes some scores away
From the great count. But love that comes too late,
Like a remorseful pardon slowly carried,
To the great sender turns a sour offence,
70   Crying, 'That's good that's gone.' Our rash faults
Make trivial price of serious things we have,
Not knowing them until we know their grave.
Oft our displeasures, to ourselves unjust,
Destroy our friends and after weep their dust.
75   Our own love waking cries to see what's done,
While shameful hate sleeps out the afternoon.
Be this sweet Helen's knell, and now forget her.

---

54 **stuck** fixed   55 **Durst** dared   **herald** messenger   56 **Where** i.e. in **my heart**   **impression**
image (of Lafew's daughter)   **infixing** was implanted/fastened onto   57 **perspective** optical
glass that produced a distorted image   58 **favour** (woman's) face   59 **fair colour** beautiful
appearance/pale complexion (considered attractive)   **expressed** deemed (it to be)   **stol'n**
i.e. falsely created with cosmetics   60 **Extended or contracted** (the **perspective**) distorted by
elongating or shortening   61 **object** spectacle/sight   62 **she** i.e. Helen   66 **scores** debts
67 **great count** large account/judgment day   68 **remorseful** compassionate   **pardon**
reprieve from death   **slowly carried** i.e. delivered too late   69 **turns** becomes   71 **Make**
trivial price undervalue   72 **knowing** acknowledging   **know their grave** i.e. lose them
73 **displeasures** wrongs   74 **weep** weep over, mourn   **dust** remains   76 **out** through
77 **knell** funeral bell

Send forth your amorous token for fair Maudlin.
The main consents are had, and here we'll stay
80 To see our widower's second marriage day,
Which better than the first, O dear heaven, bless!
Or, ere they meet, in me, O nature, cesse!

LAFEW   Come on, my son, in whom my house's name
Must be digested, give a favour from you
85 To sparkle in the spirits of my daughter,
That she may quickly come.   *Bertram gives Lafew a ring*
By my old beard,
And every hair that's on't, Helen, that's dead,
Was a sweet creature: such a ring as this,
90 The last that e'er I took her leave at court,
I saw upon her finger.

BERTRAM   Hers it was not.

KING   Now, pray you let me see it. For   *Lafew gives it to him*
mine eye,
While I was speaking, oft was fastened to't.
95 This ring was mine, and when I gave it Helen,
I bade her, if her fortunes ever stood
Necessitied to help, that by this token
I would relieve her. Had you that craft, to reave her
Of what should stead her most?

100 BERTRAM   My gracious sovereign,
Howe'er it pleases you to take it so,
The ring was never hers.

COUNTESS   Son, on my life,
I have seen her wear it, and she reckoned it
105 At her life's rate.

---

78 **Maudlin** Magdalen, Lafew's daughter; means "sorrowful" (may recall Mary Magdalene)
79 **main consents** i.e. agreements of the most important parties   82 **they meet** Bertram and
Maudlin marry/the first and second marriages become similar   **cesse** variant form of
"cease" (some editors assign the closing couplet to the countess, though with no warrant from
the Folio)   84 **digested** incorporated   **favour** love token   86 **come** yield/come forth
90 **last** last time   **took her leave** said farewell to her   96 **bade** told   97 **Necessitied to** in
dire need of   98 **reave** deprive/rob   99 **stead** help, support   104 **reckoned** valued   105 **At**
as highly as   **rate** worth

LAFEW   I am sure I saw her wear it.

BERTRAM   You are deceived, my lord. She never saw it.
In Florence was it from a casement thrown me,
Wrapped in a paper, which contained the name
110 Of her that threw it. Noble she was, and thought
I stood engaged, but when I had subscribed
To mine own fortune and informed her fully
I could not answer in that course of honour
As she had made the overture, she ceased
115 In heavy satisfaction and would never
Receive the ring again.

KING   Plutus himself,
That knows the tinct and multiplying med'cine,
Hath not in nature's mystery more science
120 Than I have in this ring. 'Twas mine, 'twas Helen's,
Whoever gave it you. Then, if you know
That you are well acquainted with yourself,
Confess 'twas hers, and by what rough enforcement
You got it from her. She called the saints to surety
125 That she would never put it from her finger,
Unless she gave it to yourself in bed,
Where you have never come, or sent it us
Upon her great disaster.

BERTRAM   She never saw it.

130 KING   Thou speak'st it falsely, as I love mine honour,
And mak'st conjectural fears to come into me
Which I would fain shut out. If it should prove
That thou art so inhuman — 'twill not prove so —
And yet I know not. Thou didst hate her deadly,
135 And she is dead, which nothing but to close
Her eyes myself could win me to believe,

---

108 casement window   111 engaged pledged (to her)   subscribed To acknowledged
113 answer . . . overture respond honorably to her advances   115 heavy satisfaction sad
resignation   117 Plutus Greek god of wealth   118 tinct tincture, elixir   multiplying
med'cine alchemical formula for turning base metals into gold   119 science knowledge
124 to surety as witness   128 Upon . . . disaster in the event of some terrible misfortune
befalling her   131 conjectural speculative   132 fain willingly

More than to see this ring. Take him away.   ↓↑*Puts ring on his*

My fore-past proofs, howe'er the matter fall,   *own finger*↓↑

Shall tax my fears of little vanity,

140 Having vainly feared too little. Away with him.

We'll sift this matter further.

BERTRAM   If you shall prove

This ring was ever hers, you shall as easy

Prove that I husbanded her bed in Florence,

145 Where yet she never was.   [*Exit, guarded*]

Enter a Gentleman [the Astringer]

KING   I am wrapped in dismal thinkings.

GENTLEMAN   Gracious sovereign,

Whether I have been to blame or no, I know not:

Here's a petition from a Florentine,

150 Who hath for four or five removes come short

To tender it herself. I undertook it,

Vanquished thereto by the fair grace and speech

Of the poor suppliant, who by this I know

Is here attending. Her business looks in her

155 With an importing visage, and she told me,

In a sweet verbal brief, it did concern

Your highness with herself.

KING   [*Reads a*] *letter*

'Upon his many protestations to marry me when his wife
was dead, I blush to say it, he won me. Now is the Count

160 Rossillion a widower. His vows are forfeited to me, and my
honour's paid to him. He stole from Florence, taking no
leave, and I follow him to his country for justice. Grant it me,
O king! In you it best lies, otherwise a seducer flourishes and
a poor maid is undone. Diana Capilet.'

---

138 fore-past former **fall** turn out   **139 Shall . . . vanity** will not reprove my fears for being
foolish; rather my fears have foolishly not been apprehensive enough   **140 vainly** stupidly/
wrongly   **141 sift** examine carefully   ***Gentleman [the Astringer]*** though no mention is
made here of his status as a hawk-keeper   **150 for** on account of   **removes** stages in a
royal progress (Helen kept missing the king)   **short** i.e. too late   **151 tender** offer
152 Vanquished won   **153 this** this time   **154 looks** manifests itself   **155 importing visage**
countenance full of urgency   **156 brief** summary   **161 honour's paid** i.e. virginity's
surrendered   **taking no leave** without saying goodbye

165 LAFEW   I will buy me a son-in-law in a fair, and toll for this.
        I'll none of him.

    KING   The heavens have thought well on thee, Lafew,
        To bring forth this discov'ry. Seek these suitors.
        Go speedily and bring again the count.

Enter Bertram [guarded]

170   I am afeard the life of Helen, lady,
        Was foully snatched.

    COUNTESS   Now, justice on the doers!

    KING   I wonder, sir, sith wives are monsters to you,
        And that you fly them as you swear them lordship,
175   Yet you desire to marry.— What woman's that?

Enter Widow [and] Diana

    DIANA   I am, my lord, a wretched Florentine,
        Derivèd from the ancient Capilet.
        My suit, as I do understand, you know,
        And therefore know how far I may be pitied.

180 WIDOW   I am her mother, sir, whose age and honour
        Both suffer under this complaint we bring,
        And both shall cease, without your remedy.

    KING   Come hither, count. Do you know these women?

    BERTRAM   My lord, I neither can nor will deny
185   But that I know them. Do they charge me further?

    DIANA   Why do you look so strange upon your wife?

    BERTRAM   She's none of mine, my lord.

    DIANA   If you shall marry,
        You give away this hand, and that is mine,
190   You give away heaven's vows, and those are mine,
        You give away myself, which is known mine,
        For I by vow am so embodied yours,

---

165 in at   fair i.e. where stolen or poor-quality goods were for sale; Lafew reasons that even
there he would receive a better deal than in accepting Bertram for his daughter   **toll for this**
sell Bertram at a market (where vendors paid a fee and entered their goods in the toll-book)
168 suitors petitioners   **170 afeard** afraid   **171 foully snatched** i.e. that she was murdered
(on Bertram's orders)   **173 sith** since   **174 that** since   **fly . . . lordship** flee them as soon as
you promise to marry them   **177 Derivèd** descended   **182 both shall cease** i.e. she will die
in dishonor   **186 strange** like a stranger   **189 this hand** i.e. Bertram's   **192 embodied
yours** made part of your body/united as one

That she which marries you must marry me,
Either both or none.

195 LAFEW   Your reputation comes too short for my   *To Bertram*
daughter. You are no husband for her.

BERTRAM   My lord, this is a fond and desp'rate creature,
Whom sometime I have laughed with. Let your highness
Lay a more noble thought upon mine honour
200 Than for to think that I would sink it here.

KING   Sir, for my thoughts, you have them ill to friend
Till your deeds gain them: fairer prove your honour
Than in my thought it lies.

DIANA   Good my lord,
205 Ask him upon his oath, if he does think
He had not my virginity.

KING   What say'st thou to her?

BERTRAM   She's impudent, my lord,
And was a common gamester to the camp.

210 DIANA   He does me wrong, my lord. If I were so,
He might have bought me at a common price.
Do not believe him. O, behold this ring,   *Shows a ring*
Whose high respect and rich validity
Did lack a parallel. Yet for all that
215 He gave it to a commoner o'th'camp,
If I be one.

COUNTESS   He blushes, and 'tis hit.
Of six preceding ancestors, that gem,
Conferred by testament to th'sequent issue,
220 Hath it been owed and worn. This is his wife,
That ring's a thousand proofs.

KING   Methought you said
You saw one here in court could witness it.

---

197 **fond** foolish   201 **you . . . friend** they are not friendly toward you   202 **gain them** win
them over again   208 **impudent** shameless, immodest   209 **gamester** sexual player,
prostitute   213 **validity** value   214 **parallel** equal   215 **commoner** prostitute   217 **'tis hit**
the mark is hit, this is true   218 **Of** by   219 **testament** will   **th'sequent issue** the successive
heir   220 **owed** owned

DIANA	I did, my lord, but loath am to produce
225	So bad an instrument: his name's Parolles.
LAFEW	I saw the man today, if man he be.
KING	Find him, and bring him hither. [*Exit an Attendant*]
BERTRAM	What of him?

He's quoted for a most perfidious slave
230 With all the spots o'th'world taxed and deboshed,
Whose nature sickens but to speak a truth.
Am I or that or this for what he'll utter,
That will speak anything?

KING   She hath that ring of yours.

235 BERTRAM   I think she has; certain it is I liked her,
And boarded her i'th'wanton way of youth.
She knew her distance and did angle for me,
Madding my eagerness with her restraint,
As all impediments in fancy's course
240 Are motives of more fancy. And in fine,
Her insuite cunning, with her modern grace,
Subdued me to her rate: she got the ring,
And I had that which any inferior might
At market-price have bought.

245 DIANA   I must be patient.
You, that have turned off a first so noble wife,
May justly diet me. I pray you yet —
Since you lack virtue, I will lose a husband —
Send for your ring, I will return it home,
250 And give me mine again.

BERTRAM   I have it not.

KING   What ring was yours, I pray you?

DIANA   Sir, much like the same upon your finger.

---

225 **instrument** agent, means   229 **quoted for** regarded as   **perfidious** treacherous
230 **With** by   **spots** stains, vices   **taxed** censured   **deboshed** debauched, corrupted
231 **but** merely   232 **or . . . for** (to be judged) one or the other according to   236 **boarded**
accosted sexually   **wanton** playful/lascivious   237 **knew her distance** knew her inferiority
of rank/knew how to tease from a distance   238 **Madding** maddening, provoking
239 **fancy's** love's/desire's   241 **insuite** possibly "unusual" (some editors emend to "infinite")
modern commonplace   242 **Subdued me** made me submit   **rate** price   246 **turned** cast
247 **diet** restrain (from what I deserve)

KING	Know you this ring? This ring was his of late.	
255	DIANA	And this was it I gave him, being abed.	
KING	The story then goes false, you threw it him	
	Out of a casement.	
DIANA	I have spoke the truth.	

Enter Parolles

BERTRAM	My lord, I do confess the ring was hers.	
260	KING	You boggle shrewdly, every feather starts you.	
	Is this the man you speak of?	
DIANA	Ay, my lord.	
KING	Tell me, sirrah — but tell me true,	*To Parolles*
	I charge you,	
	Not fearing the displeasure of your master,	
265		Which on your just proceeding I'll keep off —	
	By him and by this woman here what know you?	
PAROLLES	So please your majesty, my master hath been an	
	honourable gentleman. Tricks he hath had in him, which	
	gentlemen have.	
270	KING	Come, come, to th'purpose: did he love this woman?	
PAROLLES	Faith, sir, he did love her, but how?	
KING	How, I pray you?	
PAROLLES	He did love her, sir, as a gentleman loves a woman.	
KING	How is that?	
275	PAROLLES	He loved her, sir, and loved her not.	
KING	As thou art a knave, and no knave. What an	
	equivocal companion is this!	
PAROLLES	I am a poor man, and at your majesty's command.	
LAFEW	He's a good drum, my lord, but a naughty orator.	
280	DIANA	Do you know he promised me marriage?	
PAROLLES	Faith, I know more than I'll speak.	
KING	But wilt thou not speak all thou knowest?	
PAROLLES	Yes, so please your majesty. I did go between them,	
	as I said. But more than that, he loved her, for indeed he was	

256 **goes** is   260 **boggle** shy away (like a horse)   **shrewdly** sharply, greatly   **starts** startles
265 **just proceeding** honest speaking   266 **By** about   268 **Tricks** lustful tendencies
275 **He . . . not** i.e. wanted to have sex with her, but didn't want to marry her   277 **companion**
fellow/rascal   279 **drum** drummer   **naughty** wicked/unskilled

285   mad for her and talked of Satan and of Limbo and of Furies
        and I know not what. Yet I was in that credit with them at
        that time that I knew of their going to bed, and of other
        motions, as promising her marriage, and things which
        would derive me ill will to speak of: therefore I will not speak
290   what I know.

KING   Thou hast spoken all already, unless thou canst say
        they are married. But thou art too fine in thy evidence:
        therefore stand aside. This ring, you say, was yours?

DIANA   Ay, my good lord.

295 KING   Where did you buy it? Or who gave it you?

DIANA   It was not given me, nor I did not buy it.

KING   Who lent it you?

DIANA   It was not lent me neither.

KING   Where did you find it, then?

300 DIANA   I found it not.

KING   If it were yours by none of all these ways,
        How could you give it him?

DIANA   I never gave it him.

LAFEW   This woman's an easy glove, my lord: she goes off
305   and on at pleasure.

KING   This ring was mine, I gave it his first wife.

DIANA   It might be yours or hers, for aught I know.

KING   Take her away. I do not like her now.
        To prison with her, and away with him.
310   Unless thou tell'st me where thou hadst this ring,
        Thou diest within this hour.

DIANA   I'll never tell you.

KING   Take her away.

DIANA   I'll put in bail, my liege.

315 KING   I think thee now some common customer.

---

285 Limbo region on the border of hell for unbaptized infants and those born before the time of
Christ   **Furies** three classical goddesses of vengeance   **286 in . . . them** so trusted by
288 motions proposals/sexual movements   **289 derive** bring   **292 fine** subtle   **304 easy**
loose-fitting/sexually compliant   **glove** plays on the sense of "vagina"   **goes . . . on** plays on
the sense of "orgasms and has sex"   **305 at pleasure** at will/for sexual pleasure   **307 aught**
anything   **314 put in** provide   **315 customer** prostitute

DIANA	By Jove, if ever I knew man, 'twas you.	
KING	Wherefore hast thou accused him all this while?	
DIANA	Because he's guilty, and he is not guilty.	

He knows I am no maid, and he'll swear to't.

320   I'll swear I am a maid, and he knows not.

Great king, I am no strumpet, by my life.

I am either maid, or else this old man's wife.   *Points to Lafew*

KING   She does abuse our ears. To prison with her.

DIANA   Good mother, fetch my bail.— Stay, royal sir.

[Exit Widow]

325   The jeweller that owes the ring is sent for,

And he shall surety me. But for this lord

Who hath abused me, as he knows himself,

Though yet he never harmed me, here I quit him.

He knows himself my bed he hath defiled,

330   And at that time he got his wife with child.

Dead though she be, she feels her young one kick.

So there's my riddle: one that's dead is quick,

And now behold the meaning.

Enter Helen and Widow

KING   Is there no exorcist

335   Beguiles the truer office of mine eyes?

Is't real that I see?

HELEN   No, my good lord,

'Tis but the shadow of a wife you see,

The name and not the thing.

340   BERTRAM   Both, both. O, pardon!

HELEN   O my good lord, when I was like this maid,

I found you wondrous kind. There is your ring,

And, look you, here's your letter. This it says: *Shows letter*

'When from my finger you can get this ring

345   And are by me with child', etc. This is done:

Will you be mine, now you are doubly won?

---

316 if . . . you i.e. my virginity is intact   **knew** had sex with   **325 owes** owns   **326 surety**
act as guarantor for   **for** as for   **328 quit** acquit/repay   **332 quick** alive   **335 Beguiles**
tricks   **truer office** accurate function   **338 shadow** ghost/image/poor reflection/illusion
341 like disguised as

BERTRAM   If she, my liege, can make me know this clearly,
I'll love her dearly, ever, ever dearly.

HELEN   If it appear not plain and prove untrue,
350   Deadly divorce step between me and you!
O my dear mother, do I see you living?

LAFEW   Mine eyes smell onions. I shall weep anon:
Good Tom Drum, lend me a handkercher. So. I   *To Parolles*
thank thee. Wait on me home, I'll make sport with thee.
355   Let thy court'sies alone, they are scurvy ones.

KING   Let us from point to point this story know,
To make the even truth in pleasure flow.—
If thou be'st yet a fresh uncroppèd flower,   *To Diana*
Choose thou thy husband, and I'll pay thy dower,
360   For I can guess that by thy honest aid
Thou kept'st a wife herself, thyself a maid.—
Of that and all the progress more and less
Resolvedly more leisure shall express.
All yet seems well, and if it end so meet,
365   The bitter past, more welcome is the sweet.

Flourish

[Epilogue]
The king's a beggar now the play is done.
All is well ended if this suit be won,
That you express content, which we will pay
With strife to please you, day exceeding day.
370   Ours be your patience then, and yours our parts,
Your gentle hands lend us, and take our hearts.

Exeunt

---

347 **know** understand   350 **Deadly divorce** divorcing death   353 **handkercher** handkerchief
354 **Wait on** accompany   **make sport** joke   355 **court'sies** polite gestures/bows   357 **even**
plain, exact   362 **progress . . . less** greater and lesser details of events   363 **Resolvedly** in a
way that resolves all questions   364 **meet** fittingly   365 **past** being past   368 **express**
content i.e. with applause and calls of approval   369 **strife** striving, endeavor   **exceeding**
after   370 **Ours . . . parts** i.e. let us reverse roles: the actors will listen patiently while the
audience applaud actively   371 **Your . . . us** i.e. applaud   **hearts** gratitude

TEXTUAL NOTES

F = First Folio text of 1623, the only authority for the play
F2 = a correction introduced in the Second Folio text of 1632
F3 = a correction introduced in the Third Folio text of 1663–64
F4 = a correction introduced in the Fourth Folio text of 1685
Ed = a correction introduced by a later editor
SD = stage direction
SH = speech heading (i.e. speaker's name)

List of parts = Ed

1.1.1 SH COUNTESS = Ed. F = *Mother* **3 SH BERTRAM** = Ed. F = *Ros.*
122 got = F2. F = goe **148 wear** = Ed. F = were **159 traitress** = F2. F =
Traitoresse
1.2.4 SH FIRST LORD = Ed. F = *1.Lo.G.* **19 SH SECOND LORD** = Ed.
F = *2.Lo.E* **23 Rossillion** = F2. F = *Rosignoll*
1.3.2 SH REYNALDO = Ed. F = *Ste.* **11 SH LAVATCH** = Ed. F = *Clo.* **16 I** =
F2. F = w **22 bairns** *spelled* barnes *in* F **67** F *omits this line, but prints*
'bis' (Latin for 'twice') at the end of the *preceding line* **78 ere** = Ed. F = ore
100 Dian no queen = Ed. F = Queene **114 rightly** = Ed. F = righlie
164 t'one = F2. F = 'ton tooth **193 intenible** = F2. F = intemible
228 Haply *spelled* Happily *in* F **241 and** = F2. F = an
2.1.6 SH FIRST LORD = Ed. F = *Lord. G.* **19 SH SECOND LORD** = Ed. F =
L.G. **28 SH SECOND LORD** = Ed. F = *2.Lo.E.* **45 with his cicatrice** =
Ed. F = his sicatrice, with **65 fee** = Ed. F = see **100 SD** *Enter Helen* = Ed.
One line later in F **165 impostor** = F3. F = Impostrue **185 nay** = Ed. F =
ne **205 heaven** = Ed. F = helpe
2.2.1 SH COUNTESS = Ed. F = *Lady.* (F *also uses* Count., Lad., Old La. *and*
La.) **54 An** = Ed. F = And **59 legs** = F2. F = legegs
2.3.1 SH LAFEW = Ed. F = *Ol. Laf.* **96 her** = F2. F = heere **133 it is** = F2.
F = is is **211 thou'rt** = F3. F = th'ourt **263 SD** *Enter Count Rossillion* =
Ed. *One line earlier in* F **288 detested** = Ed. F = detected
2.5.17 Ay, 'sir', he 'Sir' 's = Ed. F = I sir, hee sirs **26 End** = Ed. F = And
28 one = Ed. F = on **30 heard** = F2. F = hard
3.1.11 SH SECOND LORD = Ed. F = *French E.* **20 SH FIRST LORD** = Ed.
F = *Fren.G.* **27 th'field** = F2. F = th the field
3.2.8 sold = F3. F = hold **18 E'en** = Ed. F = In

3.4.1 SH COUNTESS = Ed. *Not in* F **4 SH REYNALDO** = Ed. *Not in* F
  7 have = F2. F = *hane* **18 SH COUNTESS** = Ed. *Not in* F **23 SH
  REYNALDO** = Ed. F = *Ste.*
3.5.0 SD *Diana* = Ed. F = *Violenta* **30 are you** = F2. F = *are* **31 le** = Ed.
  F = la
3.6.1 SH SECOND LORD = Ed. F = *Cap. E.* **3 SH FIRST LORD** = Ed. F =
  Cap. G. **30 his** = Ed. F = this **31 ore** = Ed. F = ours
3.7.22 Resolves = F2. F = Resolve **38 After** = F. F2 = After this **46 steads**
  = F4. F = steeds
4.1.1 SH FIRST LORD = F *(1 Lord E.).* Lo.E *for remainder of scene, perhaps
  because Shakespeare has forgotten that elsewhere first lord is G and second is
  E* **6 captain** = F3. F = Captaiue **86 art** = F3. F = are
4.2.45 scar *spelled* scarre in F
4.3.128 All's . . . him *assigned to Parolles in* F **219 the** = F2. F = your
  254 cardecue = F2. F = Cardceue
4.4.18 you = F4. F = your
5.2.1 Monsieur = Ed. F = M^r **29 under her** = F2. F = vnder
5.3.67 count *spelled* compt *in* F **117 Plutus** = Ed. F = *Platus* **139 tax** = F2.
  F = taze **158 SH KING** = Ed. *Not in* F **173 sith** = Ed. F = sir **176 SD
  *Diana*** = Ed. F = *Diana, and Parolles* **241 cunning** = Ed. F = comming
  345 are = Ed. F = is **369 strife** = F2. F = *strift*

SCENE-BY-SCENE ANALYSIS

ACT 1 SCENE 1

Lines 1–74: The widowed Countess of Rossillion is saying goodbye to her son, Bertram, who has been summoned by the King of France, his legal guardian. Lafew reports that the virtuous King is very ill and has given up his doctors' attempts to cure him of a painful fistula. The Countess laments that Helen's father, the renowned physician, Gerard de Narbon, is dead, believing that his skill would have cured the King. She is full of praise for Helen, who was entrusted to the Countess' care after her father's death. Helen is weeping. The Countess offers her son advice on how to behave at court, wishes him well and leaves. Bertram asks Helen to comfort and look after his mother and then departs with Lafew.

Lines 75–215: Now alone, Helen confides that her tears are not for her father but for the departure of Bertram whom she loves. She says she cannot live without him but she might as well "love a bright particular star" and think to marry that as Bertram since "he is so above me." She's tormented by her love for one who is her social superior. Despite her pain, she enjoyed seeing him all the time and drawing a picture of him in her heart. Now she has only these "relics" to remember him by. She sees Bertram's friend Parolles and says that even though she knows he's a coward and a liar she likes him for Bertram's sake. He asks her if she's thinking about "virginity" and they conduct a bawdy exchange about its merits with Helen defending it and Parolles believing it overrated. She turns the conversation obliquely to Bertram and her wishes. Parolles is called away and Helen accuses him of cowardice. He advises her to get a husband. Once he's gone, Helen argues in a soliloquy that an individual's fate lies in their own hands. She has a plan relating to the King and is determined to carry it through.

ACT 1 SCENE 2

The King reports that Florence and Siena are at war but are equally matched. France is not going to aid the Florentines but French knights will be allowed to fight on either side if they choose. Bertram, Lafew, and Parolles arrive. The King welcomes them, praising Bertram's late father who was an old friend and regretting his own ill health, asking how long ago Bertram's father's doctor (Helen's late father) died, believing that he might have cured him.

ACT 1 SCENE 3

Lines 1–111: The Countess and Reynaldo the Steward are about to discuss Helen when the Countess notices the Clown Lavatch. He explains that he wants to get married; his reasons are desires of the flesh, repentance, and to make "friends." He goes on to offer a paradoxical justification for adultery and the Countess says she'll speak to him later. She tells him to ask Helen to come to her and Lavatch sings a song about Helen of Troy. The Countess complains about his corruption of the song and abuse of women and sends him again for Helen. When Lavatch is gone, Reynaldo explains how he recently overheard Helen saying that she loves Bertram and feels bitter that the social distance between them means they can never marry. The Countess says she is not surprised and thanks Reynaldo for his "honest care" as he leaves.

Lines 112–252: As Helen enters, the Countess exclaims in an aside, "Even so it was with me when I was young" and she goes on to register her sympathy for Helen. She calls herself Helen's "mother" but Helen rejects the idea. When asked her reason, she's confused, saying she can't be Bertram's sister, she's too humble, and he mustn't be her brother. The Countess says that Helen could be her daughter-in-law then. Helen's reaction assures her that she has discovered the secret of her love for Bertram. Helen is reluctant to confess but the Countess is determined to learn the truth. Helen admits that she loves her son and begs the Countess' pardon but says she cannot help it—her love does Bertram no harm. The Countess then asks why she wants to go to Paris. Helen admits that she believes she can cure the

King, having inherited her father's skill. The Countess gives her blessing and offers her aid for the enterprise.

ACT 2 SCENE 1

Lines 1–63: The King is saying goodbye to the young lords going to fight in the Italian wars. He encourages them to fight bravely and be honorable and warns them against love. As the King goes aside to speak with the lords, Bertram complains that he isn't allowed to go—the King's told him he's "Too young" and he can go "the next year." The other lords sympathize. Parolles recalls his previous experiences of war and, telling Bertram to be "more expressive" with his good-byes to them, they go off.

Lines 64–223: Lafew tells the King that a young woman has arrived who believes she can cure him. The King agrees to see her. Helen enters and Lafew leaves them alone. Helen explains that she's the only child of Gerard de Narbon and that on his death he left her his secret medical recipes. The King is initially reluctant but Helen eventually convinces him to let her try, guaranteeing that he will be cured within forty-eight hours and if he isn't, she's prepared to die. If she succeeds she asks only that she may be allowed to choose her own husband, promising not to choose one of royal blood. The King agrees to her terms.

ACT 2 SCENE 2

A short comic scene between the Countess and Lavatch, in which he boasts that he has an answer for all questions and occasions and she goes along with him, playing his stooge. His fit-all response turns out to be "O lord, sir!" Finally she sends him off with a letter for Helen and greetings to Bertram.

ACT 2 SCENE 3

Lines 1–149: Lafew, Bertram, and Parolles are discussing the King's recovery in terms of miracle versus science. The King, now cured, enters with Helen. He confirms the bargain they struck and has his young lords line up for Helen to choose a husband. She rejects the other young men and selects Bertram who is shocked and resentful, complaining that he wishes to choose his own wife. He knows Helen well and believes marriage to her would bring him social disgrace. The King says if that's his only objection, he can ennoble her, and goes on to point out that she is "young, wise, fair," all qualities that breed "honour," which should be derived from the individual's acts rather than noble ancestry.

Lines 150–260: When she realizes that Bertram doesn't want to marry her, Helen offers to give up the agreement, but the King insists, believing his own "honour" is "at the stake." Bertram submits to his authority and agrees to the marriage. Everyone but Parolles and Lafew leaves to witness the ceremony. Lafew compliments Parolles' "lord and master" on his "recantation," by agreeing to the King's wishes. Parolles objects to these terms to describe himself and says he'd challenge Lafew for insulting him if he weren't so old. Lafew now realizes Parolles is a fool, which he'd suspected from his showy clothes and, continuing to insult him, leaves. Parolles vows he'll be revenged, however old and however much a lord Lafew is, when the opportunity presents itself. Lafew returns to say that Bertram is married and Parolles now has a "new mistress." Parolles, however, claims that while Bertram is his "good lord," he serves the one "above," but Lafew says it's not God he serves but the devil. He tells Parolles he's a worthless "vagabond" and leaves.

Lines 261–96: Bertram returns, complaining that he's ruined and determined that even though he's married to Helen, he'll go to the wars and "never bed her." Parolles encourages him in his decision, calling France a "dog-hole" and saying that to gain honor a man should go to the wars to fight rather than hug his "kicky-wicky [wife] here at home." Bertram says he'll send Helen back to his mother, telling her how much he hates Helen, and spend the money given him by the King to equip himself for the war, since war is preferable to a "dark house" and "detested wife." Parolles tells him it's the right decision: "A young man married is a man that's marred."

ACT 2 SCENE 4

Helen is reading the letter delivered by Lavatch from the Countess. He gives a riddling response to Helen's inquiries about her. Parolles arrives and after a comic exchange with Lavatch tells Helen that she is to return to the Countess at once since Bertram is detained on "very serious business." She says she'll do whatever Bertram wishes.

ACT 2 SCENE 5

Lines 1–51: Lafew is discussing Parolles with Bertram who assures him that Parolles is a "valiant" soldier. Lafew is unconvinced and continues to mock Parolles. Bertram asks if Helen is going away as he has ordered her to and Parolles confirms that she is. Bertram says he will leave for the wars himself then. Parolles denies that there is any ill feeling between himself and Lafew and Bertram is convinced that Lafew is mistaken in his estimate of his friend. Lafew's opinion is that "The soul of this man is his clothes" though, and he warns Bertram not to trust him in important matters. Parolles dismisses Lafew as an "idle lord" and Bertram agrees. Seeing Helen coming toward him, Bertram exclaims: "Here comes my clog."

Lines 52–98: Helen says she has spoken to the King who has given her permission to leave, but he wishes to speak to Bertram. Bertram says he'll do as he asks. He then excuses himself, saying he wasn't prepared for "such a business" and is "unsettled." He asks her to go home and gives her a letter for his mother. He'll see her in two days. She repeats that she knows she isn't worthy but would ask a small thing of him. She changes her mind and then says, "Strangers and foes do sunder, and not kiss," but he tells her to hurry. After she's gone, he vows he'll never go home while he can "shake [his] sword or hear the drum."

ACT 3 SCENE 1

The Duke of Florence has explained the cause of the war to the two French lords. They agree that it seems a just war on his part but cannot say why the French king refused to ally France with Florence, however they are sure that the young French knights will all want to fight with him. The Duke says they will be welcome and he will honor them.

ACT 3 SCENE 2

Lines 1–29: Lavatch has told the Countess about recent events in Paris. She's delighted with the way things have turned out, except that Bertram hasn't returned with Helen. Lavatch describes him as "a very melancholy man." The Countess reads the letter from her son while Lavatch explains that he no longer wishes to marry, having seen the women at court. He leaves and, now alone, the Countess reads Bertram's letter aloud in which he says that he's "wedded" but not "bedded" Helen and never intends to. He has "run away" and wants her to know the truth from him first. She's disgusted by his impetuous, immature behavior, which shows contempt for the King's favor and Helen's virtue.

Lines 30–64: Lavatch returns to tell the Countess that Helen and two lords have returned with bad news. Helen says Bertram has run away and the lords confirm that he has gone to fight for the Duke of Florence. Helen relates Bertram's letter to her which says he'll never be her husband until she can "get the ring upon my finger" and prove that she's pregnant by him: "show me a child begotten of thy body that I am father to." The Countess tells Helen to cheer up—half the griefs are hers since he's her son, but now she washes her hands of him and Helen is her only child.

Lines 65–132: The Countess inquires if Bertram has gone to Florence to be a soldier and the lords confirm it and assure her that the Duke of Florence will honor him. Helen bitterly quotes another line from Bertram's letter which says, "Till I have no wife I have nothing in France." The lords try to make light of the words, but the Countess exclaims that there's nothing in France too good for him except Helen, who deserves a lord that twenty such "rude boys" might serve. She asks who is with Bertram, if it's Parolles, and when the lords admit it is, calls him "A very tainted fellow, and full of wickedness." He is a bad influence on Bertram. She gives them a message for her son, to say that he can never win "The honour that he loses" by his sword. She asks them to take a letter from her. Alone, Helen repeats Bertram's words and is shocked that her presence has driven him away to war, where he may be hurt or killed. Fearful for his safety, she decides that she must leave France that night.

ACT 3 SCENE 3

The Duke of Florence promotes Bertram to "general of our horse." Bertram says it is too great an honor but he'll try to live up to it. The Duke wishes him well and he says he will follow Mars, love war and hate love.

ACT 3 SCENE 4

The Countess questions why Reynaldo took the letter from Helen, since he must have known what she would do. She asks him to read it again. In her letter Helen says she has decided to tread the pilgrim way of Saint Jaques to repent her sin of "Ambitious love" and begs the Countess to write that her own departure has brought Bertram back safe from the war. She asks the Countess to beg Bertram's forgiveness. He is too good to die and she would prefer her own death to set him free. The Countess says Reynaldo should have brought her the letter last night so that Helen could be persuaded against this course of action, but he replies that Helen has written that pursuit would be in vain. The Countess does not believe her son—"this unworthy husband"—can thrive except through Helen's prayers. She asks Reynaldo to write to Bertram telling him of Helen's worth and her departure, in the hope that he may return and Helen may also out of "pure love." She cannot say which of the two she loves best and is overcome with sorrow.

ACT 3 SCENE 5

Lines 1–80: The Widow and her daughter, Diana, are discussing the French count's valor in the war. Mariana warns her against him and the Widow explains how she has been "solicited" by his friend. Mariana says she knows who Diana means, "One Parolles," a "filthy offi-cer," and again warns Diana to beware of them. Diana reassures her that she has no need to worry on her account. Helen enters, dis-guised as a pilgrim, asking where the "palmers" (pilgrims) lodge, and the Widow confirms it's at her house. They guess she's from France and tell her that one of her countrymen has fought valiantly in the war and name the Count of Rossillion. Helen says she knows him by name only. They report that he left France because he had been mar-ried against his will and ask Helen if she knows anything about it. Helen says she knows the lady and Diana says that Parolles speaks "but coarsely of her." Helen says the lady is chaste and honest and the women pity her. The Widow says her daughter could do the lady a "shrewd" (malicious) turn if she chose and Helen guesses that he has tried to seduce Diana. The Widow says her daughter is able to defend herself against his advances.

Lines 81–112: Bertram, Parolles, and the whole army pass across the stage. As they parade by, the Widow points out who is who and Diana points to Bertram. She asks Helen whether he is not "a hand-some gentleman" and Helen replies, "I like him well." They point out Parolles—"That jackanapes with scarves"—who is muttering about "Los[ing] our drum!" When they have passed by the Widow says she will show Helen where she is to lodge. Helen thanks her and invites mother and daughter to eat with her, at her expense, and she will give Diana some advice. They agree and go off together.

ACT 3 SCENE 6

The two French lords are trying to convince Bertram that he is deceived about Parolles, who is nothing but a coward and a liar. Bertram wonders how it can be proved and the French lords hatch a plot for him to go and recover his drum. They meanwhile will cap-ture and blindfold him, pretending to be the enemy, and they are convinced that if Bertram is present at his interrogation, he'll soon change his opinion of his friend. They convince Bertram to encourage Parolles to attempt to recover the drum. Parolles enters still complain-ing about the loss of the drum and volunteers to go and get it back.

One of the lords goes after Parolles while the other goes with Bertram to see Diana, whose only "fault" he says is that "she's honest."

ACT 3 SCENE 7

Helen has explained her true identity to the Widow, who explains that though she's poor, she's honest and was "well born." Helen reassures her that she will not be involved in anything that might damage her or Diana's reputation but begs their help in winning her husband. She wants Diana to ask Bertram for his ring and then to make an assignation with him, which she herself will keep rather than Diana. Helen has already given them money and agrees to give Diana a further "three thousand crowns" when she marries. The Widow agrees, and Helen justifies the deceit as "wicked meaning in a lawful deed / And lawful meaning in a lawful act."

ACT 4 SCENE 1

Lines 1–59: The French lord and soldiers plan to trap Parolles. They must speak in some "terrible language" so that he can't understand them. One of the soldiers, whose voice Parolles doesn't know, volunteers to act as "interpreter." Parolles enters, meditating with himself what he will say when he returns. He fears that his tongue has been "too foolhardy" and has run away with him but he is too frightened to carry out his boasts. He cannot understand how he volunteered for this mission, which they all knew was impossible. He will have to pretend to have been hurt, but they'll scorn small injuries and he daren't give himself larger ones. He decides he'll have to keep his tongue quiet in future if it gets him into trouble. Parolles works through a list of the things he might do to prove that he's been wounded, dismissing each. The soldiers meanwhile comment in satirical asides on his character.

Lines 60–94: An "Alarum" (call to arms) sounds and the soldiers jump and blindfold a terrified Parolles. They talk nonsense to him. He says he'll tell them what he knows and the soldier who volunteered to be "interpreter" conducts a comic dialogue, pretending to interpret their gobbledygook. He says he'll tell them "all the secrets of our camp." They lead him off still blindfolded and send for Bertram to witness his interrogation.

ACT 4 SCENE 2

Lines 1–46: Bertram is trying to persuade Diana that she should sleep with him, arguing that virginity is no use to the dead, that she should be like her mother, when Diana was conceived. Diana counters that her mother was doing her duty since she was married and that Bertram owes such a duty to his wife. He objects that he was forced to marry against his will but it's Diana he loves and vows he will always love and serve her. Diana says that men say that to gain their sexual desires but then such vows mean nothing. Bertram continues to try to convince her to lose her virginity to him but she refuses him, saying that men only try to trap women. Then she asks for his ring.

Lines 47–86: Bertram says he can't give her the ring since it's a family heirloom and it would be shameful to lose it. Diana counters his argument, saying that her honor's "such a ring," that her "chastity's the jewel of our house," and that it would be equally shameful to lose that. He is persuaded and gives her the ring and vows his "house," "honour," and "life" are all hers and he'll do what she asks. She tells him to come to her at midnight. After giving him her virginity, he can only remain one hour and he must not speak to her. She will explain her reasons when his ring is returned to him and she will give him a ring which will be a token of past deeds in the future. She ambiguously claims that he has "won / A wife of me." He believes he has won "A heaven on earth" and leaves. Diana reflects that her mother told her just what he'd say and do and for herself she'd rather stay single; however, she doesn't think it's a sin to deceive him in this way since he would cheat her.

ACT 4 SCENE 3

Lines 1–68: The French lords are discussing Bertram and his reaction to a letter from his mother. They say he is blamed for his treatment of Helen which has displeased the king. The first lord confides how Bertram has seduced "a young gentlewoman" in Florence and given her his ring. He will be back after midnight and they decide to postpone their interrogation of Parolles till then so that Bertram can see for himself how poor his judgment has been. In the meanwhile, peace has been concluded between the combatants. They question what Bertram will do now, whether he will continue his travels or return to France. He has been told of Helen's flight and pilgrimage to Saint Jaques and that she is now dead. They think it a pity that he will be glad of such news and reflect on the paradox that his valor as a soldier is countermanded by his domestic shame, reflecting further that "The web of our life is of a mingled yarn, good and ill together."

Lines 69–106: Bertram's servant appears and they ask where his master is. He replies that he is saying farewell to the Duke of Florence since he is going to France in the morning. Bertram then enters and explains that he has been busy saying farewell to the Duke and his friends, burying and mourning a wife, writing to his mother, organizing his return, and "many nicer deeds," concluding that the last was the "greatest" but isn't yet finished. He's now ready for the "dialogue between the fool and the soldier." Parolles, who has been in the stocks all night, is sent for. He has been weeping like a woman and has confessed everything right up to the present. Bertram is concerned about what Parolles has said of him.

Lines 107–309: They interrogate the still-blindfolded Parolles in a comic nonsense language with one soldier interpreting throughout. Parolles immediately betrays all the secrets of the army. Bertram is shocked and disgusted by his former friend and mentor's performance. They search him for letters and find a "sonnet" from Parolles to Diana about Bertram, calling him a "dangerous and lascivious boy" and advising her not to trust him. They threaten him with hanging and Parolles begs for his life, to live under any conditions. They ask him about the characters of the French lords and of Bertram and he betrays and insults them all. They finally remove his blindfold and Parolles sees that he has been duped and asks plaintively, "Who cannot be crushed with a plot?" They leave him promising to reveal his impudence in France. Parolles is undaunted, claiming he doesn't care. He's glad and won't be a captain any longer. He'll just be himself: "Simply the thing I am / Shall make me live."

ACT 4 SCENE 4

Helen assures the Widow and Diana that she has not wronged them and says that they must go and kneel before the King who is at Marseille. They willingly agree to do as she asks. Helen reflects on the strangeness of men who can "such sweet use make of what they hate." She regrets that Diana will have more to suffer for her sake but believes that her end is justified.

ACT 4 SCENE 5

Lafew and the Countess are discussing recent events with Lavatch present. Lafew claims that Bertram was led astray by Parolles. The Countess says her grief is for the death of Helen whom she could not have loved more if she'd been Helen's real mother. Lafew and Lavatch continue a conversation full of the Clown's witty banter until Lafew sends him away. The Countess says that Bertram is amused by him and he's allowed to stay but gets carried away with his wit. Lafew then says that since Helen's dead, he suggested to the King that Bertram should marry his daughter. The King agreed to his proposition and he wondered what the Countess thought of it. She too is content. The King is to arrive from Marseille the next day. Lavatch returns to say that Bertram has arrived, wearing a velvet patch on his left cheek.

ACT 5 SCENE 1

Helen, the Widow, and Diana have arrived at Marseille and Helen asks the gentleman keeper of the King's hawks (the Astringer) to present the King with a petition, only to be told that the King has already left for Rossillion. Since he's going to Rossillion himself, she asks the Astringer again to present the petition to the King for her; he'll be well rewarded and they will follow.

ACT 5 SCENE 2

Parolles asks Lavatch to deliver a letter from him to Lafew. Lavatch complains that he smells and tells him to deliver it himself since Lafew is here. Parolles asks Lafew to help him since it was he who first "found" him out. Lafew says he will see him after; he can hear the King's trumpets, but even though he's "a fool and a knave" he shall still eat.

ACT 5 SCENE 3

Lines 1–64: The King is discussing Helen with the Countess. He regrets her death and Bertram's folly. The Countess puts it down to his youth and asks for him to be forgiven. Lafew adds that he wronged everyone, especially himself, through the loss of such a wife. The King sends for Bertram and asks what his response was to the proposed match with Lafew's daughter. Lafew says Bertram was content to do as the King wished. Bertram enters and the King tells him that he is "not a day of season," meaning that his moods are changeable and now his anger has passed. Bertram begs his pardon and the King says he is forgiven. He then reminds him of Lafew's daughter. Bertram says that he always admired her before his judgment was warped by contempt. Understanding how he has misjudged things, he has finally come to love the woman everyone praised and he, since he has lost her, has learned to love.

Lines 65–116: The King is pleased to hear of Bertram's love for Helen, even though it comes too late. He reflects how often we fail to value what we have until we've lost it. And now he advises Bertram to forget Helen and think of Maudlin (Lafew's daughter). Lafew asks for a token to give his daughter from Bertram and Bertram gives him a ring. Lafew says he last saw it on Helen's hand, but Bertram denies it belonged to Helen. The King then says that he gave it to her himself, adding that if she was ever in need, by this token he would help her. The King wonders how Bertram acquired it. Bertram assures the King it didn't belong to Helen. Both the Countess and Lafew assure Bertram that they saw her wear it, but Bertram explains it was thrown to him wrapped in paper from a casement window in Florence by a lady who refused to have it back.

Lines 117–69: The King intervenes to say that he knows the ring; it was his, he gave it to Helen, and she swore that she would never take it from her finger except to give it to Bertram in her bed or to send it to the King. Bertram says she never saw it, but the King says he is lying, and the King is now full of doubt and fear about Helen's fate. He orders Bertram to be detained; he will investigate the matter further. As he is led away Bertram says the King can as easily prove the ring was Helen's as that he had sex with her in Florence, where she'd never been. The King is full of anxiety. The Gentleman hawk-keeper arrives and gives him the petition from Diana which claims that she has been seduced by Bertram. Lafew says he no longer wants Bertram for a son-in-law after this—he'd rather buy himself one "in a fair." The King sends for the Widow and Diana and for Bertram again.

Lines 170–255: The King voices his fear that Helen was murdered. Diana and her mother enter. Bertram admits that he knows them but that's all. Diana asks him why he treats his wife like a stranger, but he denies that she's his wife. When asked if he does not believe he took her virginity, he claims she's a common prostitute. She then holds up the ring that Bertram gave her. The Countess recognizes it as a family heirloom and says it's proof that Diana is his wife. Parolles is sent for as a witness to the truth of this. Bertram now says that everyone knows Parolles is a liar, but the King points out that Diana has Bertram's ring. Bertram admits he had sex with her. She says she will return his ring if he will give her hers again. When asked what ring, she says it was like the one the King is wearing and she gave it to Bertram in bed.

Lines 256–333: Bertram admits the ring was Diana's. Parolles confirms that he acted as go-between for Bertram to Diana. The King asks Diana how she came by the ring and she says she neither bought it nor was loaned nor gave it. They cannot understand her riddling words and the King is about to send her to prison when she asks her mother to "fetch my bail." She says that even though he thinks he did, Bertram never harmed her and she forgives him. He believes that he had sex with her but he actually made his wife pregnant. Even though she's dead, his wife "feels her young one kick." Her riddle is: "one that's dead is quick," and she invites them all to "behold the meaning" as Helen and the Widow appear.

Lines 334–65: Everyone is amazed. Helen tells Bertram she is the "shadow of a wife" he sees, "The name and not the thing." He replies that she is both and begs her pardon. She says that when he thought she was Diana, he was kind to her, and she shows him the letter and the ring, asking him if he will be hers now he is "doubly won." He says if she can explain it all to him, he'll love her forever. She says if it isn't clear, he can have a divorce. Lafew asks Parolles for a handkerchief and promises to joke with him. The King demands to know the full story from Diana and says that if she's a virgin, she can choose herself a husband and he'll pay her dowry, since he guesses it was with her help that Helen was able to win Bertram. They will learn the rest in due time, meanwhile everything "seems well" and since it's ending so fittingly, the bitterness of past experiences makes the present sweetness more welcome.

EPILOGUE

The King speaks a short epilogue in which he says that he is now a beggar as he asks the audience, if they are pleased with the play, for applause—"Your gentle hands"—while the players offer their "hearts."

ALL'S WELL THAT ENDS WELL IN PERFORMANCE: THE RSC AND BEYOND

The best way to understand a Shakespeare play is to see it or ideally to participate in it. By examining a range of productions, we may gain a sense of the extraordinary variety of approaches and interpretations that are possible—a variety that gives Shakespeare his unique capacity to be reinvented and made "our contemporary" four centuries after his death.

We begin with a brief overview of the play's theatrical and cinematic life, offering historical perspectives on how it has been performed. We then analyze in more detail a series of productions staged over the last half-century by the Royal Shakespeare Company. The sense of dialogue between productions that can only occur when a company is dedicated to the revival and investigation of the Shakespeare canon over a long period, together with the uniquely comprehensive archival resource of promptbooks, program notes, reviews, and interviews held on behalf of the RSC at the Shakespeare Birthplace Trust in Stratford-upon-Avon, allows an "RSC stage history" to become a crucible in which the chemistry of the play can be explored.

Finally, we go to the horse's mouth. Modern theater is dominated by the figure of the director, who must hold together the whole play, whereas the actor must concentrate on his or her part. The director's viewpoint is therefore especially valuable. Shakespeare's plasticity is wonderfully revealed when we hear directors of highly successful productions answering the same questions in very different ways. We also hear from an actor about his experience of playing Parolles in a much praised performance.

FOUR CENTURIES OF *ALL'S WELL*: AN OVERVIEW

Despite its catchy, proverbial title, the unconventional characters and plot of *All's Well That Ends Well* have won it few admirers and often evoked negative responses to the play from the time it was written in the early seventeenth century until at least the middle of the twentieth. There is no evidence of any performance before the closure of the theaters in 1642 and, although it was assigned to Thomas Killigrew's King's Company in 1660 after the Restoration, it wasn't staged until Henry Giffard's production at Goodman's Fields Theatre in 1741 when Shakespeare's comedies were becoming popular once more. Giffard played Bertram with his wife as Helen and Joseph Petersen as Parolles. The braggart soldier became a favorite part with actors thereafter and the focus on which many subsequent revivals and adaptations were based.

The following year the play acquired a reputation as "the unfortunate comedy" when it was put on at the Theatre Royal, Drury Lane, for the first time. Milward playing the King caught cold and died shortly after, while Peg Woffington as Helen was taken ill and fainted onstage. Theophilus Cibber played Parolles to great acclaim, although the part had originally been assigned to Charles Macklin which caused further ill-feeling in the company. Henry Woodward, who took over as Parolles in Giffard's Covent Garden production of 1746, was so successful that he continued to play the part for the next thirty years. He reprised the role in David Garrick's 1756 adaptation, which was built around his performance and emphasized the play's farcical elements. John Bannister's 1785 revival at the Haymarket went even further, virtually eliminating Helen and the first three acts. Neither were well received, though, and John Philip Kemble's 1793 adaptation shifted the focus back to Helen, played by Dorothy Jordan, with himself as Bertram and Bannister again playing Parolles.

Charles Kemble mounted a spectacular production in 1811 at Covent Garden, using his brother's text, which received good reviews but, despite this and an excellent cast, it was revived for only one further performance. Kemble's script had emphasized the play's romantic elements; the next adaptation, Frederick Reynolds's operatic version for Covent Garden in 1832, attempted to excise those aspects of the play considered tasteless and to replace them with musical extracts from more popular Shakespeare plays such as *A Midsummer Night's Dream* and *Twelfth Night*, but to little avail as both public and critics still found the play unacceptable.

Samuel Phelps played Parolles himself in his 1852 Sadler's Wells production to general acclaim, despite continued critical carping about the "rude nature of its plot" and "exceedingly gross" manners.[25] Henry Irving's amateur production at St. George's Hall in 1895 likewise failed to please, despite his efforts to render the play fit for Victorian audiences by extensive cuts: "The text had been so carefully bowdlerised for the Irving Club that the story would scarcely have been comprehensible to any one who did not know it beforehand."[26] George Bernard Shaw, similarly exercised about the textual cuts, was equally scathing about the leading performances:

> The cool young woman, with a superior understanding, excellent manners, and a habit of reciting Shakespear, [*sic*] presented before us by Miss Olive Kennett, could not conceivably have been even Helena's thirty-second cousin. Miss Lena Heinekey, with the most beautiful old woman's part ever written in her hands, discovered none of its wonderfully pleasant good sense, humanity, and originality . . . Mr Lewin-Mannering did not for any instant make it possible to believe that Parolles was a real person to him.[27]

The actor-manager Frank Benson finally produced *All's Well* for the Shakespeare Theatre in 1916—after thirty-five years this and *Titus Andronicus* were the only two plays which had never been produced at Stratford. Benson himself played Parolles with his wife as Helen but the production was overshadowed by the celebrations of his recent knighthood:

> The play was held up for some minutes by the unrestrained applause which greeted the appearance of the Bensons on stage. And Lady Benson noted that the audience joined with

the cast in singing "Auld Lang Syne" at the end of the play. Understandably, *All's Well* could not compete with its celebrated cast.[28]

Theater historian Joseph G. Price argues that productions of the play underwent a fundamental transformation in the twentieth century with the advent of the director, anxious to impose a coherent interpretation on the play as a whole: "The stage history of *All's Well* in the twentieth century is, with a few exceptions, a record of attempts of directors to thread the brilliant parts with a unifying, appealing theme."[29] The problem was that "theatrical tradition offered only remnants as guides, and scholarly analysis had failed to fashion a coherent pattern. The threading was difficult, and early experiments did little to change the general distaste for the play."[30]

William Poel's 1920 production at the Ethical Church, Bayswater, was certainly driven by a strong directorial line. Poel had founded the Elizabethan Stage Society which attempted to reproduce original stagings as far as possible for the plays of Shakespeare and his contemporaries. In *All's Well* though he saw a play with a contemporary social message:

> He saw a plea for the removal of class barriers where the affections between men and women were in question . . . For Poel the play had an ethical significance which gave it a place in the history of women's emancipation; in 1919 this freedom had at last been won and the exploits of Miss Sylvia Pankhurst were a recent memory.[31]

However, Poel's decision to emphasize the play's serious elements and to use low lighting gave the production a somber tone that prompted the critic of the *Athenaeum* to comment that "Helena has her counterpart in Hamlet."[32]

Robert Atkins's production for the Old Vic in 1921 was judged "both interesting and disappointing."[33] The set and lighting were praised but something was missing: "It is passionate power that Mr. Atkins fails habitually to get from his actors; he has, too, a sort of statuesque convention which he imposes on every play, as though

Shakespeare could be played in talking tableaux."[34] The pace of the production dragged; Jane Bacon's Helen was too solemn and the comedy was underplayed: "Parolles discussing virginity with Helena, for example . . . Mr Ernest Milton got through this scene without once provoking a laugh; he played it like someone skating on very thin ice, as though he were trying to spare Helena's blushes instead of provoking them."[35]

Tastes were changing slowly, and the second Stratford production directed by William Bridges-Adams in 1922 proved no more successful than the first. Birmingham Repertory Theatre staged the first modern-dress production in 1927 with "the Countess swathed in the crêpe so loved by Gallic widows, and Helena beside her in the simplest of dresses to show a dependant's humility."[36] Bernard Shaw noted the "buoyant sense of humour" of Parolles, described by the critic J. C. Trewin as "an amiable, too smart young man, a *sommelier*'s scourge," played by "a youth of nineteen, virile, heavy-eyebrowed, darkly handsome . . . His name was Laurence Olivier."[37]

In 1935 Ben Iden Payne directed the third Stratford production which again failed to please. Robert Atkins was fortunate that in 1940 at the time of his third production it was the only play in London's war-torn West End. Audience and critics were duly grateful but not bowled over. Catherine Lacey, who had played the Countess in the previous Stratford production, now played Helen to general acclaim, as "a creature from a fantastic story-book. You need not believe in her, but love her you must—and love her you will."[38] Doubts were still expressed about the play itself though: "The plot proves untrue to the title by going from bad to worse; but the poetry, intermittently, goes from good to better."[39] Needless to say, this view did not go unchallenged: "Mr. Robert Atkins should be praised and encouraged for his direction. But the play may now be put by for another twenty years without great loss. Anybody heard defending its poetry should be asked point-blank to quote two consecutive lines."[40]

It was Tyrone Guthrie in 1953 at the Stratford Festival, Ontario, who finally succeeded in capturing the play's divergent elements to create a coherent whole and establish its place in the modern repertoire:

The first [Stratford, Ontario] season's *Richard III* provided the most exciting night in the history of Canadian theatre but the second night's *All's Well That Ends Well* topped it, and every other performance at Stratford since, in sheer theatrical magic, in its discovery of breathless beauty in a dark old Shakespearean comedy.[41]

Guthrie recognized its essential modernity and saw how he might translate this insight to the stage: "Helena might be the heroine of an Existentialist drama. She refuses to be passive; she will not resign herself to be what Simone de Beauvoir, in *The Second Sex*, calls 'the prisoner of immanence.' She takes a firm line with her fate."[42] The production's modern dress "did a great deal to explain Helena to the audience."[43] Joseph G. Price expands on the point:

The fantastic turns of the plot, of Helena's traps, became much more acceptable in modern dress to a contemporary audience which had been saturated with aggressive heroines, often "career women" who had won reluctant males in innumerable romantic comedy films during the 1930s and 1940s.[44]

Its staging suggests another "modern" aspect of the production. As film has largely superseded the theater in presenting "realism," theater has returned to its roots, capitalizing on the immediacy of the actors' presence to the audience. The aim of the set designer, Tanya Moiseiwitsch, was "to offer the facilities of an Elizabethan stage, but not to attempt an Elizabethan pseudo-antique style."[45] All the performances were praised, but Irene Worth's Helen was singled out:

In his skilful placing of emphasis Dr. Guthrie was immeasurably aided by some superb playing, particularly by Irene Worth as Helena. From her first silent entrance, gazing so longingly after Bertram, Miss Worth had power to move us to tears. She convinced us of her passion before ever she spoke, and we were committed to support her in every device she found to win her love.[46]

In the same year the Old Vic mounted a less successful production directed by Michael Benthall, who was accused by one critic of turning the play into "a cross between rollicking pantomime and fairy-tale."[47] Benthall, who had set himself the task of performing all of Shakespeare's plays in his five-year tenure at the Old Vic, did not much care for the play, and in order to make it palatable for modern audiences, aimed "to remove some of the bitter taste from the play and to give it instead a fairy-tale unreality."[48] With this end in mind, he invited Osbert Lancaster (best known as a cartoonist) to design costumes and sets: "The backdrops, clear and bright like cut-outs from a child's picture book, and the fresh colours of the costumes, admirably succeeded in creating a fairy-tale atmosphere."[49] The undoubted prettiness was unconvincing though:

> The result of this approach was to divorce the play from any semblance of reality and turn it into a quick-moving farce. In this guise it won many laughs and one could hardly take seriously the match-making activities of such a high-comedy King. Yet had the more serious scenes been played with more belief the real comedy might have increased in stature . . . [50]

The honors, such as they were, went to "Mr. Michael Hordern's horribly real and truly pointed performance as the boastful cowardly militarist, Parolles, and Miss Fay Compton's Countess of Roussillon."[51]

Two years later in 1955 Noel Willman directed the play at Stratford "as a dark comedy," but

> complicated his approach by his sets, his stage business, and his interpretations of Bertram and Parolles. He placed the play in the late seventeenth century against ponderous scenery and sumptuous costumes. The heavy representative sets robbed the stage of a starkness better suited to the mood; the prettiness of the costumes conflicted with the darkness of the theme.[52]

Joyce Redman's Helen "dominated the stage, not with her vivacity, nor indeed emotional variety, but by a moral earnestness which prompted frequent appeals to heaven . . . she behaved 'like some ghastly Shavian woman . . . [demonstrating] a pertinacity worthy of the North-West Mounted Police.' "[53] The lightweight Bertram "could not be taken seriously as a partner in the 'dark comedy'" and the "sinister potentialities of Parolles were ignored as well."[54]

In 1959 Tyrone Guthrie's successful Canadian production was revived at the Stratford Memorial Theatre with Zoe Caldwell as Helen, Robert Hardy as the King, and Dame Edith Evans as the Countess. The majority of critics were enthusiastic, concurring with the judgment of the *Times*'s critic:

> His [Guthrie's] production wears Edwardian dress, but it has a real Elizabethan vitality and its vindication of Helena is under-taken with as much care as the uproariously funny "debunk-ing" of Parolles.[55]

A. Alvarez thought that "Mr Tyrone Guthrie's Stratford production of *All's Well That Ends Well* is about as perfect as we are likely to see."[56] One piece of business noted by many was Helen's curing of the King:

> Miss Caldwell makes a quick and unexpected move, stands behind the King's chair, and places her hands on his brow. He makes an impatient gesture as if to brush aside her insolent pre-sumption—their timing throughout this passage was perfec-tion—stops at her invocation of "the great'st grace" [2.1.171], relaxes, closes his eyes and listens, while with a subtle, barely perceptible rise in tone into what is practically recitative, she speaks the couplets, with their fanciful, stilted phrasing, as an incantation, a charm; and carried beyond herself, rises to the crucial answer upon which her life and fortune depend, and wrings from the so-called fustian rhymes a moment of pure the-ater magic and spell-binding. It is quite breath-taking, and com-pletely right, startling and convincing us simultaneously.[57]

There were dissenters. The critic of the *New York Times* argued that "it is apparent that Mr. Guthrie's intentions are frivolous rather than

1. Tyrone Guthrie's "watershed" production of 1959 with Zoe Caldwell as Helen and Robert Hardy as the King: "Miss Caldwell makes a quick and unexpected move, stands behind the King's chair, and places her hands upon his brow . . . It is quite breath-taking, and completely right, startling and convincing us simultaneously."

serious, and that his aim is less to reveal hidden depths in this play than to extract all possible fun."[58] While Muriel St. Clare Byrne declared Edith Evans's performance "flawless,"[59] Alan Brien characterized it thus: "Edith Evans is Edith Evans—an exiled queen locked away in a madhouse who still bestows her autumnal wisdom on the deaf zanies around her," concluding that "the play itself remains a ragbag of revue sketches."[60] Nevertheless, Guthrie's is generally regarded as the watershed production for *All's Well*, demonstrating that the play was now acceptable and could be made to work for wider audiences.

The stage history of the play in America is "astonishingly brief."[61] There was a production in 1799 at the Federal Street Theatre, Boston, in which Elizabeth Kemble-Whitlock (a sister of the Kembles) played Helen, although no reviews of the production have survived. In the nineteenth century Augustin Daly seems to have been interested in putting it on and commissioned an acting text from William Winter, but in the event he never staged it. Guthrie's was thus the first significant North American production. Price does, however, mention the "amusing fact" of its "popularity as a burlesque in American vaudeville."[62]

In 1959, the same year as the revival of Guthrie's production, John Houseman directed the play for the American Shakespeare Festival at Stratford, Connecticut. Whereas Guthrie had emphasized its comic elements, Houseman produced a dark tragicomedy: "Surprisingly, the reception by critics and audiences was almost as enthusiastic as that won by the Guthrie revival."[63] Nancy Wickwire as Helen "played the heroine with intensity," making her "the centre of the play to the exclusion of all other characters":

> The force of her character assumed a tragic intensity with Bertram's rejection of her. Her horror at the thought that she was responsible for Bertram's flight to war and at the potential danger that was threatened to him suggested that the "dark comedy" was in fact a very dark tragedy.[64]

The character of Bertram, meanwhile, was softened with stage business such as a kiss and wave to Helen in the first scene:

This kind of stage business was even more effective after the marriage when Bertram sent his bride back to Rousillon. He was not unkind to her. Somewhat overwhelmed by the force of her passion, he turned to say something to her, some kind word, but she had already begun her exit. He checked himself, showed dismay at hurting her, then recovered quickly and shouted his youthful boast.[65]

Price concluded, however, that Houseman had

paid a heavy price for his tragi-comedy. The infusion of passion changed Parolles from a braggart soldier to a coward-villain who failed to draw his first real laugh from the audience until his capture. Even then, the turnabout of his exposure was pathetic as he was knocked about by each of the departing lords in what became a repugnant scene.[66]

Nevertheless, the production was a popular success and the majority of critics agreed with Henry Hewes of the *Saturday Review* that "Houseman had 'made this unpopular play work by filling it with genuine passion.' "[67]

Since then the play has been revived at regular intervals and become, if not popular, at least a standard part of the Shakespearean repertoire. The five notable RSC productions at Stratford are discussed in more detail below.

Elijah Moshinsky's 1980 BBC television production was widely praised for the way it transferred the play to the small screen: "it seems to accept the inevitable diminution in theatrical power that the translation involves, and tries to invent new relationships which will (to some degree) compensate for that loss."[68] Jeremy Treglown describes how

Moshinsky has framed the scenes as a series of calm seventeenth-century Dutch paintings, using mirrors to give depth to his surface and filling the small screen with the interplay of grouping and of light and shade, rather than with elaborate action or tricky camerawork. It works beautifully and gives a rich visual context to the unexpectedly plausible action itself, from Helena's falling (on the rebound from her father's death) for her shifty childhood friend Bertram, to his miserably trapped duplicities in the arranged marriage which follows.[69]

Angela Down's "serenely unstoppable" Helen was praised, as was Ian Charleson's "sulkily handsome" Bertram, with Celia Johnson as his "understandably anxious old mother" and Michael Hordern as the "melancholy-wise, genial old Lafeu."[70] Donald Sinden's rather "fruity" representation of the King caused several critics concern: "one of the lapses in a usually cool and contained production."[71] The production's successful translation to television was nowhere more apparent than the televisual technique employed to handle the final reveal as Diana is being taken to prison, as described by G. K. Hunter:

At the door she stops and pleads her final stay of execution: "Good mother, fetch my bail." As the cast looks through the door music begins to play. "Behold the meaning," says Diana. But the camera does not allow us to behold. Instead it does what the camera does best—it shows us a set of mouths and eyes. As it tracks along the line we are made witness to a series of inner sunrises, as face after face responds to the miracle and lights up with understanding and relief. I confess to finding it a very moving experience.[72]

In 1993 Richard Jones directed a "mesmerizing"[73] production of the play for the New York Shakespeare Festival in Central Park, in a style "more akin" to "tragicomedy."[74] The set design was essentially abstract:

On a sea-green backing, marked by an aqua blue strip, hangs a white Rothko-like panel with a Donald Judd-like sculpture in the center that doubles as a mirror. When the action moves to Italy, the panel divides to reveal a lovely Tuscan countryside, decked with burnt umber fields and a tiny medieval town . . . Washed by Mimi Jordan Sherin's sea-change lighting, the visual impact is ravishing.[75]

The production was literally stalked by a death's head, "a little boy in a Halloween skeleton costume. Sometimes he slips, unnoticed, scythe in hand, into courtly processions at Rousillon and Paris; sometimes he peers down at the action from a perch in a row of spectators above and behind the railings."[76] The acting was strong, with "standout performances" by Miriam Healy-Louie as Helen and Joan Macintosh as the Countess; however, "The only genuine comedy [was] provided by the chorus—courtiers drilled within an inch of their lives—whether simultaneously lighting clay pipes during the interrogation scene or returning from Italy with identical suitcases."[77]

Matthew Lloyd's 1996 production at Manchester's Royal Exchange Theatre was set in "a stiff and chilly version of the 1930s . . . holding throughout to the sombre economies implied by the all-black costumes of its opening stage-direction."[78] This theme was reflected in the "unwelcoming set, the floor an expanse of dark, glassy marble fractured by numerous cracks" and the lack of "emotional warmth" with the cast deployed in "stiffly stylised groupings" displayed in "cool isolation."[79] The production's "saving grace" was Alastair Galbraith's Parolles, "blessedly exempt from the icy self-control exuded by the rest of the cast."[80]

Very different was Irina Brook's production for the Oxford Playhouse in 1997, which "attempted to create a world in which the folk-story origins of the play might operate freely by presenting it in a pastiche African world."[81] The production revealed that "the play's theatrical energy is more or less indestructible if the role that drives it has been adequately cast."[82] In this case Rachel Pickup's Helen was "so full of energy, so gracefully and intelligently spoken, and so committed in her love for Emil Marwa's boyishly naive Bertram, that much of this wonderful play's essence seemed to survive the mistaken directorial concept."[83]

Two recent productions have enjoyed critical and popular success; Marianne Elliott's in 2009 for the National Theatre and Stephen Fried's 2010 production for the Shakespeare Theatre of New Jersey. Elliott offered a "picture-book romance" that evolved into a story about "the attainment of maturity."[84] In critic Michael

Billington's view its strength was the way in which the production balanced "romance and realism," with Michelle Terry's "fine performance" as Helen "holding the evening together": "We see her growth from fairy princess into real woman. And even though hero and heroine are finally united, there is a look of aghast bewilderment as they pose for the cameras. In short Elliott gives us a fairytale for grown-ups."[85]

Stephen Fried's inspired decision to set the play in the Edwardian period of the "New Woman" enabled beautiful, flowing art nouveau sets and elegant costumes, while making Ellen Adair's combination of "girlish modesty with the passion and wiles of a determined go-getter"[86] seem plausible. The versatile cast of nine played all twenty-three parts in this lively, warmly received production, with some notable doubling by John Ahlin as the King of France and the Clown Lavatch, and Tamara Tunie, the Countess and Widow Capilet. The three actors who played single roles were Adair as "an engagingly outgoing and energetically upbeat"[87] Helen; Clifton Duncan softening the unlovable Bertram by making him appear "blandly clueless";[88] and Clark Carmichael playing Parolles with "dandified comic flair . . . Ostentatiously grooming his mustache and eyebrows while peering into a hand-held mirror, he is the ultimate braggart and prevaricator, itching for a comeuppance."[89]

The conclusion of the *New York Times*'s review seems to sum up the theatrical fate of the play: "Though you leave the theater wondering about the long-term viability of Helena and Bertram's union, you hope for the best. In the meantime, you can't help loving this show."[90]

AT THE RSC

The play's historical unpopularity and paucity of performances over the years has offered modern directors a particular sort of challenge:

> *All's Well That Ends Well* is for us virtually a new play, and in this it is not unlike another problem comedy that has only recently found an audience, *Troilus and Cressida*. The "indeli-

cacy" of the central story, in which a woman pursues a man all the way into his bed, has ensured that the play has no theatrical history worth mentioning until a few years ago.[91]

John Barton (1967)

John Barton's production with Estelle Kohler as Helen (Lynn Farleigh took over the role the following year) to Ian Richardson's Bertram offers a striking set of ambiguities. From the start, Kohler presents a bright, witty young woman, sincere in her devotion to Bertram, while Richardson, stunned by her effrontery, recoils in anger at the "betrothal" and storms, "I cannot *love* her." The critic of the *Birmingham Mail* acknowledged the dilemma for an audience faced with a likable Helen and a justifiably angry Bertram:

> She does the early debate with Parolles on virginity with wit, and for the rest of the evening she has so completely won our sympathies as a young woman in love with her social superior that I doubt whether we give much thought to the lack of scruple in her tactics. It is much to Ian Richardson's credit, in the face of this attack, that he can make Bertram's resentment and defiance reasonably understandable.[92]

The theater program suggests that Bertram's conduct "has recently been viewed with less repulsion. It is realised that his attitude to a match with a poor girl below his rank would have seemed normal and not snobbish in Shakespeare's time." Accordingly, taking its cue from Stuart Hall's discussion in the theater program of a struggle in the play between the old order, represented by the King, Lafew, and the Countess, and a counterculture where "the young make up the rules," the play could be appraised as "an unromantic analysis of sex and station in life": "In John Barton's splendidly simple production the modernity of the play is appreciated."[93] Timothy O'Brien's simple wooden set, together with the Jacobean costumes, emphasized the historical and cultural contexts against which the sexual politics were played out.

A change in critical perceptions of Helen is evident from remarks by the critic J. C. Trewin:

Estelle Kohler does very little indeed that could win me to Helena but Bertram is transformed by one of the finest Royal Shakespeare actors, Ian Richardson: making no excuses for the man's weakness and arrogance, he does get us to listen.[94]

While Milton Schulman argues that Bertram "is one of the most abused young men in Shakespeare" and that John Barton's produc-

2. John Barton's 1967 RSC production with Ian Richardson as Bertram and Clive Swift as Parolles: "As interpreted by Ian Richardson, Bertram is harmless rather than wilful, amiable rather than cruel, weak rather than venal. He just doesn't want to get married."

tion "seems determined, as far as Bertram is concerned, to correct a critical wrong": "As interpreted by Ian Richardson, Bertram is harmless rather than wilful, amiable rather than cruel, weak rather than venal. He just doesn't want to get married."[95] Praise was extended to "Catherine Lacey's beautifully autumnal Countess," Elizabeth Spriggs (the Widow), Helen Mirren (Diana), and Brewster Mason (Lafew).[96]

Trevor Nunn (1981)

Michael Billington in the *Guardian* described Trevor Nunn's production, with Mike Gwilym as Bertram and Harriet Walter as Helen, "a total masterpiece":

> Indeed, Nunn's great achievement is to have endowed a fairy-tale plot about a miracle-curing heroine and her defecting husband, with a total emotional reality. Partly he does this by updating the play to a precise Edwardian world in which class differences are crucial: thus the keys around Helena's waist tell us that she is a working girl down on the Countess of Rossillion's humane Chekhovian estate while Bertram, the object of her affection, is an aristocratic scion who at the Paris court becomes one of a bevy of fencing, vaulting, brandy-swilling St Cloud* junior officers.[97]

In Billington's view, Harriet Walter "is no ruthless opportunist," but rather "a love-struck heroine who knows she is up against an inflexible class-system," while Mike Gwilym's Bertram is "a savage Strindbergian monster" (Philip Franks played a less monstrous, more "caddish" Bertram when the production transferred to the Barbican).

Tom Vaughan praised John Gunter's "Crystal Palace-style setting" as "brilliantly ingenious and evocative" but felt "a vital ingredient gets lost; this society is really medieval and the King and possibly the Countess as well have life and death powers over their subjects."[98]

---

* St. Cloud: a suburb of Paris, known for wealth and high living.

Helen was played as "a sombre, governessy girl"[99] who faltered at the first hurdle when Bertram rejects her:

In the scene of choosing a husband, she had tried to prevent the King from joining their hands, and when she made her final appearance, Bertram "went to take her hand, but didn't actually do so; instead he spoke that cryptic, conditioned couplet.* This wary meeting between husband and wife contrasted strikingly with Helena's intensely moving reunion with the Countess . . . Left alone, Bertram and Helena walked upstage together, their hands still apart, the final image of an unequal marriage."[100]

Sympathy for Helena can be detected in James Fenton's review: "In terms of the play, Helena's tricking of Bertram is a legitimate response to the challenge he issues to her. Helena never wrongs Bertram, however much he may feel wronged."[101]

Others were less impressed with the moral turnaround:

There is a slight snag about such realism and this is that the bad characters are so much more likeable than the good ones. Harriet Walter's Helena is an admirable performance, but by God what a dull person this Helena turns out to be. The Florentine Diana, who lures the unfaithful Bertram to her bed but substitutes Helena in the dark . . . is twice as much fun and Cheryl Campbell has a splendid time with her.[102]

The performances were likewise praised of Parolles (Stephen Moore); the "higher grade" comedy of Lafew (Robert Eddison) and Lavatch (Geoffrey Hutchings), "bent double like Rigoletto and, like Rigoletto, pretty contemptuous of the upper classes"; and Peggy Ashcroft's "true dignity" as the Countess. Ashcroft, whose performance was described as "perfect, noble, maternal, affectionate by

---

* The lines of the "conditioned couplet" are: "If she, my liege, can make me know this clearly, / I'll love her dearly, ever, ever dearly" (5.3.347–48).

3. Trevor Nunn's RSC production (1981) with Harriet Walter as "a sombre, governessy" Helen and Peggy Ashcroft as the Countess: "perfect, noble, maternal, affectionate by turn," she imbued her words "with a sure, sad knowledge of the world."

turn,"[103] imbued her words "with a sure, sad knowledge of the world."[104]

Barry Kyle (1989)

The theater program for Barry Kyle's 1989 production illustrates a world of toy soldiers, some marching to the beat of a drum and others blowing the bugle, astride a rocking horse. As Waller remarks, "Kyle opened the play with Bertram playing with toy soldiers, taking up the description of war as 'a nursery to our gentry' [1.2.20]."[105]

Kyle offers a perfectly plausible account of two children growing up together, but unfortunately Patricia Kerrigan's Helen matures earlier than her playfellow, Bertram (Paul Venables). She is ready for a relationship but he is young and seeks adventure and glory with other boy soldiers. The potential tragedy of their situation is insisted upon by Chris Dyer's permanent set, "a child's nursery complete with huge hobby-horse and three toy soldiers."[106] One critic praised "the achievement of coherence, remarkable in a play which sometimes appears to be a patchwork of fragments culled from other Shakespeare plays."[107] Kyle presents Helen's "sturdy self-assertion" in choosing Bertram for her husband as "an acceptable error" and shows her immediate "agonised realisation of her miscalculation." For the "choosing" scene, the suitors had each a full-length mirror "by which they could set their images."[108] The illusory attraction of the world of toy soldiers became apparent when the angry King of France (Hugh Ross) struck Bertram for refusing Helen, forced their hands together and then threatened him with his sword. Bertram had no option but to take her hand and exit.

Michael Billington felt that the director had imposed an "artificial visual unity" on the play but that "Mr Kyle's most original idea is to preface the court scenes with images of Elizabeth and James I implying that Shakespeare, writing around 1603, was lamenting the loss of a vanished Golden Age."[109] In one interview Kyle admitted that he

4. Barry Kyle's 1989 RSC production with Patricia Kerrigan as Helena: for the "choosing" scene, the suitors had each a full-length mirror "by which they could set their images." The illusory attraction of the world of toy soldiers became apparent.

had toyed with the idea of setting *All's Well That Ends Well* in the City of London in 1989, with characters setting off to the wars by helicopter. The themes he finds in the play, of "an old world being supplanted by a new world and new values, new money," had obvious and tempting parallels with 1980s Britain.[110] Opinions were divided over Paul Venables as Bertram who was accused of giving "an over-diagrammatic performance," which suggested that "buried deep down, Bertram may harbour a secret affection for his enforced bride."[111] The production was described as a "cop-out" that offered the spectator "a boring compromise."[112] Certainly, the unambiguous ending showed Bertram, Helen, and the Countess locked in embrace.

While Gwen Watford delivered the Countess's "embittered grief," Bruce Alexander's "admirable braggart Parolles" was not only "exactly costumed (his cross-hatched finery is precisely the 'window of lattice' described by Lafew) but even in decline retains the clipped accents of the Sandhurst saloon-bar military poseur."[113]

Peter Hall (1992)

Reviewing Peter Hall's production at The Swan in 1992, Michael Billington noted a particular problem with the play: "Shakespeare's psychological realism often bursts through the fairy tale structure." He remarked that Hall, returning to the Royal Shakespeare Company after a twenty-year absence, had solved the difficulties "by giving the play the elegant formality of a spoken opera staged in Caroline costumes," a device he considered "very much classical, late Peter Hall."[114]

Martin Dodsworth in his review for the *Times Literary Supplement* found the production "intense and powerful": "The bare stage of the Swan puts all the emphasis in how characters relate to one another. Body language throughout is significant. It rarely signifies happiness."[115] Helen (Sophie Thompson) entered "radiant with success" to dance with the cured King (Richard Johnson) in "a splendid scene."[116] When Bertram (Toby Stephens) rejected her, with an angry emphasis on "Disdain / Rather corrupt me ever!" (2.3.118–19), the court, as one, moved to protect the King. In this production, courtly etiquette demanded that Bertram quickly repair the breach of decorum, accede to the King's command and exit holding Helen's hand.

Charles Spencer thought the production smacked of "dogged conscientiousness rather than real inspiration," the Caroline costumes made the play "something of a museum piece," and that "too few of the characters take on a life of their own."[117] While conceding the latter point, Dodsworth considered, "The price paid for coherence is a certain thinning-out of character" and "Helena is made to seem simpler than she is." Hall's "through-line" for Helen was that of "a wide-eyed innocent":

> She is very close to a child and has the power to impose her childish conviction on others. When, at the end of it all, she has fulfilled the impossible conditions for her reunion with Bertram, she had the absolute faith of a child in the written word: "And look you, here's your letter. This it says . . ."[118]

5. Peter Hall's RSC production, 1992: the city wall and view of Florence with Andrée Evans as the Widow, "an example of how to play a small part to perfection," Emily Raymond as Mariana, Sophie Thompson "a wide-eyed innocent" Helen, and Rebecca Saire as a "sparky" Diana.

Other performances drew praise; for example, Barbara Jefford's performance as the Countess was "full of poise and a sense of reflective wisdom, which is matched for weight by Richard Johnson's powerful King of France."[119] Michael Siberry's "rollicking Parolles" possessed "the right energy and elan,"[120] and Rebecca Saire's Diana was "sparky,"[121] while Andrée Evans as the Widow was commended as "an example of how to play a small part to perfection."[122]

Hall kept some interesting surprises for the ending:

As interpreted by Hall, the conclusion loses any refulgent, romance-like glow. When the lights dim and Helena enters dressed in white, the gathered people don't respond to her as some symbol of harmonising fecundity but start back in terror, realistically, as at the approach of a ghost.[123]

Finally there was the "beautiful moment" when the childlike Helen grows up:

She starts to read the letter, pointing with her finger at every significant word: "When from my finger you can get this ring. And are by me with child . . . " Then suddenly, and at last, an adult understanding takes over, the rest of the letter is summed up in a comprehensive and dismissive "etcetera" and she tears it in half, cancelling the bond to which Bertram had subscribed, inviting him at last to commit himself to her freely and afresh.[124]

Helen moved directly to the Countess, leaving Bertram free to choose. He held out his hand as she hoped he would.

Gregory Doran (2003)

Judi Dench played the Countess in Gregory Doran's production at the Swan (2003), returning to Stratford for the first time in twenty-four years. Michael Billington observed, "It is Dench who is drawing the crowds, but the triumph lies in the restoration of an unforgivably neglected play."[125]

The set for the Rossillion estate had "an elegiac quality," captured in Stephen Brimson Lewis's "spare, effective design of wintry trees etched on sheets of silvery, scoured glass."[126] Costumes were seventeenth-century and Judi Dench was the "winter queen."[127] Kate Kellaway recalls the effect of Dench's performance:

> Tears started into my eyes as she threw herself into the speech that she—or Doran—sees as pivotal to the play. It is the moment when she first learns of Helena's love for her son—lines that could just as easily have been thrown away. But Dench brings to the speech an urgency, as though her words were the last flowering of everything she had ever felt—age's passionate identification with youth: "Even so it was with me when I was young. / If ever we are nature's, these are ours: this thorn / Doth rightly belong. / Our blood to us, this to our blood is born."[128]

A note of caution was sounded, however: "She gives an authoritative performance, as one would expect, but it is Helena and Bertram who matter," and Bertram (Jamie Glover) "has no character change."[129] There was universal acclaim for Claudie Blakley's performance as Helen: "she's feisty and forlorn at the same time, vulnerable when riding high, courageous in deepest misery."[130] Nicholas de Jongh described how the Countess "scathingly dismisses her heir as a chronic disappointment and passionately upholds Helena as a cherishable daughter-in-law."[131]

The production had tilted approbation toward Helen in such a way that everything she did appeared "perfectly normal" while Bertram had nowhere to go at the end:

> Glover gave a superb rendering here of an unimaginative, unreflective and largely inarticulate young man realizing too late that his attempts at achieving liberty have only betrayed him into a permanent version of exactly the "subjection" he had resented back in I.I: his performance never made the mistake of trying to make Bertram likeable, but I've never seen the young Count's situation illuminated so fully and so desolately.[132]

The play ended with the lights fading on Helen and Bertram "looking warily at one another, circling each other, a pace apart, in a recapitulation of the choosing scene's dance."[133]

Turning to the rest of the cast, there was praise for "the wonderfully accomplished" performance of Gary Waldhorn as the King of France, while "Guy Henry as Parolles is bliss: tall as a hollyhock, trailing hippy scarves from unexpected quarters of his body and glitteringly garrulous. Thank goodness that the play, like life, is sorrow *and* joy."[134]

THE DIRECTOR'S CUT: INTERVIEWS WITH GREGORY DORAN AND STEPHEN FRIED

Gregory Doran, born in 1958, studied at Bristol University and the Bristol Old Vic theater school. He began his career as an actor, before becoming associate director at the Nottingham Playhouse. He played some minor roles in the RSC ensemble before directing for the company, first as a freelance, then as associate and subsequently chief associate director. His productions, several of which have starred his partner Antony Sher, are characterized by extreme intelligence and lucidity. He has made a particular mark with several of Shakespeare's lesser-known plays and the revival of works by his Elizabethan and Jacobean contemporaries. His much-acclaimed 2003 production of *All's Well That Ends Well* discussed here featured Dame Judi Dench as the Countess of Rossillion and Guy Henry as Parolles.

Stephen Fried has a BA in history and drama from Stanford University and an MFA in directing from the Yale School of Drama. He teaches acting at the Shakespeare Theatre of New Jersey and is on the directing faculty for the New School for Drama. He is the recipient of the Drama League Director's Fellowship as well as the Jacob Javitz Fellowship, and has trained at the Center for Theatre Studies in Gardzienice, Poland, and with the Double Edge Theatre troupe. He now works as a freelance director in New York after three years as resident assistant director with the Shakespeare Theatre Company.

Apart from his many innovative productions of the plays of Shakespeare and other classic writers, he has also created productions of new writing with contemporary playwrights. His successful *Much Ado About Nothing* in 2010 for the Trinity Shakespeare Festival led to his being hailed as a contemporary "Defining director." Stephen is talking here about his 2010 *All's Well That Ends Well* for the Shakespeare Theatre of New Jersey, which successfully cast a total of nine actors for all twenty-three parts.

There are different views as to whether this is an early Shakespeare play (perhaps revised later) or a late play; did you have any preconceptions about this and were they confirmed or confounded by your production?

Doran: I had a very precise impression of what period the play was, because it seemed to have a relationship with the Sonnets. There is something about the ambiguity of the language that reminded me in a very particular way of the Sonnets. Sometimes the language is dense and gnarled; there are times when Helen, in trying to describe her love for Bertram, describes it in a very compressed way. The Sonnets are all about compression; they keep feelings in check with language, whereas in *All's Well That Ends Well* feelings are released through language. That gave me a strong sense that the play would have been written around about the early 1600s. The Sonnets were first published in 1609 but clearly were written before that.

Fried: Throughout my time working on *All's Well That Ends Well*, I never felt that it could have been an early play. My experience with the early comedies—having directed both *The Comedy of Errors* and *Love's Labour's Lost*—is that those plays radiate a youthful exuberance and naiveté. You feel in the early comedies that Shakespeare identifies himself principally with his youthful protagonists. In *All's Well That Ends Well*, he seems to take a much more critical look at the subject of youth—he points our attention in the play's first half not only to Bertram's pride and recklessness and Parolles' self-absorption, but also to Helen's inexperience and her mistaking of obsession for mature love. The adult characters—the Countess and the King—function as the play's moral centers, and provide the play with its mature, almost Chekhovian outlook. Take, for example, the Countess's speech from Act 1 Scene 3:

> Even so it was with me when I was young.
> If ever we are nature's, these are ours. This thorn
> Doth to our rose of youth rightly belong.
> Our blood to us, this to our blood is born:
> It is the show and seal of nature's truth,
> Where love's strong passion is impressed in youth.
> By our remembrances of days foregone,
> Such were our faults, or then we thought them none.

I find it difficult to imagine that this could have been the work of a young writer. It's in passages like this one that Shakespeare seems to be identifying more with the older characters in the play, which isn't the case in the earlier plays.

In addition to this, the play's ambiguities, both in content and form, always suggested to me the work of a playwright who had grown so experienced in his craft that he was now experimenting with the comedic genre. In terms of content, the play's complicated moral questions regarding the possibility of redemption and the ability to love someone who may not deserve your love place it in close relation to the other mid-career problem plays *Troilus and Cressida* and *Measure for Measure.* In addition to this, the blending of comedic and dramatic tones seemed to me to connect *All's Well* with later plays—particularly *Cymbeline*—and so it never really seemed possible to me that this could be an early play.

The language of *All's Well That Ends Well* also distances it from the early-career works. In the early plays, Shakespeare frequently seems to be showing off through bold displays of his verbal dexterity. The language in those plays feels youthful and exuberant. *All's Well*, on the other hand, has a more mature, subtle, and complicated feeling to it. The imagery is more delicate and nuanced. To put it simply, the play sounds so different from the early comedies, and feels much more connected in tone to the great tragedies and problem plays that Shakespeare wrote in the middle and later phases of his career.

The play seems to draw attention to the role of language with its high incidence of rhyming couplets, of proverbs and sayings, on "telling" rather than "showing" and the inclusion of a character called Parolles; how did you cope with this emphasis on language in the play?

Doran: The language in the central scene of the first part, when Helen cures the King, has an incantatory quality. In performance there is a sense that the rhymes themselves are curing the King. There is something very deliberate about the spell and the enchantment that it evokes.

Fried: While there certainly are a great number of proverbs and rhymes in the play, in production and in terms of what the play is really about, I didn't find *All's Well That Ends Well* to be significantly more concerned with the role of language than any other of Shakespeare's plays. Human beings' relationship with language and words was a constant fascination of Shakespeare's, and appears as a theme in almost every play he wrote, probably most explicitly in *Love's Labour's Lost.*

That said, the play's emphasis on "telling" rather than "showing" is certainly one of the great challenges that it presents to a director. Many of the play's most significant events—Helen's curing of the King, her discovery that Bertram has run away, the complicated maneuvering of the rings, and of course the infamous "bed trick," all occur offstage, and we're given complicated conversational scenes such as the beginning of Act 2 Scene 3 between Lafew, Bertram, and Parolles, or the opening of Act 4 Scene 3 between the two Dumaine brothers to learn of the momentous events that have taken place out of our view. As a result, I felt it was important at certain points to delicately weave visual storytelling into places where it wasn't explicitly called for by the playwright. An example of this was the ring plot—which is one of those aspects of the play that is endlessly talked about but barely shown onstage. I felt that the audience's appreciation for the significance of these rings would benefit from seeing a bit of their traffic, and so in the first scene, as the Countess bade farewell to Bertram, she presented his father's ring to him as a sort of "going away present." In Act 2 Scene 3, the King grandly presented his ring to Helen in gratitude for her curing him. These small moments enabled the audience to follow the conversation over these rings a little more closely in the final scene, I think.

Yet I also felt that the play's emphasis on telling rather than showing was somewhat by design, and I tried not to betray this aspect of the play. The result of this focus on the aftermath of an event, I found, is that the audience's attention is pulled off of the events themselves and onto the way that the play's characters respond to them. Thus, the real "story" of the play lies in the characters' subtle shifts in outlook and behavior as they react to what's happening around them. It's this aspect of the text that I think gives the play its almost Chekhovian tone; there is frequently a sensation of distance between the characters and the events they are responding to, and so the characters are able to reveal aspects of their humanity that they wouldn't if they were right in the middle of the event. For this reason, while we did show certain things when I felt that it might improve narrative clarity without betraying the play's structural intentions (such as the ring exchanges described above), I also tried to honor the play's impulse against showing certain events. I think many directors might be tempted to stage the bed trick in the interest of narrative clarity, but it felt intentional to me that the audience not be allowed to see that. As that moment of consummation represents such a major transformation for both Helen and Bertram, it seemed somehow perfect that Shakespeare leads us right up to that scene, then suddenly takes the characters away to somewhere where we can't see exactly what they go through—where a miracle can occur—and then brings them back radically changed. Both Helen and Bertram's speech and behavior change fundamentally from Act 4 Scene 3 on—after the point in the play where the bed trick would occur. So we come to understand what has happened not by seeing the event itself, but by seeing how it has changed the human beings that were involved in it. By keeping the bed trick offstage, Shakespeare allows the event to assume a more mythic size than anything that could be shown onstage.

The absence of so many of the play's events from the stage also pulls our focus to the events that actually do occur onstage— Bertram's rejection of Helen, his decision to run away, Parolles' betrayal of Bertram, and Helen's eventual acceptance of him following his pleas of "pardon." These are the events that really delineate that play's most significant journey—the evolution of the relationships between Helen, Bertram, and Parolles—and this journey becomes so much clearer because so many of the other events occur outside of our view.

In terms of how all of this affected our production, I think it was this emphasis on human behavior that led me to take a decidedly Chekhovian approach to the production. The autumn became a major reference point in terms of the physical world, and it was important to me that the play finish in a sort of "magical fall," which captured not only the play's particular pensiveness and its emphasis on time and age, but also its capacity for miraculous redemption. The actors' work also focused on the exploration of those fine details and nuances of human behavior that we frequently associate with Chekhov. All of this, I believe, stems in some degree from the play's emphasis on language, and its tendency to talk about an event rather than to show it directly.

Shakespeare often yokes together seemingly incompatible plot elements; is *All's Well* a radical play about the removal of class barriers and a woman's right to choose her partner, or a fairy tale with its roots in folklore, or something between the two?

Doran: It's a bittersweet play, a sort of realistic fairy tale. It has fairy-tale elements, but I think you have to root it in reality. We didn't heighten the sense of fairy tale. I took a rather historicist point of view about the play, again in relationship to the Sonnets. It seemed to me that you could quite easily connect Bertram to either the Earl of Pembroke or Henry Wriothesley, the Earl of Southampton, two of Shakespeare's patrons, both of whom, like Bertram, had refused marriages to women who they thought were not right for them. I was also fascinated by the possibility that Shakespeare and the King's Men, in order to avoid the plague in 1603, had come to Wilton House, where Mary Pembroke, Sidney's sister, ran this sort of Academy and patronized many poets, writers, and scientists. This was the world of the Countess of Rossillion. We were therefore quite specific and set our production absolutely in 1603/1604.

It's a Blackfriars play rather than a Globe play. It has a concentration of thought and an ambiguity of character which is interesting. From one point of view, Helen is a stalker: she wants her man and she stalks him all the way to Paris and he finds himself stuck with marrying her. That's not the basis for a great relationship, is it? On the other hand, she recognizes something profound about her love for him.

We were interested in the class element in the Sonnets, where the poet is devoted to the young man who is way beyond him in terms of social standing. Shakespeare was just an ordinary boy from Warwickshire, and perhaps in the portrait of Helen there was something autobiographical. Also in Parolles—from the French word *parole*: what better way for Shakespeare to disguise himself than to call himself "words"? Parolles is a spectacular wordsmith. He is also a pompous braggart, but he learns something very precise about living life.

Fried: I think it's something between the two. When I first encountered *All's Well That Ends Well*, what initially appealed to me was the way that it begins very much like a fairy tale, but that as the young characters go out into the world and actually experience life, the fairy tale breaks down. Shakespeare pushes the story beyond its fairy-tale roots into a far more complicated exploration of human behavior, and also of the flaws in each of us and in the world we live in.

That said, I don't think that the play ever really becomes so direct as to be called "a radical play about the removal of class barriers and a woman's right to choose her partner." Helen's "right" to choose Bertram isn't really the central question of the play—as the Countess gives Helen her blessing in the play's third scene, and the King sanctions the union three scenes after that. While class barriers certainly play a huge role in the play, I think Shakespeare is trying to get at something even deeper and more universal, and the barriers between Helen and Bertram are simply a device Shakespeare uses to get at the idea of an "impossible dream." He seems to be asking, "What do you do when you achieve your dream and it turns out to be something less perfect than you imagined it to be?" Is the thing you have always aspired toward worth pursuing if it reveals itself to be flawed? In this way, Shakespeare seems to be interrogating the idea of a fairy tale quite brilliantly. The world will never live up to our happily-ever-after aspirations, he seems to be saying, so how should we cope with the inevitable disappointments of human existence? In this way, the play's tone becomes almost Shavian: an idealistic and somewhat naive heroine pursues a goal obsessively, only to discover that that goal isn't all that she thought it would be, and as a result, she's forced to mature and develop a more nuanced and pragmatic worldview.

It has been suggested that *All's Well* is the "lost" Shakespeare play, *Love's Labour's Won*; did you give any credence to this theory and did your production glance at the idea at all?

Doran: No. I know what *Love's Labour's Won* is, I am absolutely certain of it: it's *Much Ado About Nothing.* When I did *Love's Labour's Lost* with David Tennant and Nina Sosanya, the relationship between Rosaline and Berowne is left at the end with the imposition of one year in which they have to be apart from each other. Berowne has to go and tend the sick. So as the relationship ends you don't know when or whether these people are going to get back together.

At the beginning of *Much Ado About Nothing* Beatrice and Benedick have this past history. They have been wounded. Maybe he didn't come back after the year apart, or she believed his promises but he didn't quite live up to them. But he's still a wit and the relationship between Rosaline and Berowne transmogrifies into Benedick and Beatrice. So I am sure that *All's Well That Ends Well* is not *Love's Labour's Won*, but *Much Ado About Nothing* is. It never occurred to us that this had any relationship to *Love's Labour's Won*, because ultimately the love's labors *aren't* won.

Fried: I can't say that I ever thought about this while working on *All's Well That Ends Well*. I had heard a theory that *Much Ado About Nothing* was actually the lost *Love's Labour's Won*, and the similarities between that play and *Love's Labour's Lost*, and particularly between Berowne and Rosaline and Benedick and Beatrice, always gave this theory a little more plausibility for me.

Helen's often seen as a problematic heroine; many have questioned why someone so clever and lively falls for and then has the bad taste to foist herself on an unattractive spoiled brat, using

the morally dubious bed trick. How did you reconcile the different aspects of her character?

Doran: I think she has a certainty about her: she knows this is right. The bed trick is seen from her perspective as a sort of corrective for Bertram's bad behavior. Bertram is immature; he doesn't want to be shackled by marriage or by the society of the French court. Going off and becoming General of the Horse is liberating for him; he wants to sow his wild oats and play the field. Diana realizes how attractive this young man is and although she resists him he has a kind of charisma that is irresistible to somebody like Helen. She firmly believes she is the one who can solve his problems; she will make him fall in love with her. His mother, the Countess, sees that this love is there, does not object to it on class grounds because she sees the virtue and integrity in Helen and therefore allows the depth of her love to prosper.

Fried: As I was working on *All's Well That Ends Well*, I frequently found myself defending the play against critics who took issue with Helen's love for the seemingly undeserving Bertram. Without question, Helen's flight from Rossillion at the end of Act 3 Scene 2, and her continued pursuit of Bertram in Florence even after he has so harshly rejected her, pose a problem for any postfeminist reading of the play. Yet I feel quite strongly that to look at the play as the story of a "clever and lively heroine who falls for an unattractive spoiled brat" denies the possibility that both Helen and Bertram must change and mature over the course of the play. I think it's very important to recognize—as I strove to make clear through my production—that Helen begins the play as a fairly sheltered and somewhat naive girl who confuses childlike obsession and idol worship with mature love. It is only after her idol rejects her that she must then confront reality and mature into the woman who, presented with Bertram at the end of the play, is able to define the terms by which she is to be wed rather than simply giving herself over unquestioningly.

This doesn't completely solve the problem of why Helen continues to pursue Bertram even after he rejects her. Yet I think it's unfair to expect that Helen should behave rationally when it comes to Bertram. How often is love rational? And how frequently has each of us fallen head over heels for someone completely undeserving of that love? Is Helen's love for Bertram easy to watch? Certainly not. But does it reveal a deeply honest truth about the irrational and inexplicable actions of the human heart? Without a doubt. In my production, when Helen mused in Act 4 Scene 4, "But, O strange men, / That can such sweet use make of what they hate," she seemed to recognize both the irrationality and also the inevitability of her love. Fully aware of Bertram's disdain for her, she was nonetheless filled with wonder over the sweetness of their night together.

Regarding the bed trick, by the time it appears in the play we've seen Helen put through so much abuse that I think most audience members are willing to forgive the moral questions that this tactic raises. More importantly, this shockingly cynical and pragmatic approach to winning a husband represents an important stage of Helen's maturation—gone are her more noble fantasies of how a man ought to be won, and she is now willing to face the world with all of its ugliness, to roll up her sleeves, and to do whatever she needs to do to get what she wants. In her bold disregard for the conventional morality that would stop such actions, there is, ironically, a unique sort of feminism. She doesn't particularly care about the morality behind what she's doing; for better or for worse, she's out to win Bertram, and understands that she must beat him at his own game in order to do so.

Bertram seems to have no redeeming qualities as a character and when cornered performs a one-line volte-face; how did you handle him and his sudden change of heart?

Doran: I think he is young, and I know that is often an excuse, but I think his youth and his hot temper make him behave impulsively. Such is the strength of Helen's love that I think that Bertram is moved in the final moments to realize that here is a good woman who loves him, and could he really ask for more than that? But there is still at the end a question of whether or not the marriage is going to be happy. Has she tamed him? Is that morally acceptable? That ambiguity is at the heart of the play and is what makes it one of the "problem plays," as they used to be called, of that middle period.

Fried: As unpleasantly pragmatic as it sounds, the first advice that I would give to any director of *All's Well That Ends Well* is to be sure when casting Bertram to find a dazzlingly charismatic young man whose charm and allure radiate even when he has nothing to say, and even in spite of the many unpleasant things that Shakespeare has given him to say. Without this, the audience will have a very hard time understanding and sympathizing with Helen's obsession with him, and in order for the play to "work," I think that we must be able to sympathize with Helen.

I also think that it's crucial that, like Helen, Bertram be allowed to mature and develop over the course of the production, and not be played as fully formed at the beginning. We must meet him not as a confirmed cad, but as a young man who still has a huge amount to learn, whose head is filled with misconceptions as to what "honour" and "nobility" really mean, and who is heading out into the world seeking these ideals having put all of his trust in the hands of a rascal named Parolles. It is easy for a production to dismiss Parolles as simply a clownish jokester, but I think that Bertram's ultimate redemption (and thus, the play's resolution and our ability to believe in Helen) is only possible if we understand that Bertram starts the play misguidedly trusting Parolles with his life. For this reason, I pushed Parolles away from a clownish fool and toward a more believably cynical and self-serving young man with great charisma, huge ambitions, and few, if any, scruples. In this way, Bertram's admiration and trust in him becomes more real and, as a result, Parolles' betrayal becomes a crushing event for Bertram. It forces him to reassess his estimation of the people around him, and ultimately to transform into a man that we can tolerate Helen ending up with. When Bertram enters into Act 4 Scene 3, since the last time we have seen him he has received news of both Helen's supposed death and his mother's approbation, he has slept with a woman he believed to be Diana, and he has also been informed that his best friend has offered to betray the secrets of the camp, so the man who enters into this scene is a very different Bertram than the man we last saw wooing Diana. It was important to me that his speech, "I have tonight dispatched sixteen businesses, a month's length apiece . . . ," be filled with a sort of distracted wonder, as if the sheer volume of life experience he has acquired in the last several hours has forced him to reconsider the life choices he has made thus far in the play. By the end of this scene, his dearest friend will be revealed to him as even more insidious than he previously thought possible, so Bertram leaves Florence a shaken man, eager to create himself anew upon his return to Rossillion.

Bertram's lies and harsh lines toward Diana in the play's final scene do seem to problematize his redemption, but in the context of Act 5 Scene 3, these flagrant displays of his still deeply fault-ridden character function as the final purging of his moral recklessness. Here, at the end of the play, Bertram reveals just how repugnant he is capable of being. His ugly display crests in its finale of calling Diana "that which any inferior might / At market-price have bought." And yet, as heinous as his behavior is, it is now out in the open. He no longer has Parolles to blame his sins on, and must now take full responsibility for his actions and suffer the disdain of every other character onstage (as well as of the audience) in a way that he hasn't been forced to until now. The young man who left home five acts ago in pursuit of honor and nobility must now feel what it means to be publicly stripped of both. From this moment in which his lies are

6. Stephen Fried's 2010 production for the Shakespeare Theatre of New Jersey with Clifton Duncan as Bertram, "not . . . a confirmed cad, but . . . a young man who still has a huge amount to learn," and Ellen Adair as Helen, "a somewhat naive girl" who has to "confront reality" in order to "mature into the woman."

revealed and he confesses to having slept with Diana (as he believes himself to have done), Bertram then remains mysteriously silent until the moment when Helen reappears. This silence, I believe, bespeaks his recognition of his own moral failure, so that when Helen reappears, and he is presented, after suffering such public shame, with the woman he believes himself to have killed, his only recourse is to beg the pardon of Helen and everyone else around him. We must believe that his "O, pardon!" comes from the very depths of his soul, as he has now achieved full recognition of his sins and is prepared to reform.

George Bernard Shaw famously thought the Countess "the most beautiful old woman's part ever written"; is that what you found?

Doran: I told Judi Dench that, although I think I left out the "old" part! It is a beautiful part; the Countess is the moral heart of the play. I think Trevor Nunn knew that when he cast Peggy Ashcroft. That production was meant to open the Swan Theatre, although the opening was delayed so it ended up playing in the main house. Judi Dench was attracted to the role partly to come back to Stratford and to the Swan, but the Countess is the still center of the play and of Rossillion, which makes her a deeply attractive character. She found expression even in the silences of the Countess; there was one moment when Helen is revealed at the end to have come back and Judi simply opened her hands, giving a gesture of acceptance, relief, and acknowledgment, which was very, very beautiful. But she also conveyed the rage of the Countess, the sense of fun in the Countess's relationship with Lavatch, and the depth of her own loss when she loses her son to Court.

Fried: I would agree wholeheartedly. At some point during rehearsals we realized that she might be the only example (or at least one of the few) of a truly good parent in all of Shakespeare. Shakespeare's parental figures generally tend to have some major flaw. Capulet has a violent temper. Eleanor, Elizabeth, and Constance all seem out for political gain. Henry IV is somewhat ineffective. Volumnia (while fabulous) seems a bit manipulative. Even Prospero can seem a little overly protective of Miranda. But the Countess seems to be motivated simply by pure love for both her son and for Helen. And it's for this reason that it is so incredibly heartbreaking when her son disap-

7. Gregory Doran's 2003 RSC production in the Swan Theatre with Judi Dench as the Countess of Rossillion and Claudie Blakley as Helena: "The Countess is the still center of the play and of Rossillion, which makes her a deeply attractive character. She [Judi] found expression even in the silences of the Countess."

points her. When she laments, in Act 3 Scene 4, that "My heart is heavy and mine age is weak. / Grief would have tears, and sorrow bids me speak," we are forced to consider every wound that we have ever inflicted upon our own parents.

All's Well That Ends Well is a comforting thought, but how well does the play end and what does it mean by "end" anyway?

Doran: We always felt that it should be called *All's Well That Ends Well?* with a question mark, because the ending is so ambiguous. There's a chill to the play. It is perhaps not Shakespeare's most congenial play. It fits into that middle period; it doesn't have the snarl of *Troilus and Cressida* or the decadence of *Measure for Measure*, but it does have this ache in it, which fits very much in that period. "All's well that ends well" is an aspiration that rather than a certainty.

Fried: I see the title as a somewhat open question that the play asks of its audience: if we find our way toward ultimate redemption, can we forgive the sins committed along the way? Helen seems quite resolute that "all's well that ends well," as she twice argues to the Widow and Diana, but I think that Shakespeare intended to leave the question of whether the end really does justify the means somewhat ambiguous.

In a more abstract sense, the notion that "all's well that ends well" also gets at the possibility of salvation. It's what we're asked to consider when assessing both Bertram's and Parolles' characters; these two young men both commit gross acts of misjudgment causing great pain to those around them, and yet they each (Bertram through Helen and Parolles through Lafew) find their way toward self-recognition and reformation. They both, in essence, "end well." So can we forgive them for everything they did along the way? The play forces us to consider how much we believe that a human being is actually capable of change, and how much we are willing to forgive in other people.

GUY HENRY ON PLAYING PAROLLES

Guy Henry was born in 1960 and trained at the Royal Academy of Dramatic Art in London. In 1982 he played the title role in ITV's

Young Sherlock Holmes series. He has since enjoyed wide success as an actor on stage, in radio, film, and television. He first joined the RSC in 1991 and has played many well-known Shakespearean roles, including Sir Andrew Aguecheek (1996), Dr. Caius (*The Merry Wives of Windsor* 1997), Malvolio (2001), and the title role in *King John* (2001), the same year in which he won the TMA/Barclays Best Supporting Actor award for his Mosca in *Volpone* (1999), directed by Lindsay Posner. Guy is probably most widely known for his film role as Pius Thicknesse in the film *Harry Potter and the Deathly Hallows*. He has also worked with Cheek by Jowl and at the National Theatre as Turgenev in Tom Stoppard's *The Coast of Utopia* (2002). He is here discussing his much lauded performance as Parolles in the 2003 *All's Well That Ends Well* directed by Gregory Doran.

Why do you think Parolles is such a large part in the play, second only to Helen in terms of lines? Is it something to do with the play's emphasis on language: the high incidence of rhyming couplets, proverbs, and sayings, "telling" rather than "showing," apart from a character·actually called Parolles ("words")?

I think Shakespeare probably knew when he was on to a good thing. He invented a character that is full of warmth and eccentricity, foibles and failings, and has an extraordinary range of humanity; he must have wanted to put him into all sorts of situations. I think he knew that he'd created a character that was going to be very watchable and very interesting. He is also very different; he's not like anyone else in the play, indeed I suspect he's not like many other characters who have ever been written. He was an invented character and doesn't appear in the source material, so there must have been an element of creating this firework character, who is a catalyst in the play. He loves words. He's a liar and a braggart, a fantasist who lives in his own world. So he can go any which way: he can say or do almost anything that Shakespeare wants him to. Once that character has come to a writer, it must be rather a gift.

"Simply the thing I am / Shall make me live." A fantastic line— how did you deliver it? And what "thing" do you think Parolles is or was and does he change?

8. Guy Henry in Gregory Doran's 2003 production in the Swan Theatre in his "fantastic costume of rags and tatters." His Parolles "was obsessed with his scarves: that was all part of the pretence—anything to take the eye away from what's really going on. He loved anything flashy, he was like a magpie."

At the time Greg Doran asked me to do it I was working with Trevor Nunn at the National on *The Coast of Utopia*. I told Trevor and he said that if anyone ever doubted that Shakespeare was a great humanitarian and the great understander of human behavior, then he'd only have to point at the character of Parolles to show how Shakespeare believes humans are capable of change and redemption and generosity of spirit. I think that's right. That line comes after he's been beaten and tormented, and his mask has been ripped away. I was on my knees, sat back on my haunches, alone on the stage. Greg Doran quite rightly kept emphasizing the need to make it as simple as possible, because all the lying is gone. He sees a way to be much happier if he no longer piles layers of lies upon what he is and just tells the truth. It's a lovely thing to be able to play a character that has what some people call a journey, a change. He does. He goes very simply back to the court and I think all his lies and nonsense are forgiven. I remember thinking what a relief it must be not to have to bother to pretend anymore. That's one of the great moments in the play. It's interesting that a supposed upstanding and honorable gentleman like Bertram is in fact revealed as less generous-spirited than Parolles turns out to be.

How does Parolles compare with other Shakespearean parts you've played?

He is unique. He's not as stupid as Sir Andrew Aguecheek and he's not as wise as Feste. He reminds me more of Mosca in *Volpone*, in that he's a chancer and liar. He's nowhere near as clever as Mosca, but in terms of flashiness and extraordinary braggadocio behavior they are similar.

There's a lot of discussion in the text of his clothes—how was that realized in production?

I had a fantastic costume of rags and tatters. He was obsessed with his scarves: that was all part of the pretense—anything to take the eye away from what's really going on. He loved anything flashy: he was like a magpie. The first scene he has, with Helen, has a lot of rather dense, jokey stuff about virginity. I'm quite neurotic and I can get quite inhibited in rehearsal, which is not particularly helpful to the director or anyone else! That's a very naked scene to do, to come on and launch into all that stuff. So Greg Doran gave me something to do. He gave me a great big trunk with scarves hanging out of it. Parolles was going away with the soldiers so he was taking everything he could from his wardrobe. I would pull this trunk onstage and be packing a few things into it and then sit on it. Having something to tie the scene to and then having somewhere to sit naturally on a bare stage gave the scene, and the rehearsal of the scene, an anchor. And I think visually it told quite a bit about Parolles that out of everybody he had the biggest trunk!

Your Parolles was very funny and widely praised—how did you handle the scenes in which he's captured, blindfolded, and then mercilessly exposed?

He was brought in blindfolded on a cart. It was a really hard scene to make work. He is changed by it. He's stripped of all his braggadocio behavior. He thinks he's going to die and experiences abject terror. It's a difficult scene to play because you should try to make it as cruel and as unpleasant and frightening for him as possible. Of course it's also funny as well. It needs to be played with nothing held back.

Do you think the designation of *All's Well* as a "problem" play is justified and why do you think it's so rarely been performed?

In the same way that *The Taming of the Shrew* has its problems with modern sensibilities, I think people find the character of Bertram and his rejection of Helen difficult. It was very well played by Jamie Glover in our production, although I think he did consider it one of the more thankless parts because everybody hates you! Bertram's fiendishly difficult for a modern audience to like and that might be part of the reason for its comparative rarity in performance. But I've done several plays with Greg [Doran]—*Henry VIII, King John, All's Well*—that are all very rarely performed but, without wishing to sound arrogant, when we had a go at them and tried to play the truth and the humor of them, you couldn't see why people think they are problematic. Audiences love them and I think it's exciting to explore the plays that are done less frequently.

SHAKESPEARE'S CAREER IN THE THEATER

BEGINNINGS

William Shakespeare was an extraordinarily intelligent man who was born and died in an ordinary market town in the English Midlands. He lived an uneventful life in an eventful age. Born in April 1564, he was the eldest son of John Shakespeare, a glove maker who was prominent on the town council until he fell into financial difficulties. Young William was educated at the local grammar in Stratford-upon-Avon, Warwickshire, where he gained a thorough grounding in the Latin language, the art of rhetoric, and classical poetry. He married Ann Hathaway and had three children (Susanna, then the twins Hamnet and Judith) before his twenty-first birthday: an exceptionally young age for the period. We do not know how he supported his family in the mid-1580s.

Like many clever country boys, he moved to the city in order to make his way in the world. Like many creative people, he found a career in the entertainment business. Public playhouses and professional full-time acting companies reliant on the market for their income were born in Shakespeare's childhood. When he arrived in London as a man, sometime in the late 1580s, a new phenomenon was in the making: the actor who is so successful that he becomes a "star." The word did not exist in its modern sense, but the pattern is recognizable: audiences went to the theater not so much to see a particular show as to witness the comedian Richard Tarlton or the dramatic actor Edward Alleyn.

Shakespeare was an actor before he was a writer. It appears not to have been long before he realized that he was never going to grow into a great comedian like Tarlton or a great tragedian like Alleyn. Instead, he found a role within his company as the man who patched up old plays, breathing new life, new dramatic twists, into tired repertory pieces. He paid close attention to the work of the university-educated dramatists who were writing history plays and tragedies for the public stage in a style more ambitious, sweeping, and poetically grand than anything that had been seen before. But he may also have noted that what his friend and rival Ben Jonson would call "Marlowe's mighty line" sometimes faltered in the mode of comedy. Going to university, as Christopher Marlowe did, was all well and good for honing the arts of rhetorical elaboration and classical allusion, but it could lead to a loss of the common touch. To stay close to a large segment of the potential audience for public theater, it was necessary to write for clowns as well as kings and to intersperse the flights of poetry with the humor of the tavern, the privy, and the brothel: Shakespeare was the first to establish himself early in his career as an equal master of tragedy, comedy, and history. He realized that theater could be the medium to make the national past available to a wider audience than the elite who could afford to read large history books: his signature early works include not only the classical tragedy *Titus Andronicus* but also the sequence of English historical plays on the Wars of the Roses.

He also invented a new role for himself, that of in-house company dramatist. Where his peers and predecessors had to sell their plays to the theater managers on a poorly paid piecework basis, Shakespeare took a percentage of the box-office income. The Lord Chamberlain's Men constituted themselves in 1594 as a joint stock company, with the profits being distributed among the core actors who had invested as sharers. Shakespeare acted himself—he appears in the cast lists of some of Ben Jonson's plays as well as the list of actors' names at the beginning of his own collected works—but his principal duty was to write two or three plays a year for the company. By holding shares, he was effectively earning himself a royalty on his work, something no author had ever done before in England. When the Lord Chamberlain's Men collected their fee for performance at court in the Christmas season of 1594, three of them went along to the Treasurer of the Chamber: not just Richard Burbage the tragedian and Will Kempe the clown, but also Shakespeare the scriptwriter. That was something new.

The next four years were the golden period in Shakespeare's

career, though overshadowed by the death of his only son, Hamnet, aged eleven, in 1596. In his early thirties and in full command of both his poetic and his theatrical medium, he perfected his art of comedy, while also developing his tragic and historical writing in new ways. In 1598, Francis Meres, a Cambridge University graduate with his finger on the pulse of the London literary world, praised Shakespeare for his excellence across the genres:

> As Plautus and Seneca are accounted the best for comedy and tragedy among the Latins, so Shakespeare among the English is the most excellent in both kinds for the stage; for comedy, witness his *Gentlemen of Verona*, his *Errors*, his *Love Labours Lost*, his *Love Labours Won*, his *Midsummer Night Dream* and his *Merchant of Venice*: for tragedy his *Richard the 2*, *Richard the 3*, *Henry the 4*, *King John*, *Titus Andronicus* and his *Romeo and Juliet*.

For Meres, as for the many writers who praised the "honey-flowing vein" of *Venus and Adonis* and *Lucrece*, narrative poems written when the theaters were closed due to plague in 1593–94, Shakespeare was marked above all by his linguistic skill, by the gift of turning elegant poetic phrases.

PLAYHOUSES

Elizabethan playhouses were "thrust" or "one-room" theaters. To understand Shakespeare's original theatrical life, we have to forget about the indoor theater of later times, with its proscenium arch and curtain that would be opened at the beginning and closed at the end of each act. In the proscenium arch theater, stage and auditorium are effectively two separate rooms: the audience looks from one world into another as if through the imaginary "fourth wall" framed by the proscenium. The picture-frame stage, together with the elaborate scenic effects and backdrops beyond it, created the illusion of a self-contained world—especially once nineteenth-century developments in the control of artificial lighting meant that the auditorium could be darkened and the spectators made to focus on the lighted stage. Shakespeare, by contrast, wrote for a bare platform stage with a standing audience gathered around it in a courtyard in full daylight. The audience were always conscious of themselves and their fellow spectators, and they shared the same "room" as the actors. A sense of immediate presence and the creation of rapport with the audience were all-important. The actor could not afford to imagine he was in a closed world, with silent witnesses dutifully observing him from the darkness.

Shakespeare's theatrical career began at the Rose Theatre in Southwark. The stage was wide and shallow, trapezoid in shape, like a lozenge. This design had a great deal of potential for the theatrical equivalent of cinematic split-screen effects, whereby one group of characters would enter at the door at one end of the tiring-house wall at the back of the stage and another group through the door at the other end, thus creating two rival tableaux. Many of the battle-heavy and faction-filled plays that premiered at the Rose have scenes of just this sort.

At the rear of the Rose stage, there were three capacious exits, each over ten feet wide. Unfortunately, the very limited excavation of a fragmentary portion of the original Globe site, in 1989, revealed nothing about the stage. The first Globe was built in 1599 with similar proportions to those of another theater, the Fortune, albeit that the former was polygonal and looked circular, whereas the latter was rectangular. The building contract for the Fortune survives and allows us to infer that the stage of the Globe was probably substantially wider than it was deep (perhaps forty-three feet wide and twenty-seven feet deep). It may well have been tapered at the front, like that of the Rose.

The capacity of the Globe was said to have been enormous, perhaps in excess of three thousand. It has been conjectured that about eight hundred people may have stood in the yard, with two thousand or more in the three layers of covered galleries. The other "public" playhouses were also of large capacity, whereas the indoor Blackfriars theater that Shakespeare's company began using in 1608—the former refectory of a monastery—had overall internal dimensions of a mere forty-six by sixty feet. It would have made for a much more intimate theatrical experience and had a much smaller capacity, probably of about six hundred people. Since they paid at least six-pence a head, the Blackfriars attracted a more select or "private" audience. The atmosphere would have been closer to that of an indoor performance before the court in the Whitehall Palace or at Richmond. That Shakespeare always wrote for indoor production at court as well as outdoor performance in the public theater should make us cautious about inferring, as some scholars have, that the opportunity provided by the intimacy of the Blackfriars led to a sig-nificant change toward a "chamber" style in his last plays—which, besides, were performed at both the Globe and the Blackfriars. After the occupation of the Blackfriars a five-act structure seems to have become more important to Shakespeare. That was because of artifi-cial lighting: there were musical interludes between the acts, while the candles were trimmed and replaced. Again, though, something similar must have been necessary for indoor court performances throughout his career.

Front of house there were the "gatherers" who collected the money from audience members: a penny to stand in the open-air yard, another penny for a place in the covered galleries, sixpence for the prominent "lord's rooms" to the side of the stage. In the indoor "private" theaters, gallants from the audience who fancied making themselves part of the spectacle sat on stools on the edge of the stage itself. Scholars debate as to how widespread this practice was in the public theaters such as the Globe. Once the audience were in place and the money counted, the gatherers were available to be extras on-stage. That is one reason why battles and crowd scenes often come later rather than early in Shakespeare's plays. There was no formal prohibition upon performance by women, and there certainly were women among the gatherers, so it is not beyond the bounds of possi-bility that female crowd members were played by females.

The play began at two o'clock in the afternoon and the theater had to be cleared by five. After the main show, there would be a jig—which consisted not only of dancing but also of knockabout comedy (it is the origin of the farcical "afterpiece" in the eighteenth-century theater). So the time available for a Shakespeare play was about two and a half hours, somewhere between the "two hours' traffic" men-tioned in the prologue to *Romeo and Juliet* and the "three hours' spectacle" referred to in the preface to the 1647 Folio of Beaumont and Fletcher's plays. The prologue to a play by Thomas Middleton refers to a thousand lines as "one hour's words," so the likelihood is that about two and a half thousand, or a maximum of three thousand lines, made up the performed text. This is indeed the length of most of Shakespeare's comedies, whereas many of his tragedies and histories are much longer, raising the possibility that he wrote full scripts, possibly with eventual publication in mind, in the full knowledge that the stage version would be heavily cut. The short Quarto texts published in his lifetime—they used to be called "Bad" Quartos— provide fascinating evidence as to the kind of cutting that probably took place. So, for instance, the First Quarto of *Hamlet* neatly merges two occasions when Hamlet is overheard, the "Fishmonger" and the "nunnery" scenes.

The social composition of the audience was mixed. The poet Sir John Davies wrote of "A thousand townsmen, gentlemen and whores, / Porters and servingmen" who would "together throng" at the public playhouses. Though moralists associated female play-going with adultery and the sex trade, many perfectly respectable citizens' wives were regular attendees. Some, no doubt, resembled the modern groupie: a story attested in two different sources has one citizen's wife making a post-show assignation with Richard Burbage and ending up in bed with Shakespeare—supposedly eliciting from the latter the quip that William the Conqueror was before Richard III. Defenders of theater liked to say that by witnessing the comeuppance of villains on the stage, audience members would repent of their own wrongdoings, but the reality is that most people went to the theater then, as they do now, for entertainment more than moral edification. Besides, it would be foolish to suppose that audiences behaved in a homogeneous way: a pamphlet of the 1630s tells of how two men went to see *Pericles* and one of them laughed while the other wept. Bishop John Hall complained that people went to church for the same reasons that they went to the theater: "for company, for custom, for recreation . . . to feed his eyes or his ears . . . or perhaps for sleep."

Men-about-town and clever young lawyers went to be seen as much as to see. In the modern popular imagination, shaped not least by *Shakespeare in Love* and the opening sequence of Laurence Olivier's *Henry V* film, the penny-paying groundlings stand in the yard hurling abuse or encouragement and hazelnuts or orange peel at the actors, while the sophisticates in the covered galleries appreciate Shakespeare's soaring poetry. The reality was probably the other way around. A "groundling" was a kind of fish, so the nickname suggests the penny audience standing below the level of the stage and gazing in silent open-mouthed wonder at the spectacle unfolding above them. The more difficult audience members, who kept up a running commentary of clever remarks on the performance and who occasionally got into quarrels with players, were the gallants. Like Hollywood movies in modern times, Elizabethan and Jacobean plays exercised a powerful influence on the fashion and behavior of the young. John Marston mocks the lawyers who would open their lips, perhaps to court a girl, and out would "flow / Naught but pure Juliet and Romeo."

THE ENSEMBLE AT WORK

In the absence of typewriters and photocopying machines, reading aloud would have been the means by which the company got to know a new play. The tradition of the playwright reading his complete script to the assembled company endured for generations. A copy would then have been taken to the Master of the Revels for licensing. The theater book-holder or prompter would then have copied the parts for distribution to the actors. A partbook consisted of the character's lines, with each speech preceded by the last three or four words of the speech before, the so-called "cue." These would have been taken away and studied or "conned." During this period of learning the parts, an actor might have had some one-to-one instruction, perhaps from the dramatist, perhaps from a senior actor who had played the same part before, and, in the case of an apprentice, from his master. A high percentage of Desdemona's lines occur in dialogue with Othello, of Lady Macbeth's with Macbeth, Cleopatra's with Antony, and Volumnia's with Coriolanus. The roles would almost certainly have been taken by the apprentice of the lead actor, usually Burbage, who delivers the majority of the cues. Given that

9. Hypothetical reconstruction of the interior of an Elizabethan playhouse during a performance.

apprentices lodged with their masters, there would have been ample opportunity for personal instruction, which may be what made it possible for young men to play such demanding parts.

After the parts were learned, there may have been no more than a single rehearsal before the first performance. With six different plays to be put on every week, there was no time for more. Actors, then, would go into a show with a very limited sense of the whole. The notion of a collective rehearsal process that is itself a process of discovery for the actors is wholly modern and would have been incomprehensible to Shakespeare and his original ensemble. Given the number of parts an actor had to hold in his memory, the forgetting of lines was probably more frequent than in the modern theater. The book-holder was on hand to prompt.

Backstage personnel included the property man, the tire-man who oversaw the costumes, call boys, attendants, and the musicians, who might play at various times from the main stage, the rooms above, and within the tiring-house. Scriptwriters sometimes made a nuisance of themselves backstage. There was often tension between the acting companies and the freelance playwrights from whom they purchased scripts: it was a smart move on the part of Shakespeare and the Lord Chamberlain's Men to bring the writing process in-house.

Scenery was limited, though sometimes set pieces were brought on (a bank of flowers, a bed, the mouth of hell). The trapdoor from below, the gallery stage above, and the curtained discovery-space at the back allowed for an array of special effects: the rising of ghosts and apparitions, the descent of gods, dialogue between a character at a window and another at ground level, the revelation of a statue or a pair of lovers playing at chess. Ingenious use could be made of props, as with the ass's head in *A Midsummer Night's Dream.* In a theater that does not clutter the stage with the material paraphernalia of everyday life, those objects that are deployed may take on powerful symbolic weight, as when Shylock bears his weighing scales in one hand and knife in the other, thus becoming a parody of the figure of Justice who traditionally bears a sword and a balance. Among the more significant items in the property cupboard of Shakespeare's company, there would have been a throne (the "chair of state"), joint stools, books, bottles, coins, purses, letters (which are brought onstage, read, or referred to on about eighty occasions in the complete works), maps, gloves, a set of stocks (in which Kent is put in *King Lear*), rings, rapiers, daggers, broadswords, staves, pistols, masks and vizards, heads and skulls, torches and tapers and lanterns which served to signal night scenes on the daylit stage, a buck's head, an ass's head, animal costumes. Live animals also put in appearances, most notably the dog Crab in *The Two Gentlemen of Verona* and possibly a young polar bear in *The Winter's Tale.*

The costumes were the most important visual dimension of the play. Playwrights were paid between £2 and £6 per script, whereas Alleyn was not averse to paying £20 for "a black velvet cloak with sleeves embroidered all with silver and gold." No matter the period of the play, actors always wore contemporary costume. The excitement for the audience came not from any impression of historical accuracy, but from the richness of the attire and perhaps the transgressive thrill of the knowledge that here were commoners like themselves strutting in the costumes of courtiers in effective defiance of the strict sumptuary laws whereby in real life people had to wear the clothes that befitted their social station.

To an even greater degree than props, costumes could carry symbolic importance. Racial characteristics could be suggested: a breastplate and helmet for a Roman soldier, a turban for a Turk, long robes for exotic characters such as Moors, a gabardine for a Jew. The figure of Time, as in *The Winter's Tale*, would be equipped with hourglass, scythe, and wings; Rumour, who speaks the prologue of *2 Henry IV*, wore a costume adorned with a thousand tongues. The wardrobe in the tiring-house of the Globe would have contained much of the same stock as that of rival manager Philip Henslowe at the Rose: green gowns for outlaws and foresters, black for melancholy men such as Jaques and people in mourning such as the Countess in *All's Well That Ends Well* (at the beginning of *Hamlet*, the prince is still in mourning black when everyone else is in festive garb for the wedding of the new king), a gown and hood for a friar (or a feigned friar like the duke in *Measure for Measure*), blue coats and tawny to distinguish the followers of rival factions, a leather apron and ruler for a carpenter (as in the opening scene of *Julius Caesar*—and in *A Midsummer Night's Dream*, where this is the only sign that Peter Quince is a carpenter), a cockle hat with staff and a pair of sandals for a pilgrim or palmer (the disguise assumed by Helen in *All's Well*), bodices and kirtles with farthingales beneath for the boys who are to be dressed as girls. A gender switch such as that of Rosalind or Jessica seems to have taken between fifty and eighty lines of dialogue—Viola does not resume her "maiden weeds," but remains in her boy's costume to the end of *Twelfth Night* because a change would have slowed down the action at just the moment it was speeding to a climax. Henslowe's inventory also included "a robe for to go invisible": Oberon, Puck, and Ariel must have had something similar.

As the costumes appealed to the eyes, so there was music for the ears. Comedies included many songs. Desdemona's willow song, perhaps a late addition to the text, is a rare and thus exceptionally poignant example from tragedy. Trumpets and tuckets sounded for ceremonial entrances, drums denoted an army on the march. Background music could create atmosphere, as at the beginning of *Twelfth Night*, during the lovers' dialogue near the end of *The Mer-*

chant of Venice, when the statue seemingly comes to life in *The Win-ter's Tale,* and for the revival of Pericles and of Lear (in the Quarto text, but not the Folio). The haunting sound of the hautboy sug-gested a realm beyond the human, as when the god Hercules is imag-ined deserting Mark Antony. Dances symbolized the harmony of the end of a comedy—though in Shakespeare's world of mingled joy and sorrow, someone is usually left out of the circle.

The most important resource was, of course, the actors them-selves. They needed many skills: in the words of one contemporary commentator, "dancing, activity, music, song, elocution, ability of body, memory, skill of weapon, pregnancy of wit." Their bodies were as significant as their voices. Hamlet tells the player to "suit the action to the word, the word to the action": moments of strong emo-tion, known as "passions," relied on a repertoire of dramatic ges-tures as well as a modulation of the voice. When Titus Andronicus has had his hand chopped off, he asks, "How can I grace my talk, / Wanting a hand to give it action?" A pen portrait of "The Character of an Excellent Actor" by the dramatist John Webster is almost cer-tainly based on his impression of Shakespeare's leading man, Richard Burbage: "By a full and significant action of body, he charms our attention: sit in a full theatre, and you will think you see so many lines drawn from the circumference of so many ears, whiles the actor is the centre. . . ."

Though Burbage was admired above all others, praise was also heaped upon the apprentice players whose alto voices fitted them for the parts of women. A spectator at Oxford in 1610 records how the audience were reduced to tears by the pathos of Desdemona's death. The puritans who fumed about the biblical prohibition upon cross-dressing and the encouragement to sodomy constituted by the sight of an adult male kissing a teenage boy onstage were a small minority. Little is known, however, about the characteristics of the leading apprentices in Shakespeare's company. It may perhaps be inferred that one was a lot taller than the other, since Shakespeare often wrote for a pair of female friends, one tall and fair, the other short and dark (Helena and Hermia, Rosalind and Celia, Beatrice and Hero).

We know little about Shakespeare's own acting roles—an early allusion indicates that he often took royal parts, and a venerable tradition gives him old Adam in *As You Like It* and the ghost of old King Hamlet. Save for Burbage's lead roles and the generic part of the clown, all such castings are mere speculation. We do not even know for sure whether the original Falstaff was Will Kempe or another actor who specialized in comic roles, Thomas Pope.

Kempe left the company in early 1599. Tradition has it that he fell out with Shakespeare over the matter of excessive improvisation. He was replaced by Robert Armin, who was less of a clown and more of a cerebral wit: this explains the difference between such parts as Lancelet Gobbo and Dogberry, which were written for Kempe, and the more verbally sophisticated Feste and Lear's Fool, which were written for Armin.

One thing that is clear from surviving "plots" or storyboards of plays from the period is that a degree of doubling was necessary. *2 Henry VI* has over sixty speaking parts, but more than half of the characters appear only in a single scene and most scenes have only six to eight speakers. At a stretch, the play could be performed by thirteen actors. When Thomas Platter saw *Julius Caesar* at the Globe in 1599, he noted that there were about fifteen. Why doesn't Paris go to the Capulet ball in *Romeo and Juliet?* Perhaps because he was doubled with Mercutio, who does. In *The Winter's Tale,* Mamillius might have come back as Perdita and Antigonus been doubled by Camillo, making the partnership with Paulina at the end a very neat touch. Titania and Oberon are often played by the same pair as Hippolyta and Theseus, suggesting a symbolic matching of the rulers of the worlds of night and day, but it is questionable whether there would have been time for the necessary costume changes. As so often, one is left in a realm of tantalizing speculation.

THE KING'S MAN

On Queen Elizabeth's death in 1603, the new king, James I, who had held the Scottish throne as James VI since he had been an infant, immediately took the Lord Chamberlain's Men under his direct patronage. Henceforth they would be the King's Men, and for the rest of Shakespeare's career they were favored with far more court performances than any of their rivals. There even seem to have been rumors early in the reign that Shakespeare and Burbage were being considered for knighthoods, an unprecedented honor for mere actors—and one that in the event was not accorded to a member of the profession for nearly three hundred years, when the title was bestowed upon Henry Irving, the leading Shakespearean actor of Queen Victoria's reign.

Shakespeare's productivity rate slowed in the Jacobean years, not because of age or some personal trauma, but because there were frequent outbreaks of plague, causing the theaters to be closed for long periods. The King's Men were forced to spend many months on the road. Between November 1603 and 1608, they were to be found at various towns in the south and Midlands, though Shakespeare probably did not tour with them by this time. He had bought a large house back home in Stratford and was accumulating other property. He may indeed have stopped acting soon after the new king took the throne. With the London theaters closed so much of the time and a large repertoire on the stocks, Shakespeare seems to have focused his energies on writing a few long and complex tragedies that could have been played on demand at court: *Othello, King Lear, Antony and Cleopatra, Coriolanus,* and *Cymbeline* are among his longest and poetically grandest plays. *Macbeth* survives only in a shorter text, which shows signs of adaptation after Shakespeare's death. The bitterly satirical *Timon of Athens,* apparently a collaboration with Thomas Middleton that may have failed on the stage, also belongs to this period. In comedy, too, he wrote longer and morally darker works than in the Elizabethan period, pushing at the very bounds of the form in *Measure for Measure* and *All's Well That Ends Well.*

From 1608 onward, when the King's Men began occupying the indoor Blackfriars playhouse (as a winter house, meaning that they only used the outdoor Globe in summer?), Shakespeare turned to a more romantic style. His company had a great success with a revived and altered version of an old pastoral play called *Mucedorus.* It even featured a bear. The younger dramatist John Fletcher, meanwhile, sometimes working in collaboration with Francis Beaumont, was pioneering a new style of tragicomedy, a mix of romance and royalism laced with intrigue and pastoral excursions. Shakespeare experimented with this idiom in *Cymbeline,* and it was presumably with his blessing that Fletcher eventually took over as the King's Men's company dramatist. The two writers apparently collaborated on three plays in the years 1612–14: a lost romance called *Cardenio* (based on the love-madness of a character in Cervantes' *Don Quixote*), *Henry VIII* (originally staged with the title "All Is True"), and *The Two Noble Kinsmen,* a dramatization of Chaucer's "Knight's Tale." These were written after Shakespeare's two final solo-authored plays, *The Winter's Tale,* a self-consciously old-fashioned work dramatizing the pastoral romance of his old enemy Robert Greene, and *The Tempest,* which at one and the same time drew together multiple theatrical traditions, diverse reading, and contemporary interest in the fate of a ship that had been wrecked on the way to the New World.

The collaborations with Fletcher suggest that Shakespeare's career ended with a slow fade rather than the sudden retirement supposed by the nineteenth-century Romantic critics who read Prospero's epilogue to *The Tempest* as Shakespeare's personal farewell to his art. In the last few years of his life Shakespeare certainly spent more of his time in Stratford-upon-Avon, where he became further involved in property dealing and litigation. But his London life also continued. In 1613 he made his first major London property purchase: a freehold house in the Blackfriars district, close to his company's indoor theater. *The Two Noble Kinsmen* may have been written as late as 1614, and Shakespeare was in London on business a little over a year before he died of an unknown cause at home in Stratford-upon-Avon in 1616, probably on his fifty-second birthday.

About half the sum of his works were published in his lifetime, in texts of variable quality. A few years after his death, his fellow actors began putting together an authorized edition of his complete *Comedies, Histories and Tragedies.* It appeared in 1623, in large "Folio" format. This collection of thirty-six plays gave Shakespeare his immortality. In the words of his fellow dramatist Ben Jonson, who contributed two poems of praise at the start of the Folio, the body of his work made him "a monument without a tomb":

> And art alive still while thy book doth live
> And we have wits to read and praise to give . . .
> He was not of an age, but for all time!

SHAKESPEARE'S WORKS: A CHRONOLOGY

1589–91	? *Arden of Faversham* (possible part authorship)
1589–92	*The Taming of the Shrew*
1589–92	? *Edward the Third* (possible part authorship)
1591	*The Second Part of Henry the Sixth*, originally called *The First Part of the Contention betwixt the Two Famous Houses of York and Lancaster* (element of coauthorship possible)
1591	*The Third Part of Henry the Sixth*, originally called *The True Tragedy of Richard Duke of York* (element of co-authorship probable)
1591–92	*The Two Gentlemen of Verona*
1591–92; perhaps revised 1594	*The Lamentable Tragedy of Titus Andronicus* (probably cowritten with, or revising an earlier version by, George Peele)
1592	*The First Part of Henry the Sixth*, probably with Thomas Nashe and others
1592/94	*King Richard the Third*
1593	*Venus and Adonis* (poem)
1593–94	*The Rape of Lucrece* (poem)
1593–1608	*Sonnets* (154 poems, published 1609 with *A Lover's Complaint*, a poem of disputed authorship)
1592–94/ 1600–03	*Sir Thomas More* (a single scene for a play originally by Anthony Munday, with other revisions by Henry Chettle, Thomas Dekker, and Thomas Heywood)
1594	*The Comedy of Errors*
1595	*Love's Labour's Lost*

1595–97   *Love's Labour's Won* (a lost play, unless the original title for another comedy)

1595–96   *A Midsummer Night's Dream*

1595–96   *The Tragedy of Romeo and Juliet*

1595–96   *King Richard the Second*

1595–97   *The Life and Death of King John* (possibly earlier)

1596–97   *The Merchant of Venice*

1596–97   *The First Part of Henry the Fourth*

1597–98   *The Second Part of Henry the Fourth*

1598   *Much Ado About Nothing*

1598–99   *The Passionate Pilgrim* (20 poems, some not by Shakespeare)

1599   *The Life of Henry the Fifth*

1599   "To the Queen" (epilogue for a court performance)

1599   *As You Like It*

1599   *The Tragedy of Julius Caesar*

1600–01   *The Tragedy of Hamlet, Prince of Denmark* (perhaps revising an earlier version)

1600–01   *The Merry Wives of Windsor* (perhaps revising version of 1597–99)

1601   "Let the Bird of Loudest Lay" (poem, known since 1807 as "The Phoenix and Turtle" [turtledove])

1601   *Twelfth Night, or What You Will*

1601–02   *The Tragedy of Troilus and Cressida*

1604   *The Tragedy of Othello, the Moor of Venice*

1604   *Measure for Measure*

1605   *All's Well That Ends Well*

1605   *The Life of Timon of Athens*, with Thomas Middleton

1605–06   *The Tragedy of King Lear*

1605–08   ? contribution to *The Four Plays in One* (lost, except for *A Yorkshire Tragedy*, mostly by Thomas Middleton)

1606	*The Tragedy of Macbeth* (surviving text has additional scenes by Thomas Middleton)
1606–07	*The Tragedy of Antony and Cleopatra*
1608	*The Tragedy of Coriolanus*
1608	*Pericles, Prince of Tyre*, with George Wilkins
1610	*The Tragedy of Cymbeline*
1611	*The Winter's Tale*
1611	*The Tempest*
1612–13	*Cardenio*, with John Fletcher (survives only in later adaptation called *Double Falsehood* by Lewis Theobald)
1613	*Henry VIII (All Is True)*, with John Fletcher
1613–14	*The Two Noble Kinsmen*, with John Fletcher

FURTHER READING
AND VIEWING

CRITICAL APPROACHES

Calderwood, James L., "Styles of Knowing in *All's Well*," *Modern Language Quarterly* 25, September 1964, pp. 272–94. Examines the play's various problems in relation to Shakespeare's narrative poem, *Venus and Adonis*, and the importance of literal, symbolic, and self-knowledge.

Cole, Howard C., *The All's Well Story from Boccaccio to Shakespeare* (1981). Thorough review of all the source material.

Findlay, Alison, *A Feminist Perspective on Renaissance Drama* (1999). Discusses *All's Well* in relation to female self-fashioning, pp. 91–100.

Frye, Northrop, *The Myth of Deliverance: Reflections on Shakespeare's Problem Comedies* (1983). Brilliant analysis of comedy in terms of mythic structures and cultural history across a broad terrain of classical literary texts, arguing that *All's Well* is untypical in its emphasis on social change.

Haley, David, *Shakespeare's Courtly Mirror: Reflexivity and Prudence in All's Well That Ends Well* (1993). Argues the play offers a critical analysis of courtly society.

Hopkins, Lisa, *The Shakespearean Marriage: Merry Wives and Heavy Husbands* (1998). Examines all aspects of contemporary marriage and its significance in Shakespeare's plays: *All's Well* is treated at pp. 56–62 and *passim*.

McCandless, David, "Helena's Bed-Trick: Gender and Performance in *All's Well That Ends Well*," *Shakespeare Quarterly* 45 (1994), pp. 449–68. Theoretically informed exploration of the problematic nature of Helen's physical desire and its representation in performance, including the possibility of staging the bed trick.

Muir, Kenneth, ed., *Shakespeare: The Comedies* (1965). Collection of distinguished earlier critical essays, including M. C. Bradbrook, "Virtue Is the True Nobility: A Study in the Structure of *All's Well*," pp. 119–32, and G. Wilson Knight's "Helena," pp. 133–51.

Price, Joseph G., *The Unfortunate Comedy: A Study of All's Well That Ends Well and Its Critics* (1968). Dated but still useful: Part I covers stage history, including chapters on the Kemble "Text" and "All's Well in America." Part II discusses the critical history to 1964.

Rossiter, A. P., *Angel with Horns, and Other Shakespeare Lectures*, ed. Graham Storey (1961). Chapter 5 on *All's Well*, pp. 82–107, discusses the significance of Shakespeare's various "additions" and "alterations" to his source material in order to elucidate its problematic nature and deeper philosophical strain.

Waller, Gary, "From 'the Unfortunate Comedy' to 'this Infinitely Fascinating Play,' the Critical and Theatrical Emergence of *All's Well That Ends Well*," in *All's Well That Ends Well: New Critical Essays* (2007), pp. 1–56. Excellent, varied collection of essays, covering aspects of the play from structure to genre, religion, gender politics, and performance.

Zitner, Sheldon P., *All's Well That Ends Well: Harvester New Critical Introductions to Shakespeare* (1989). Good overview of play's critical reception and discussion of its status as a "problem play."

THE PLAY IN PERFORMANCE

Dobson, Michael, "Shakespeare Performances in England, 2004," in *Shakespeare Survey* 58 (2005), pp. 268–297. Detailed, thoughtful discussion.

Magoulias, Michael, ed., *Shakespearean Criticism* 26 (1995). Useful overview of stage history with a good selection of reviews.

Price, Joseph G., *The Unfortunate Comedy: A Study of All's Well That Ends Well* (1968). Dated but still useful: Part I covers stage history, including chapters on the Kemble "Text" and "All's Well in America." Part II discusses the critical history to 1964.

Styan, J. L., *Shakespeare in Performance: All's Well that Ends Well* (1984). Detailed analysis of the play in performance, focusing on important twentieth-century productions.

Waller, Gary, "The Critical and Theatrical Emergence of *All's Well That Ends Well*," in *All's Well That Ends Well: New Critical Essays* (2007), pp. 1–56. Excellent, varied collection of essays, covering aspects of the play from structure to genre, religion, gender politics, and performance.

AVAILABLE ON DVD

All's Well that Ends Well directed by Elijah Moshinsky for BBC Shakespeare (1981, DVD 2006). Starring Angela Down, Ian Charleson, Michael Hordern, Celia Johnson, and Donald Sinden, it won both BAFTA and RTS awards and was considered one of the best of the BBC Shakespeare series.

REFERENCES

1. *The Works of Shakespeare*, ed. Samuel Johnson (1765), vol. 3, p. 399.
2. A. W. Schlegel, *Lectures on Dramatic Art and Literature* (1808–11), in *The Romantics on Shakespeare*, ed. Jonathan Bate (1992), p. 260.
3. George Bernard Shaw, letter to Janet Achurch, 23 April 1895. On Helen as proto-Ibsenite heroine, see The *"Shakespearean Law,"* in *Shaw on Shakespeare: An Anthology of Bernard Shaw's Writings on the Plays and Production of Shakespeare*, ed. Edwin Wilson (1961), p. 240.
4. Samuel Taylor Coleridge, *Lectures and Notes on Shakspere and Other English Poets*, ed. T. Ashe (1900), p. 298.
5. Coleridge, from *Table-Talk*, 1 July 1833, in *Coleridge's Criticism of Shakespeare: A Selection*, ed. R. A. Foakes (1989), p. 176.
6. Anna Jameson, *Characteristics of Women: Moral, Poetical, and Historical* (1832, reprinted 1879), p. 125.
7. Ellen Terry, *Four Lectures on Shakespeare* (1932), cited by Joseph G. Price, *The Unfortunate Comedy: A Study of All's Well That Ends Well and its Critics* (1968), pp. 99–100.
8. Coleridge, *Table-Talk*, p. 176.
9. Sheldon P. Zitner, *All's Well That Ends Well* (1989), p. 13.
10. Price, *The Unfortunate Comedy*, p. 134.
11. Price, *The Unfortunate Comedy*, p. 135.
12. James L. Calderwood, "Styles of Knowing in *All's Well*," *Modern Language Quarterly* 25 (1964), p. 274.
13. W. W. Lawrence, *Shakespeare's Problem Comedies* (1931), p. 32.
14. David McCandless, "Helena's Bed-Trick: Gender and Performance in *All's Well That Ends Well*," *Shakespeare Quarterly*, 45 (1994), p. 450.
15. Barbara Everitt, ed., *All's Well That Ends Well* (1970), p. 16.
16. A. P. Rossiter, *Angel with Horns, and other Shakespeare Lectures* (1961), p. 87.
17. R. B. Parker, "War and Sex in *All's Well That Ends Well*," *Shakespeare Survey* 37 (1984), p. 105.
18. Northrop Frye, *The Myth of Deliverance: Reflections on Shakespeare's Problem Comedies* (1983), p. 49.
19. Frye, *The Myth of Deliverance*, p. 55.
20. Rossiter, *Angel with Horns*, p. 85.

21. J. Dennis Huston, "'Some Stain of Soldier': The Functions of Parolles in *All's Well That Ends Well*," *Shakespeare Quarterly* 21 (1970), p. 433.

22. Frye, *The Myth of Deliverance*, p. 52.

23. Calderwood, "Styles of Knowing in *All's Well*," p. 274.

24. John Barton, in "Directing Problem Plays: John Barton talks to Gareth Lloyd Evans" (1972), in *Aspects of Shakespeare's "Problem Plays,"* ed. Kenneth Muir and Stanley Wells (1982), p. 5.

25. *Athenaeum*, No. 1297, 4 September 1852, p. 955.

26. William Archer, review of *All's Well That Ends Well*, in *The Theatrical "World" of 1895* (1896), pp. 37–41.

27. George Bernard Shaw, "Poor Shakespear!," in *Our Theatres in the Nineties*, Vol. I (1932), pp. 24–30.

28. Joseph G. Price, "The Director and the Search for Unity," in *The Unfortunate Comedy: A Study of All's Well That Ends Well and Its Critics* (1968), pp. 43–72.

29. Price, "The Director and the Search for Unity."

30. Price, "The Director and the Search for Unity."

31. Robert Speaight, *William Poel and the Elizabethan Revival* (1954), quoted in Price, "The Director and the Search for Unity."

32. T. Moult, *Athenaeum*, 4 June 1920, quoted in Price, "The Director and the Search for Unity."

33. John Francis Hope, *The New Age*, Vol. XXX, No. 7, 15 December 1921, p. 82.

34. Hope, *The New Age*.

35. Hope, *The New Age*.

36. J. C. Trewin, *The Birmingham Repertory Theatre: 1913–63* (1963), p. 90.

37. Trewin, *The Birmingham Repertory Theatre*.

38. Ivor Brown, *Punch*, Vol. CXCIX, No. 5, 195, 16 October 1940, p. 388.

39. Brown, *Punch*, Vol. CXCIX, No. 5, 195, 16 October 1940, p. 388.

40. Alan Dent, *Manchester Guardian*, October 1940, reprinted in *Preludes & Studies* (1942), pp. 102–29 and 121–22.

41. Herbert Whittaker, *The Stratford Festival 1953–1957* (1958), pp. x–xv.

42. Tyrone Guthrie, "First Shakespeare Festival at Stratford, Ontario," in *Renown at Stratford: A Record of the Shakespeare Festival in Canada, 1953* (1953), p. 49.

43. Guthrie, "First Shakespeare Festival at Stratford, Ontario."

44. Price, "The Director and the Search for Unity."

45. Tyrone Guthrie, "Shakespeare at Stratford, Ontario," in *Shakespeare Survey* 8 (1955), pp. 127–31.

46. Whittaker, *The Stratford Festival 1953–1957*.
47. Derek Monsey, *Spectator* 191(6535), 25 September 1953, pp. 322–23.
48. Roger Wood and Mary Clarke, *Shakespeare at the Old Vic* (1954), pp. 12–16.
49. Wood and Clarke, *Shakespeare at the Old Vic*.
50. Wood and Clarke, *Shakespeare at the Old Vic*.
51. Monsey, *Spectator*.
52. Price, "The Director and the Search for Unity."
53. Price, "The Director and the Search for Unity."
54. Price, "The Director and the Search for Unity."
55. *The Times* (London), 22 April 1959.
56. A. Alvarez, *New Statesman* LVII(1,467), 25 April 1959.
57. M. St. Clare Byrne, "The Shakespeare Season at The Old Vic, 1958–59 and Stratford-upon-Avon, 1959," *Shakespeare Quarterly* X, Autumn 1959, pp. 545–67.
58. Patrick Gibbs, *New York Times*, 22 April 1959.
59. St. Clare Byrne, "The Shakespeare Season at The Old Vic, 1958–59 and Stratford-upon-Avon, 1959."
60. Alan Brien, *Spectator* 202(6826), 1959, pp. 577, 579.
61. Joseph G. Price, "*All's Well* in America and in the Minor Theatres," in *The Unfortunate Comedy: A Study of All's Well That Ends Well and Its Critics* (1968), pp. 43–72.
62. Price, "*All's Well* in America and in the Minor Theatres."
63. Price, "*All's Well* in America and in the Minor Theatres."
64. Price, "*All's Well* in America and in the Minor Theatres."
65. Price, "*All's Well* in America and in the Minor Theatres."
66. Price, "*All's Well* in America and in the Minor Theatres."
67. Henry Hewes, quoted in *Shakespearean Criticism* 26, 1995, p. 3.
68. G. K. Hunter, "A Review of *All's Well that Ends Well*," in *Shakespeare on Television: An Anthology of Essays and Reviews*, ed. J. C. Bulman and H. R. Coursen (1988), pp. 185–87.
69. Jeremy Treglown, "Camera Cuts," *Times Literary Supplement*, 9 January 1981, p. 33.
70. Treglown, "Camera Cuts."
71. Hunter, "A Review of *All's Well that Ends Well*."
72. Hunter, "A Review of *All's Well that Ends Well*."
73. Jeremy Gerard, *Variety* 352(2), 23 August 1993, p. 23.
74. Robert Brustein, *New Republic* 209(14), 14 October 1993, pp. 32–34.
75. Brustein, *New Republic*.
76. Gerard, *Variety*.

77. Brustein, *New Republic*.

78. Grevel Lindop, "Cold Wars and Boors," *Times Literary Supplement* 4878, 27 September 1996, p. 19.

79. Lindop, "Cold Wars and Boors."

80. Lindop, "Cold Wars and Boors."

81. Robert Smallwood, "Shakespeare Performances in England, 1997," *Shakespeare Survey* 51 (1998), pp. 219–55.

82. Smallwood, "Shakespeare Performances in England, 1997."

83. Smallwood, "Shakespeare Performances in England, 1997."

84. Michael Billington, *Guardian*, 29 May 2009.

85. Billington, *Guardian*, 29 May 2009.

86. Naomi Siegel, *New York Times*, Theater Review/NY Region, 24 September 2010.

87. Bob Rendell, *Talkin' Broadway*, 29 September 2010.

88. Rendell, *Talkin' Broadway*, 29 September 2010.

89. Siegel, *New York Times*, Theater Review/NY Region, 24 September 2010.

90. Siegel, *New York Times*, Theater Review/NY Region, 24 September 2010.

91. J. L. Styan, *Shakespeare in Performance: All's Well That Ends Well* (1984), p. 1.

92. *Birmingham Mail*, 2 June 1967.

93. Desmond Pratt, *Yorkshire Post*, 2 June 1967.

94. J. C. Trewin, *Illustrated London News*, 10 June 1967.

95. Milton Schulman, *Evening Standard*, 2 June 1967.

96. Schulman, *Evening Standard*, 2 June 1967.

97. Michael Billington, *Guardian*, 7 July 1982.

98. Tom Vaughan, *Morning Star*, 8 July 1982.

99. Christopher Hudson, *Standard*, 7 July 1982.

100. J. L. Styan, *Shakespeare in Performance: All's Well that Ends Well* (2007), pp. 115–16, quoting Roger Warren, *Shakespeare Quarterly* 34(1) (1983), p. 80.

101. James Fenton, *Sunday Times* (London), 11 July 1982.

102. B. A. Young, *Financial Times*, 6 July 1982.

103. Young, *Financial Times*, 6 July 1982.

104. John Barber, *Daily Telegraph*, 7 July 1982.

105. Gary Waller, *All's Well that Ends Well: New Critical Essays* (2007), p. 23.

106. Charles Osborne, *Daily Telegraph*, 12 October 1989.

107. Paul Lapworth, *Stratford Herald*, 13 October 1989.

108. Waller, *All's Well That Ends Well*, p. 23.
109. Michael Billington, *Guardian*, 12 October 1989.
110. Terry Grimley, *Birmingham Post*, 10 October 1989.
111. Paul Taylor, *Independent*, 12 October 1989.
112. Michael Coveney, *Financial Times*, 11 October 1989.
113. Billington, *Guardian*, 12 October 1989.
114. Michael Billington, *Guardian*, 3 July 1992.
115. Martin Dodsworth, *Times Literary Supplement*, 10 July 1992.
116. Margaret Ingram, *Stratford Herald*, 10 July 1992.
117. Charles Spencer, *Daily Telegraph*, 2 July 1992.
118. Dodsworth, *Times Literary Supplement*, 10 July 1992.
119. Terry Grimley, *Birmingham Post*, 2 July 1992.
120. Nicholas de Jongh, *Evening Standard*, 1 July 1992.
121. Billington, *Guardian*, 3 July 1992.
122. Malcolm Rutherford, *Financial Times*, 2 July 1992, p. 19.
123. Paul Taylor, *Independent*, 2 July 1992.
124. Dodsworth, *Times Literary Supplement*, 10 July 1992.
125. Michael Billington, *Guardian*, 12 December 2003.
126. Paul Taylor, *Independent*, 15 December 2003.
127. Robert Hewison, *Sunday Times*, 21 December 2003.
128. Kate Kellaway, *Observer*, 14 December 2003.
129. Hewison, *Sunday Times*, 21 December 2003.
130. Alastair Macaulay, *Financial Times*, 15 December 2003.
131. Nicholas de Jongh, *Evening Standard*, 12 December 2003.
132. Michael Dobson, *Shakespeare Survey* 58 (2005), p. 270.
133. Dobson, *Shakespeare Survey* 58, pp. 273–74.
134. Kellaway, *Observer*, 14 December 2003.

ACKNOWLEDGMENTS AND PICTURE CREDITS

Preparation of *"All's Well That Ends Well* in Performance" was assisted by a generous grant from the CAPITAL Centre (Creativity and Performance in Teaching and Learning) of the University of Warwick for research in the RSC archive at the Shakespeare Birthplace Trust. The second half of the introduction, "The Critics Debate," draws extensively on a longer survey prepared for us by Sarah Carter.

Thanks as always to our indefatigable and eagle-eyed copy editor Tracey Day and to Ray Addicott for overseeing the production process with rigor and calmness.

Picture research by Michelle Morton. Grateful acknowledgment is made to the Shakespeare Birthplace Trust for assistance with picture research (special thanks to Helen Hargest) and reproduction fees.

Images of RSC productions are supplied by the Shakespeare Centre Library and Archive, Stratford-upon-Avon. This library, maintained by the Shakespeare Birthplace Trust, holds the most important collection of Shakespeare material in the UK, including the Royal Shakespeare Company's official archive. It is open to the public free of charge.

For more information see www.shakespeare.org.uk.

1. Directed by Tyrone Guthrie (1959). Angus McBean © Royal Shakespeare Company
2. Directed by John Barton (1967). Tom Holte © Shakespeare Birthplace Trust
3. Directed by Trevor Nunn (1981). Joe Cocks Studio Collection © Shakespeare Birthplace Trust
4. Directed by Barry Kyle (1989). Joe Cocks Studio Collection © Shakespeare Birthplace Trust

MODERN LIBRARY IS ONLINE AT
WWW.MODERNLIBRARY.COM

MODERN LIBRARY ONLINE IS YOUR GUIDE
TO CLASSIC LITERATURE ON THE WEB

THE MODERN LIBRARY E-NEWSLETTER

Our free e-mail newsletter is sent to subscribers, and features sample chapters, interviews with and essays by our authors, upcoming books, special promotions, announcements, and news. To subscribe to the Modern Library e-newsletter, visit **www.modernlibrary.com**

THE MODERN LIBRARY WEBSITE

Check out the Modern Library website at
www.modernlibrary.com for:

- The Modern Library e-newsletter
- A list of our current and upcoming titles and series
- Reading Group Guides and exclusive author spotlights
- Special features with information on the classics and other paperback series
- Excerpts from new releases and other titles
- A list of our e-books and information on where to buy them
- The Modern Library Editorial Board's 100 Best Novels and 100 Best Nonfiction Books of the Twentieth Century written in the English language
- News and announcements

Questions? E-mail us at **modernlibrary@randomhouse.com**.
For questions about examination or desk copies, please visit
the Random House Academic Resources site at
www.randomhouse.com/academic